BESSIE STRINGFIELD:
TALES
OF THE
TALENTED
TENTH

WORDS AND PICTURES
JOEL CHRISTIAN GILL

FULCRUM

Library of Congress Cataloging-in-Publication Data

Names: Gill, Joel Christian, author.
Title: Bessie Stringfield / words and pictures by Joel Christian Gill.
Description: Golden, CO : Fulcrum Publishing, [2016] | Series: Tales of the talented tenth ; volume 2 | Audience: Ages 12 and up.
Identifiers: LCCN 2016030231 | ISBN 9781938486944 (paperback)
Subjects: LCSH: Stringfield, Bessie, 1911-1993--Comic books, strips, etc. | Women motorcyclists--United States--Biography--Comic books, strips, etc. | Motorcyclists--United States--Biography--Comic books, strips, etc. | United States--Description and travel--Comic books, strips, etc. | African American women--Biography--Comic books, strips, etc. | African Americans--Biography--Comic books, strips, etc. | Messengers--United States--Biography--Comic books, strips, etc. | United States. Army--Civilian employees--Biography--Comic books, strips, etc. | Graphic novels. | BISAC: JUVENILE NONFICTION / Comics & Graphic Novels / Biography. | JUVENILE NONFICTION / Comics & Graphic Novels / History. | JUVENILE NONFICTION / People & Places / United States / African American.
Classification: LCC GV1060.2.S87 G45 2016 | DDC 796.7/5092 [B] --dc23
LC record available at https://lccn.loc.gov/2016030231

Production assistant: Shannon Scott
Editors: Alison Auch and Rebecca McEwen

Printed in the United States
0 9 8 7 6 5 4 3 2 1

Fulcrum Publishing
4690 Table Mountain Dr., Ste. 100
Golden, CO 80403
800-992-2908 • 303-277-1623
https://fulcrum.bookstore.ipgbook.com

Contents

Praise for *Bessie Stringfield*

"Gill's presentation of Bessie Stringfield to the world is much needed. Her life is a great story that should be heard by all, starting with our youngest generations."

— J.A. Micheline, contributor to A.V. Club
and Women Write About Comics

"Joel Christian Gill has gifted us yet again with a beautifully crafted comic art narrative that pictures the experiences of people of African descent and their history as heartfelt, visually stunning, and fun to read. Bessie Stringfield was a hero who struggled with and overcame both racial and gender barriers as a military dispatch rider during WWII, and Gill delivers the story of her diasporic roots and struggle from childhood to adulthood with artistic brilliance and compelling wit. Like Stringfield, Gill asserts himself as a messenger; he is bringing together multiple generations of readers who now have an opportunity to read and view Blackness and Black historical figures anew."

— Deborah Elizabeth Whaley, author of
Black Women in Sequence: Reinking Comics, Graphic Novels, and Anime

"Joel Christian Gill brings the story of Bessie Stringfield to roaring, colorful life. I'd never heard of this pioneering motorcyclist, but in Joel's telling, she lays out her own story with humor, grace and a uniquely American sense that in this country, anything is possible. Bessie Stringfield roams and races through these pages, and readers of all ages will marvel at her true-life adventures. I thoroughly enjoyed this book!"

— Tony Puryear, co-writer, artist, *Concrete Park*

"Joel Christian Gill is a modern-day graphic griot. His mastery of visual storytelling coupled with his tireless research make him one of the most important artist/scholars working today."

— John Jennings, Eisner-nominated comics scholar
and award-winning graphic novelist

'Bessie Stringfield's story is a call to adventure. Joel Christian Gill's gorgeous artwork depicts her dynamic heroics throughout America's lush and beautiful landscapes."

— Box Brown, *New York Times* best-selling artist of
Andre the Giant: Life and Legend

Praise for Joel Christian Gill

Still more thoughtful reflections come from Joel Christian Gill's graphic novel *Strange Fruit: Uncelebrated Narratives from Black History*, which unpacks its power through drawings and pointed text that chronicle the trials and triumphs of black Americans who struggled against prejudice more than a century ago. At a moment when racial inequities have ignited this nation, Mr. Gill offers direction for the road ahead from the road behind.

— *The New York Times*

The short narratives [in *Strange Fruit*] are conversational in tone and the accompanying detailed images convey tragic beauty. Gill doesn't shy away from portraying brutal scenes, but does so without sensationalism.

— *School Library Journal*

Gill's graphic novel series is a tool with which to discuss African Americans, social justice and a shared history.

— *The Philadelphia Tribune*

Gill's book [*Strange Fruit*] fills a definite void in America's painfully white history books, but on top of that, it's just a really good read. Gill doesn't sugarcoat — not everyone gets a happy ending — but the book is visually witty, engaging, and well researched. History truly comes to life under Gill's skillful hand.

— *Foreword Reviews*

Gill [*Strange Fruit*] launches the Tales of the Talented Tenth series, about notable figures in African American history, with an entry outlining the life of Bass Reeves, among the first black Deputy U.S. Marshals. Over seven chapters, Gill skillfully shifts (and draws parallels) between Reeves's childhood as a slave and his adult service as a marshal.

— *Publisher's Weekly*

By the time I finished reading *Strange Fruit*, I thought, let the comic-book sellers have their mythic superheroes; through Joel Gill, we can have our own. But, instead of flying around in capes or spinning webs, the superheroes in *Strange Fruit* are extraordinary-ordinary black folks making — "a way out of no way." The difference: they really lived.

— Dr. Henry Louis Gates, Jr.
Alphonse Fletcher University Professor, Harvard University

Foreword

There is much archival and activist work happening within and across the comics industry. Some are using comics to challenge gendered and racial inequalities, some are using comics to reimagine an industry that has historically stereotyped Black people, and some are using comics to tell complex stories about social, political, and economic issues. In *Bessie Stringfield: Tales of the Talented Tenth*, Joel Christan Gill is pioneering a comics movement that not only addresses the aforementioned, but also reminds readers that Black history in America is indeed *American* history.

This graphic novel, accompanied by Gill's existing body of work, is inter-generational and interdisciplinary, where the book is educational and entertaining, whilst filling a void in American history literature. That void is the telling of stories about African Americans who remain outside of classroom textbooks, outside of many of the stories told in our own homes, and outside of those stories normally highlighted during Black History Month, or other discussions about American history.

After reading *Bessie Stringfield: Tales of the Talented Tenth*, I was inspired by Bessie Stringfield's courage, wit, and sense of freedom during a time in American history that was turbulent and perilous for Blacks in America. She lived through the Great Depression, Jim Crow, and World War II, becoming the first African American woman to ride across the United States on her motorcycle in 1927. The book you hold in your hands depicts the adventures of a true American Heroine — Bessie Stringfield, the Motorcycle Queen of Miami.

Stringfield was not only a motorcycle rider, but also a symbol of strength and resilience, as she challenged not only the racial confines of society, but the gendered confines as well. Bessie Stringfield left her home in Boston to ride solo across parts of Canada and the northern United States, even riding as a U.S. military dispatcher through the Jim Crow South, where the lynching of

Blacks was common. Between 1880 and 1930, during the time period Bessie was riding, thousands of Black men, women, and children were lynched, yet Bessie Stringfield, in all of her courage and audacity, followed her dreams. Joel Christian Gill uses his artistic talent and meticulous research and writing skills to delve not only into Bessie Stringfield's adventures but also the fabric of who she was, her childhood, her life, and her story.

Joel Christian Gill continues on his quest to provide a resource and stage for Black American superheroes and -heroines, who are not fictional characters but real-life people, who are indeed extraordinary. The tale of Bessie Stringfield is beautifully imagined, chronicled, and envisioned in this graphic novel. I completed this book inspired, enlightened, and encouraged, and I know you will too.

Sheena C. Howard
Associate Professor of Communication Studies
Author, Producer, Comics Scholar

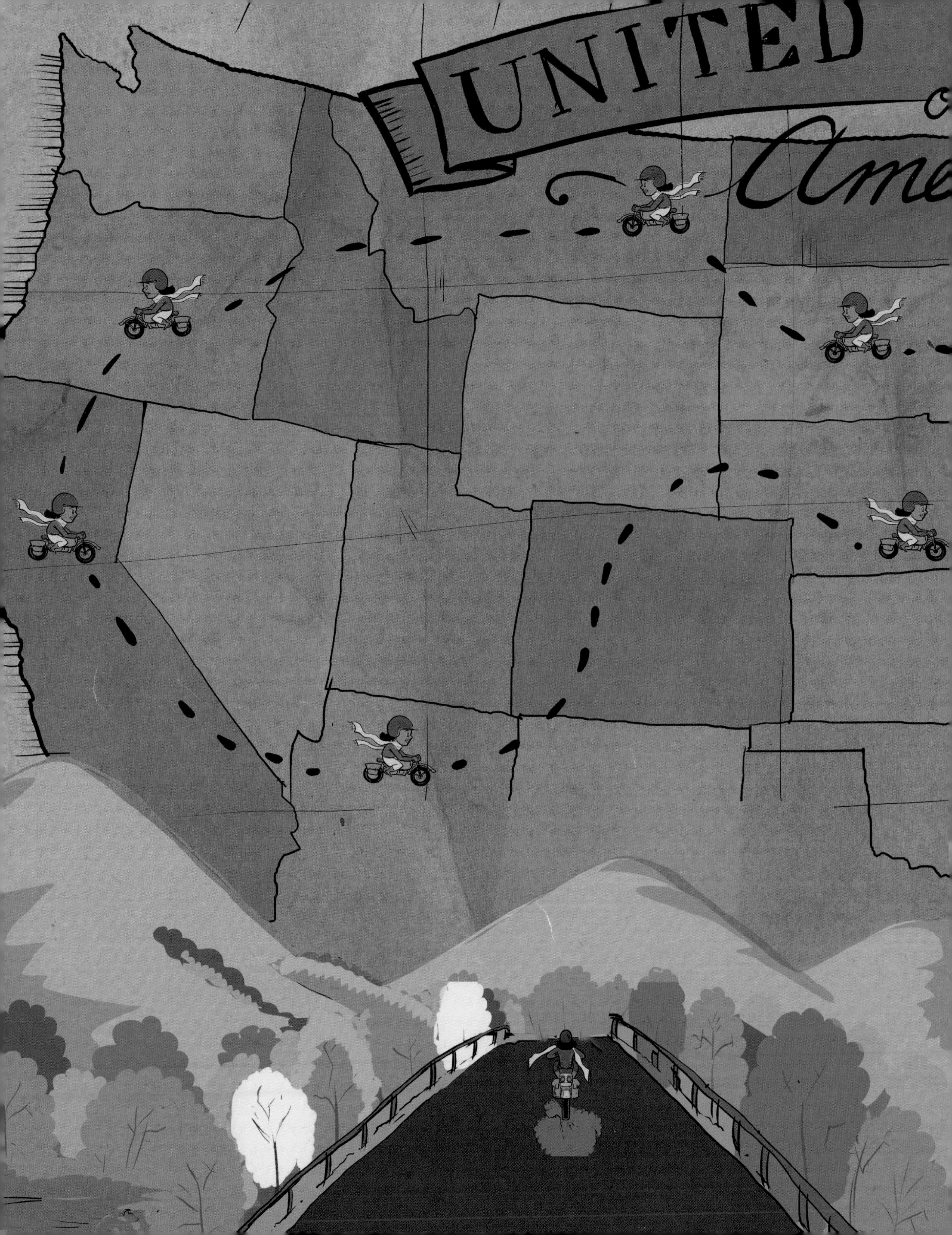
UNITED

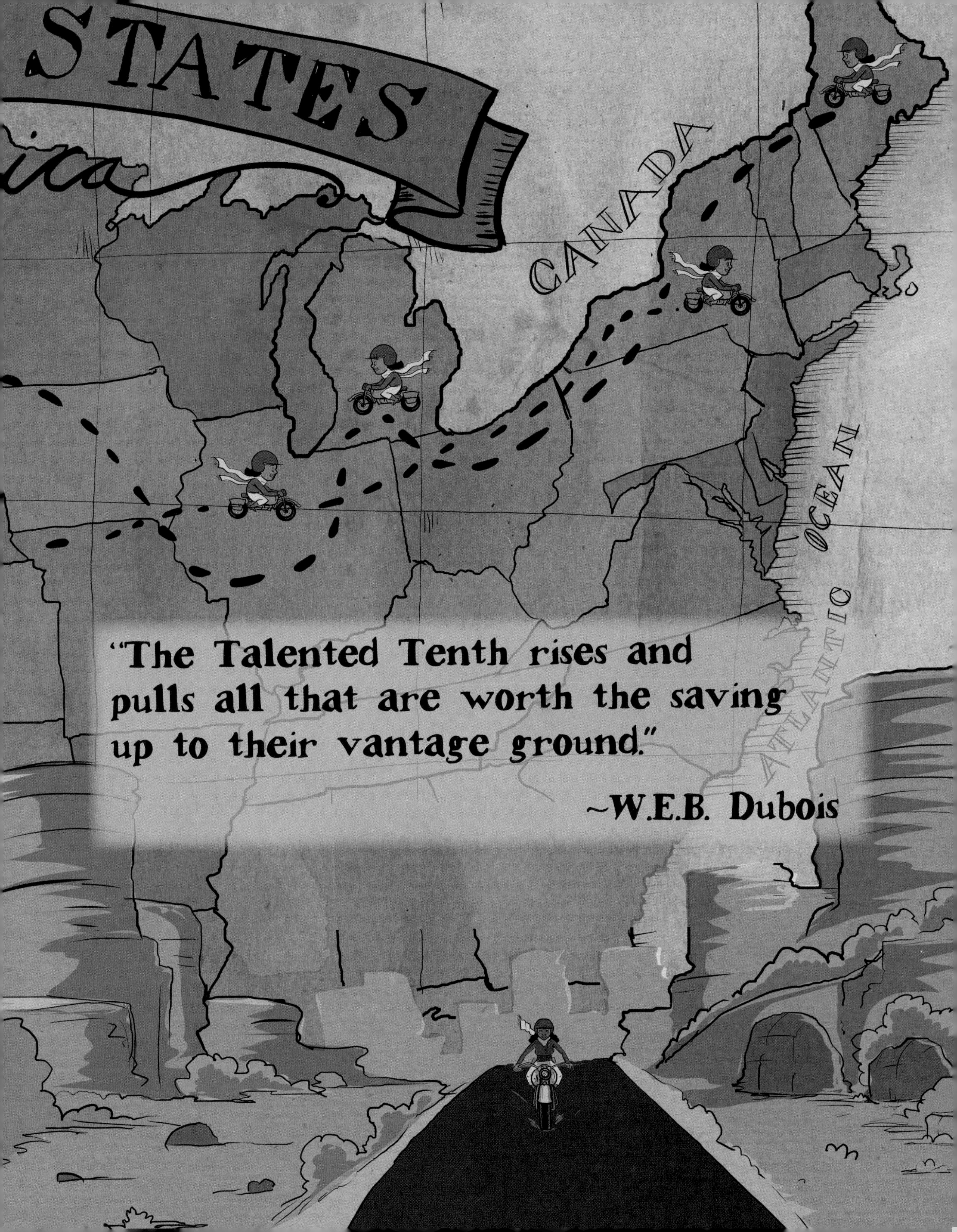
STATES
CANADA
ATLANTIC OCEAN
"The Talented Tenth rises and pulls all that are worth the saving up to their vantage ground."
~W.E.B. Dubois

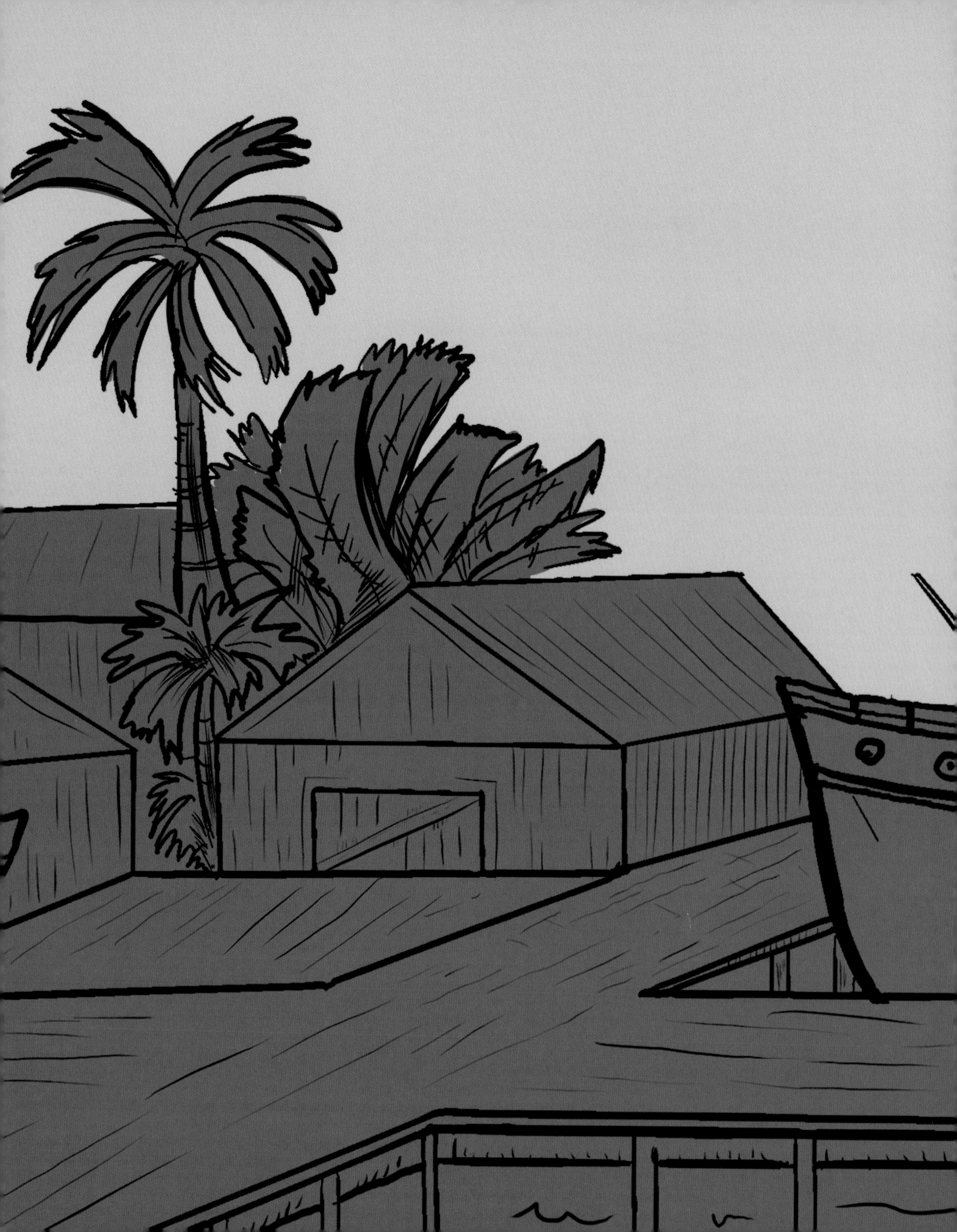

CHAPTER 1

VOYAGE

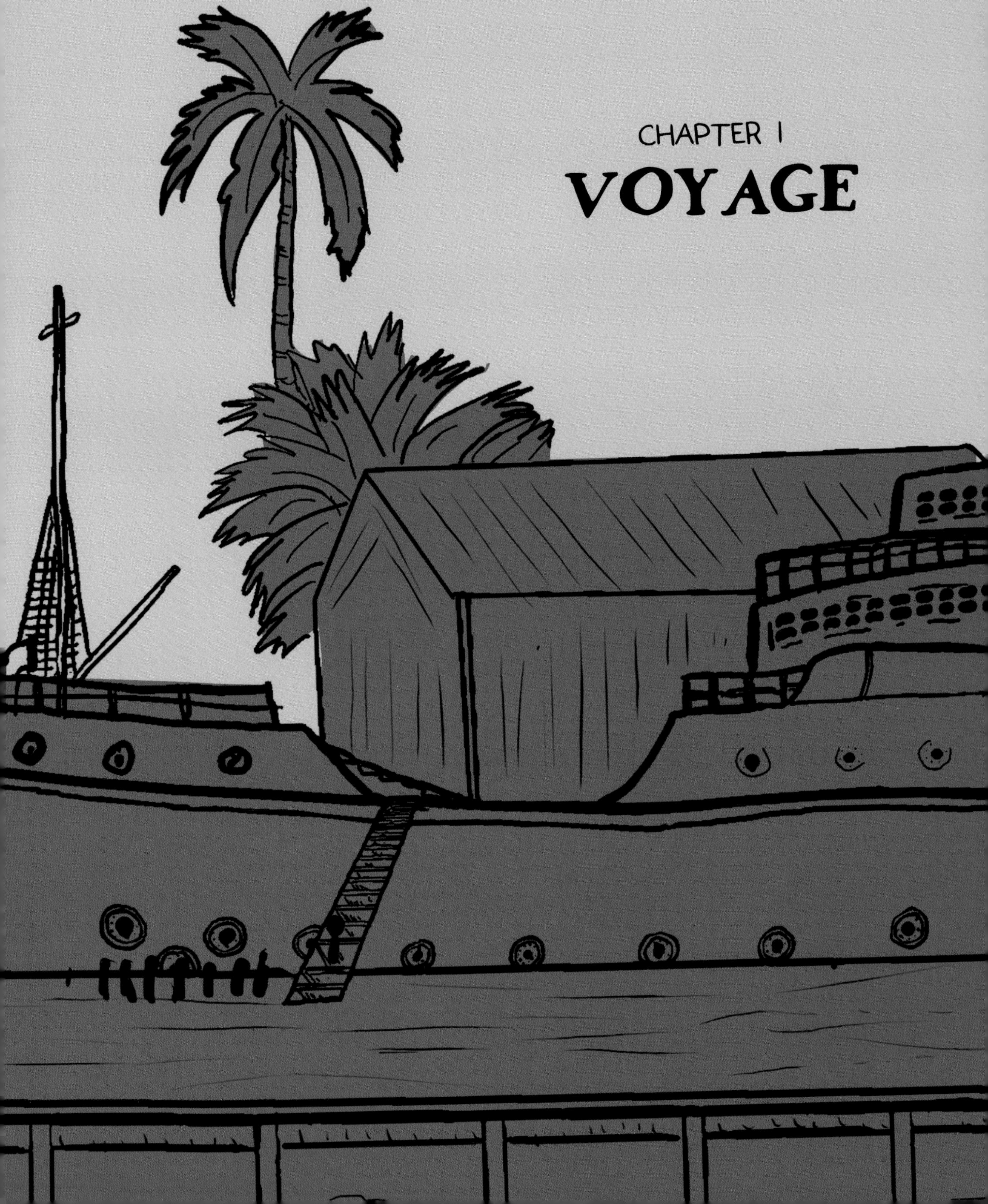

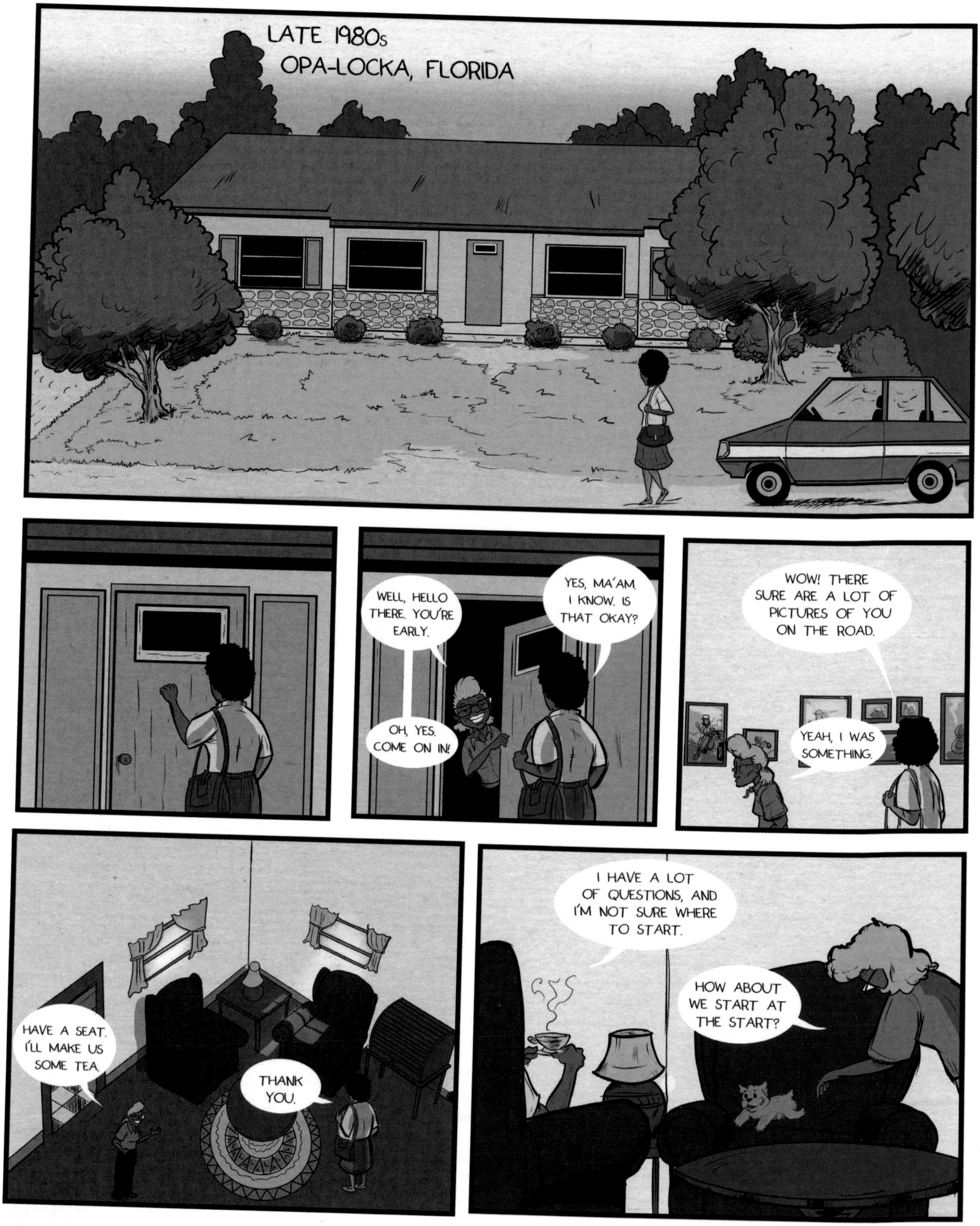
LATE 1980s
OPA-LOCKA, FLORIDA
WELL, HELLO THERE. YOU'RE EARLY.
YES, MA'AM. I KNOW. IS THAT OKAY?
OH, YES. COME ON IN!
WOW! THERE SURE ARE A LOT OF PICTURES OF YOU ON THE ROAD.
YEAH, I WAS SOMETHING.
HAVE A SEAT. I'LL MAKE US SOME TEA.
THANK YOU.
I HAVE A LOT OF QUESTIONS, AND I'M NOT SURE WHERE TO START.
HOW ABOUT WE START AT THE START?

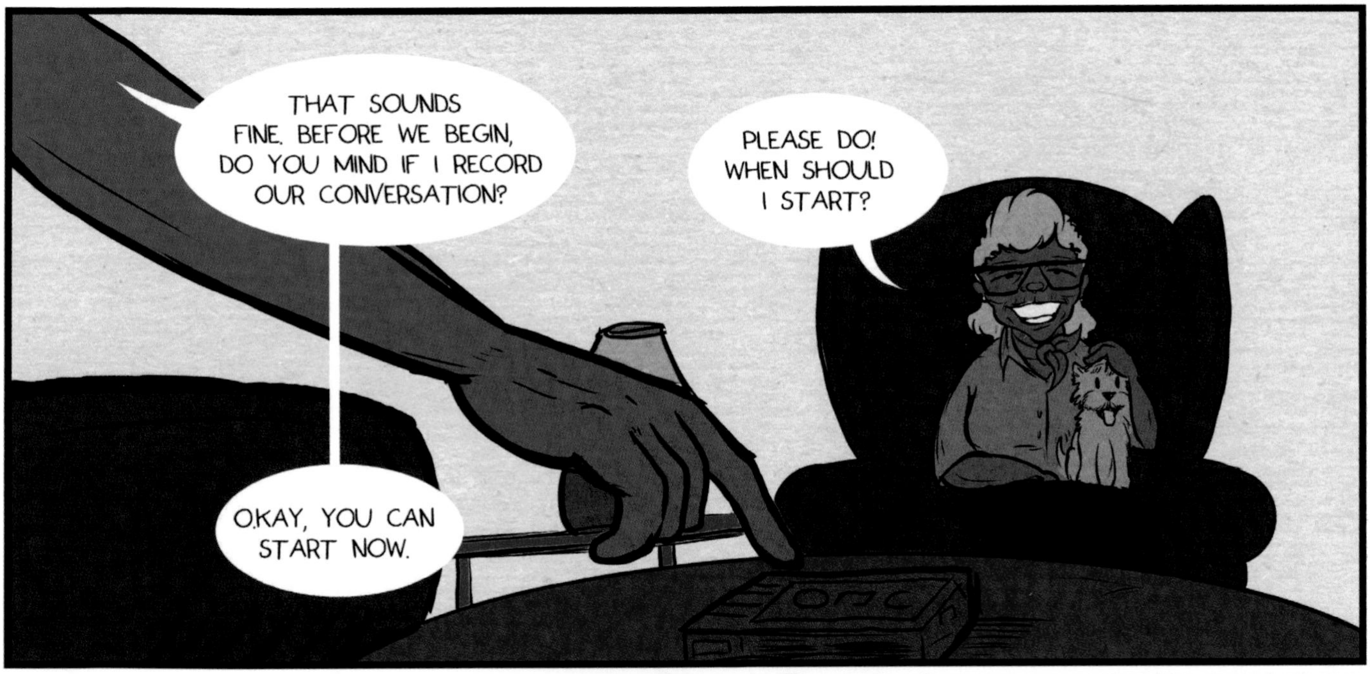
THAT SOUNDS FINE. BEFORE WE BEGIN, DO YOU MIND IF I RECORD OUR CONVERSATION?
PLEASE DO! WHEN SHOULD I START?
O.KAY, YOU CAN START NOW.

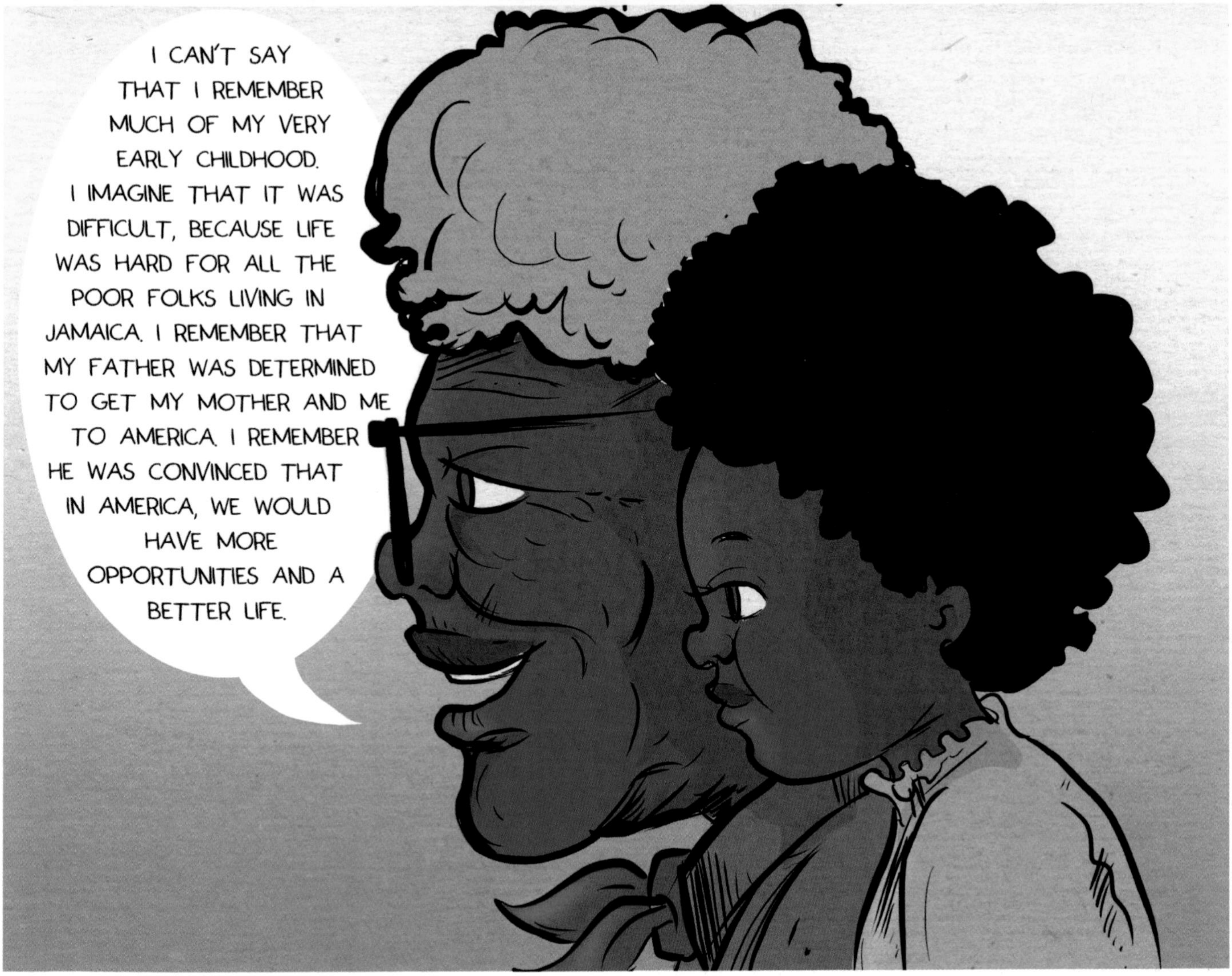
I CAN'T SAY THAT I REMEMBER MUCH OF MY VERY EARLY CHILDHOOD. I IMAGINE THAT IT WAS DIFFICULT, BECAUSE LIFE WAS HARD FOR ALL THE POOR FOLKS LIVING IN JAMAICA. I REMEMBER THAT MY FATHER WAS DETERMINED TO GET MY MOTHER AND ME TO AMERICA. I REMEMBER HE WAS CONVINCED THAT IN AMERICA, WE WOULD HAVE MORE OPPORTUNITIES AND A BETTER LIFE.

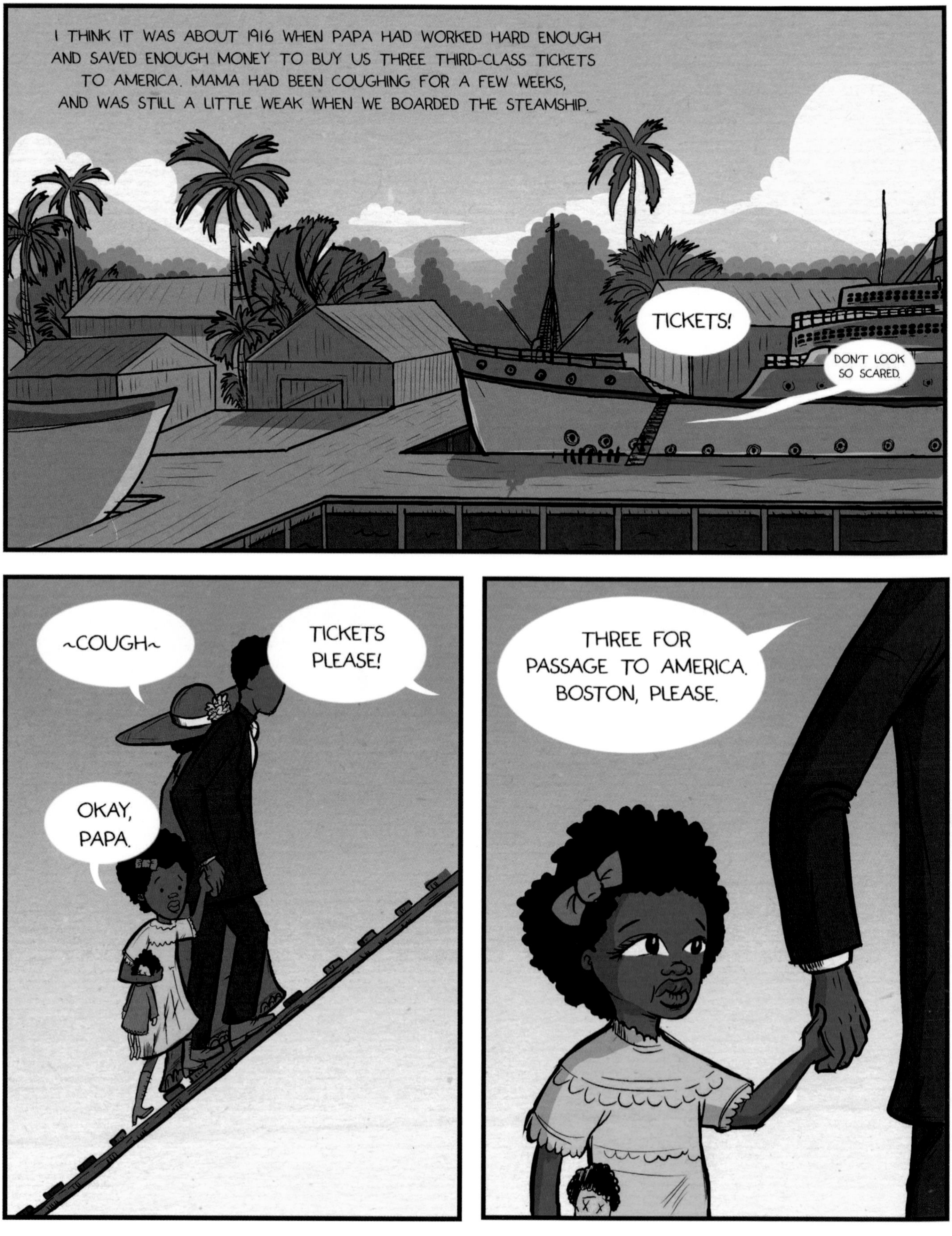
I THINK IT WAS ABOUT 1916 WHEN PAPA HAD WORKED HARD ENOUGH AND SAVED ENOUGH MONEY TO BUY US THREE THIRD-CLASS TICKETS TO AMERICA. MAMA HAD BEEN COUGHING FOR A FEW WEEKS, AND WAS STILL A LITTLE WEAK WHEN WE BOARDED THE STEAMSHIP.
TICKETS!
DON'T LOOK SO SCARED.
~COUGH~
TICKETS PLEASE!
OKAY, PAPA.
THREE FOR PASSAGE TO AMERICA. BOSTON, PLEASE.

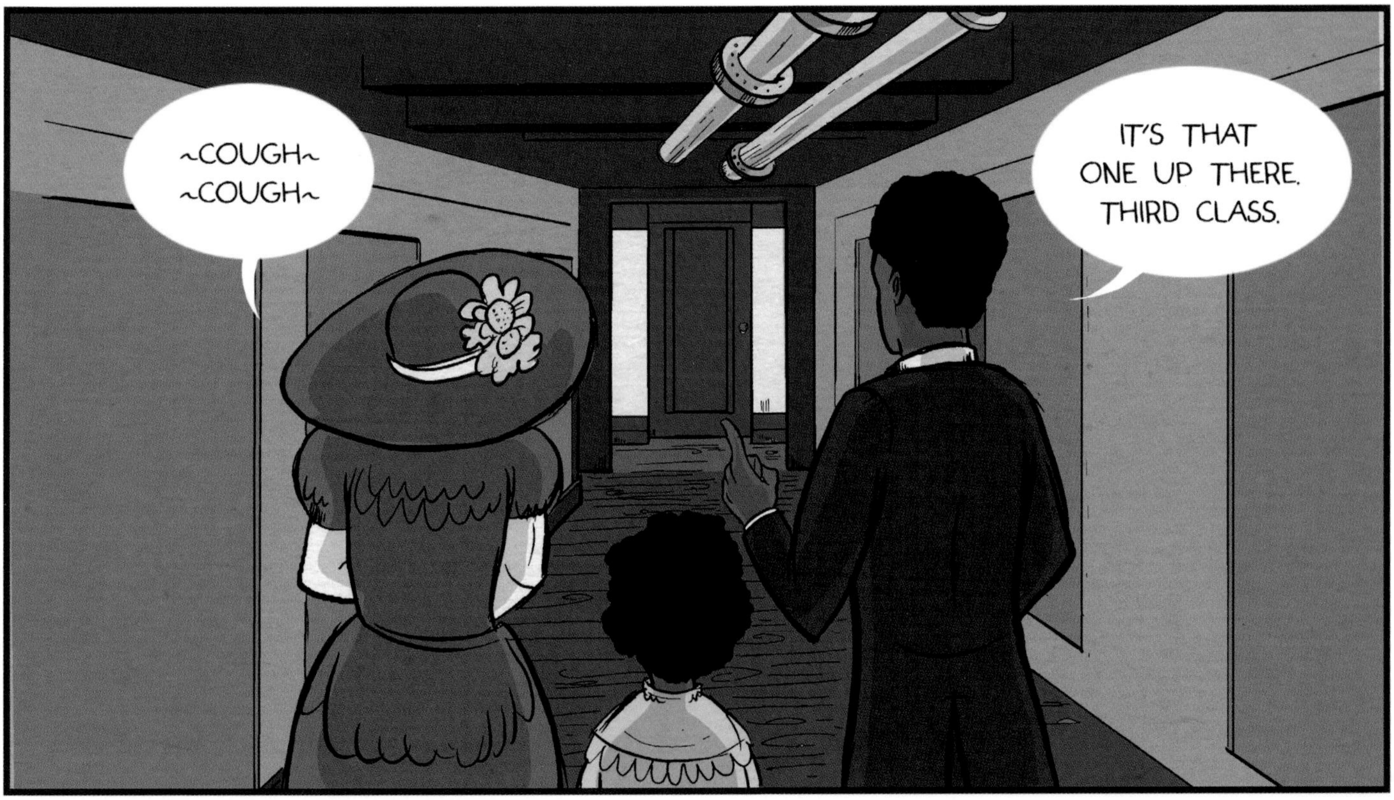
~COUGH~
~COUGH~
IT'S THAT ONE UP THERE. THIRD CLASS.

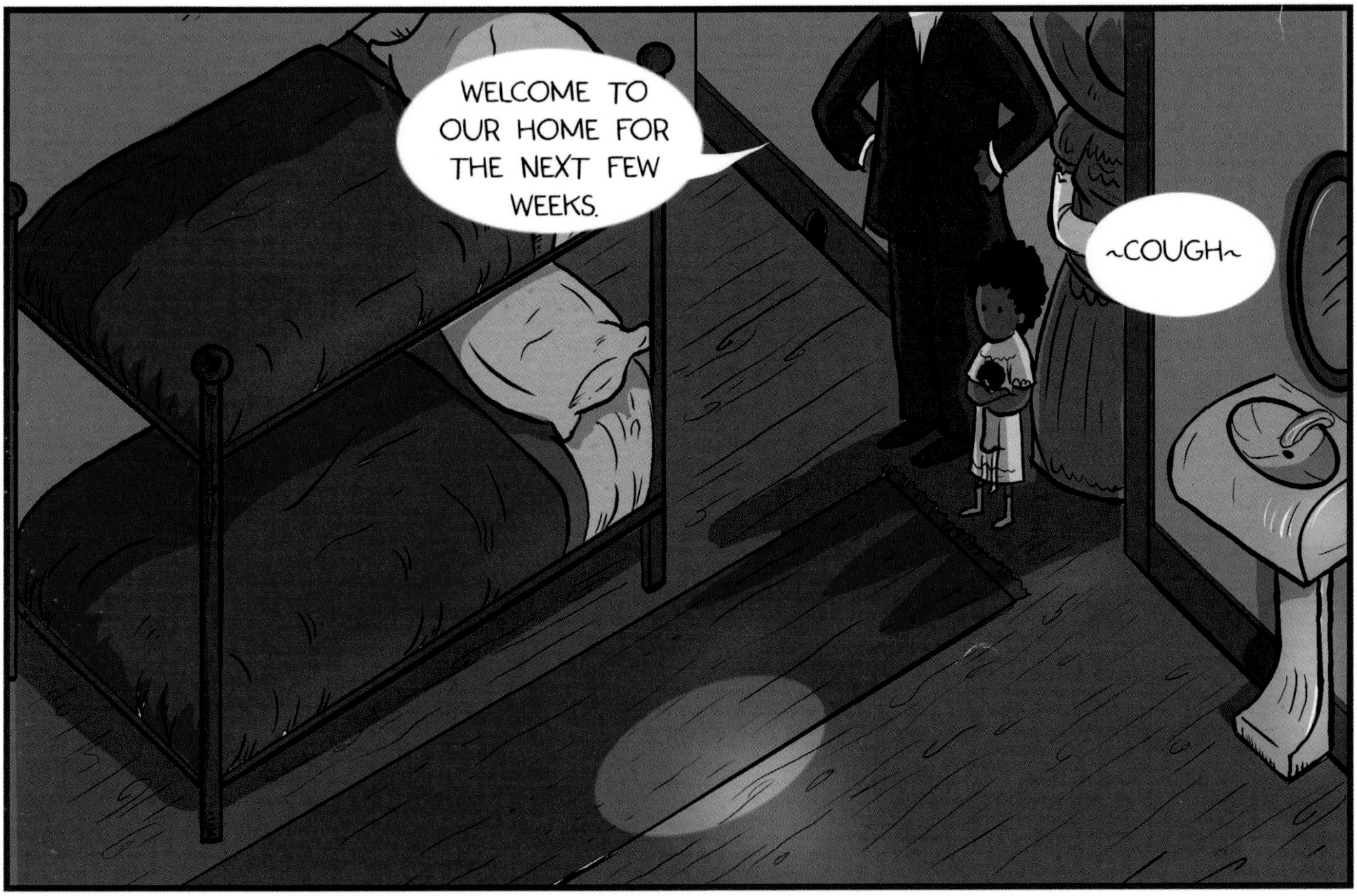
WELCOME TO OUR HOME FOR THE NEXT FEW WEEKS.
~COUGH~

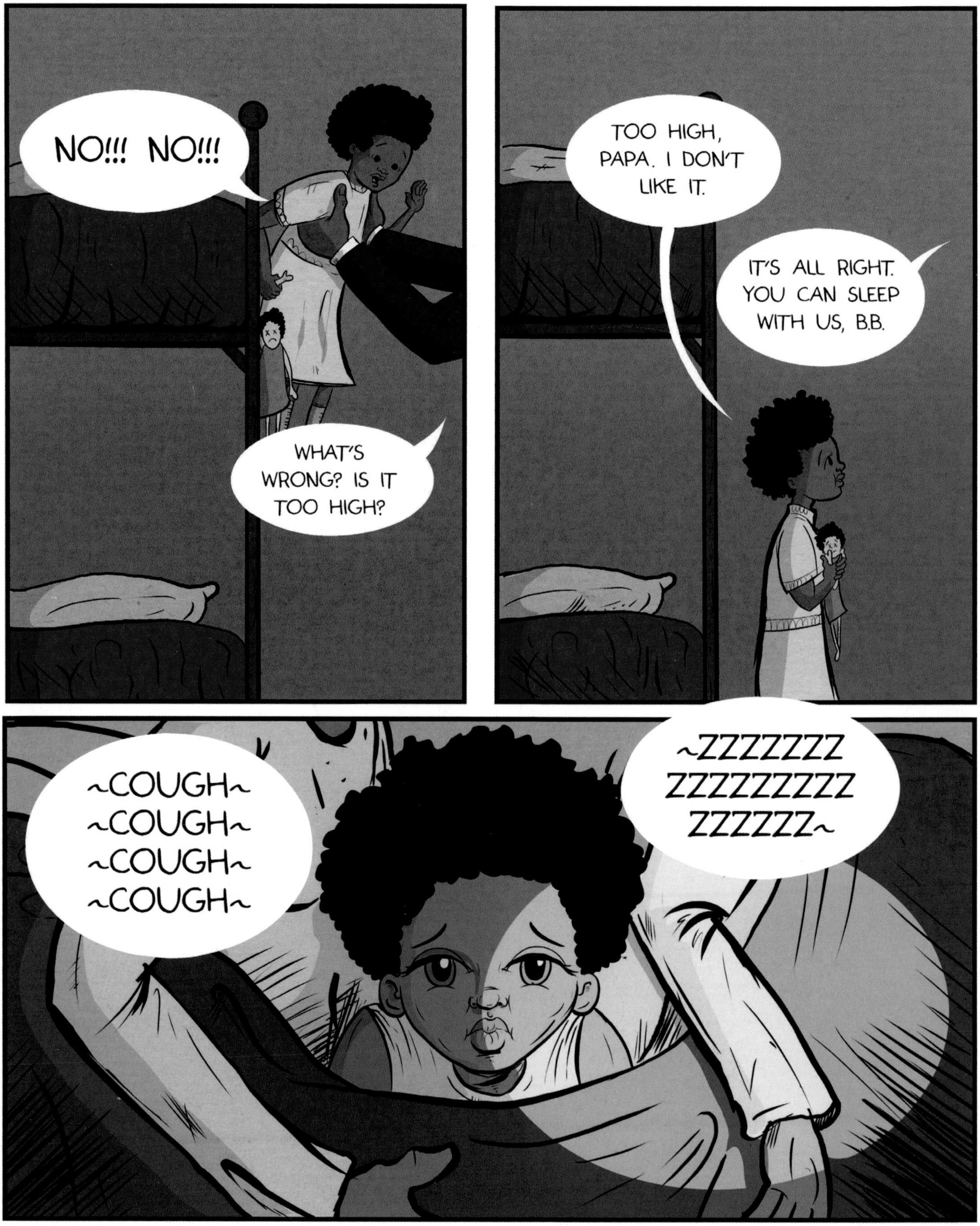
NO!!! NO!!!
WHAT'S WRONG? IS IT TOO HIGH?
TOO HIGH, PAPA. I DON'T LIKE IT.
IT'S ALL RIGHT. YOU CAN SLEEP WITH US, B.B.
~COUGH~ ~COUGH~ ~COUGH~ ~COUGH~
~ZZZZZZZ ZZZZZZZZZ ZZZZZZ~

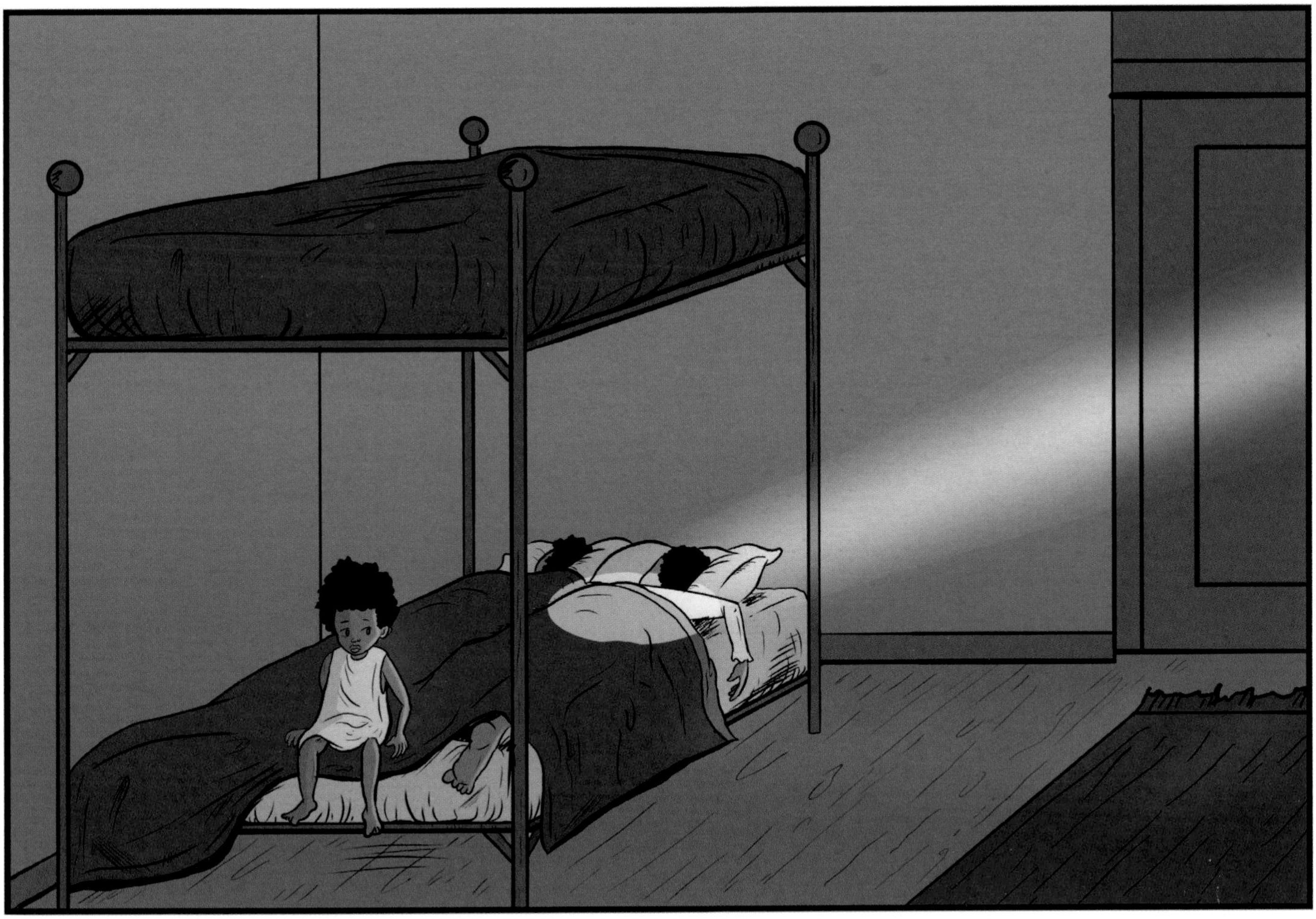

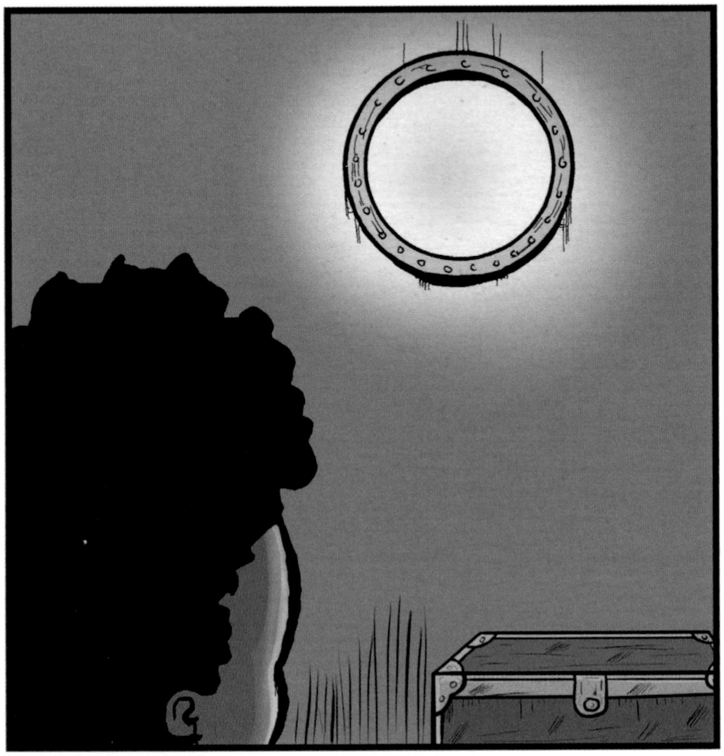

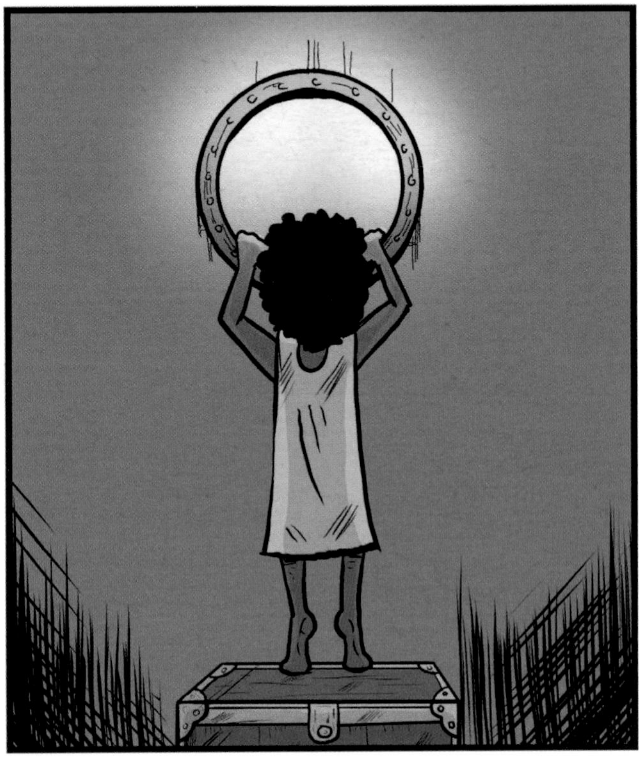

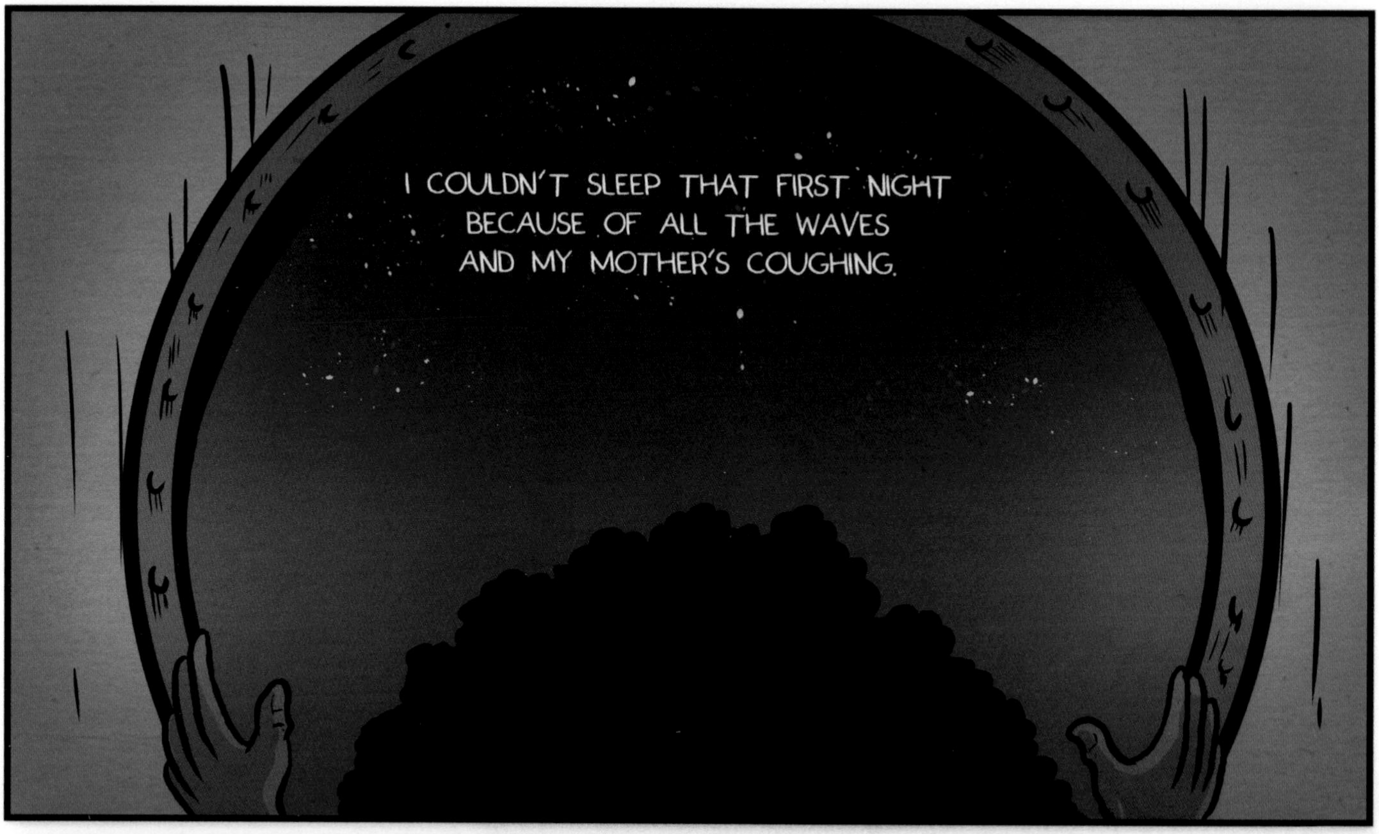
I COULDN'T SLEEP THAT FIRST NIGHT
BECAUSE OF ALL THE WAVES
AND MY MOTHER'S COUGHING.

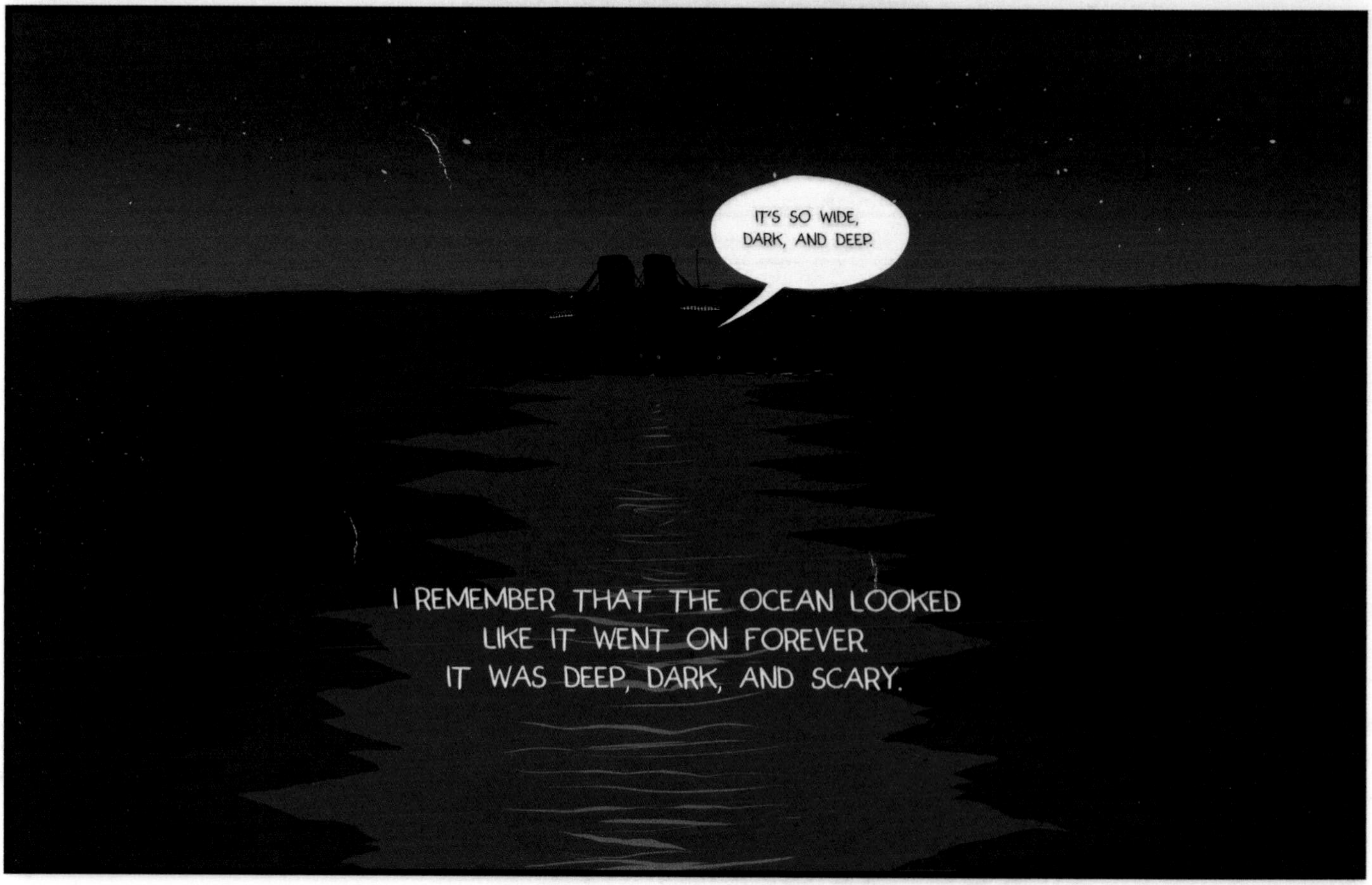
IT'S SO WIDE,
DARK, AND DEEP.
I REMEMBER THAT THE OCEAN LOOKED
LIKE IT WENT ON FOREVER.
IT WAS DEEP, DARK, AND SCARY.

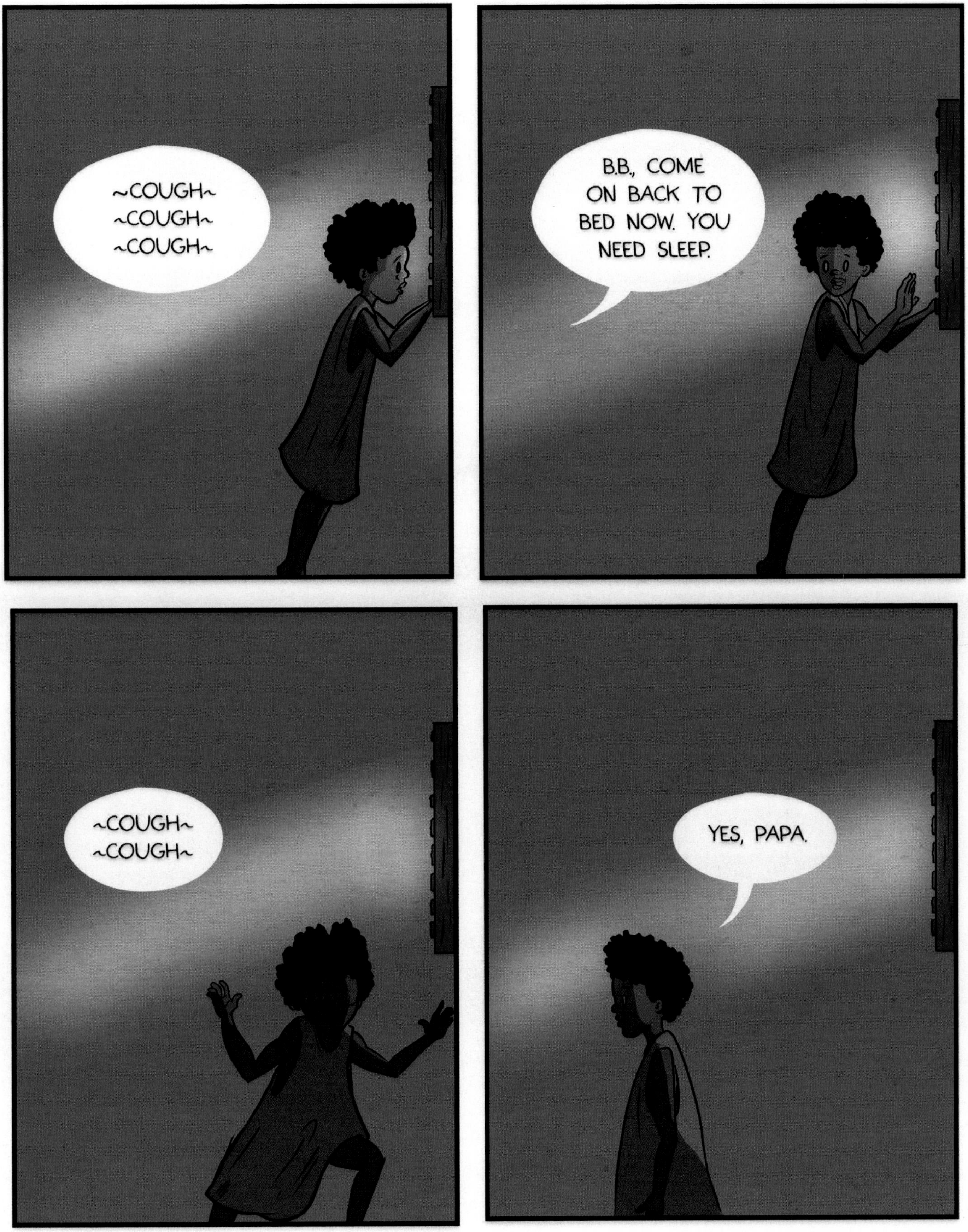
~COUGH~
~COUGH~
~COUGH~
B.B., COME ON BACK TO BED NOW. YOU NEED SLEEP.
~COUGH~
~COUGH~
YES, PAPA.

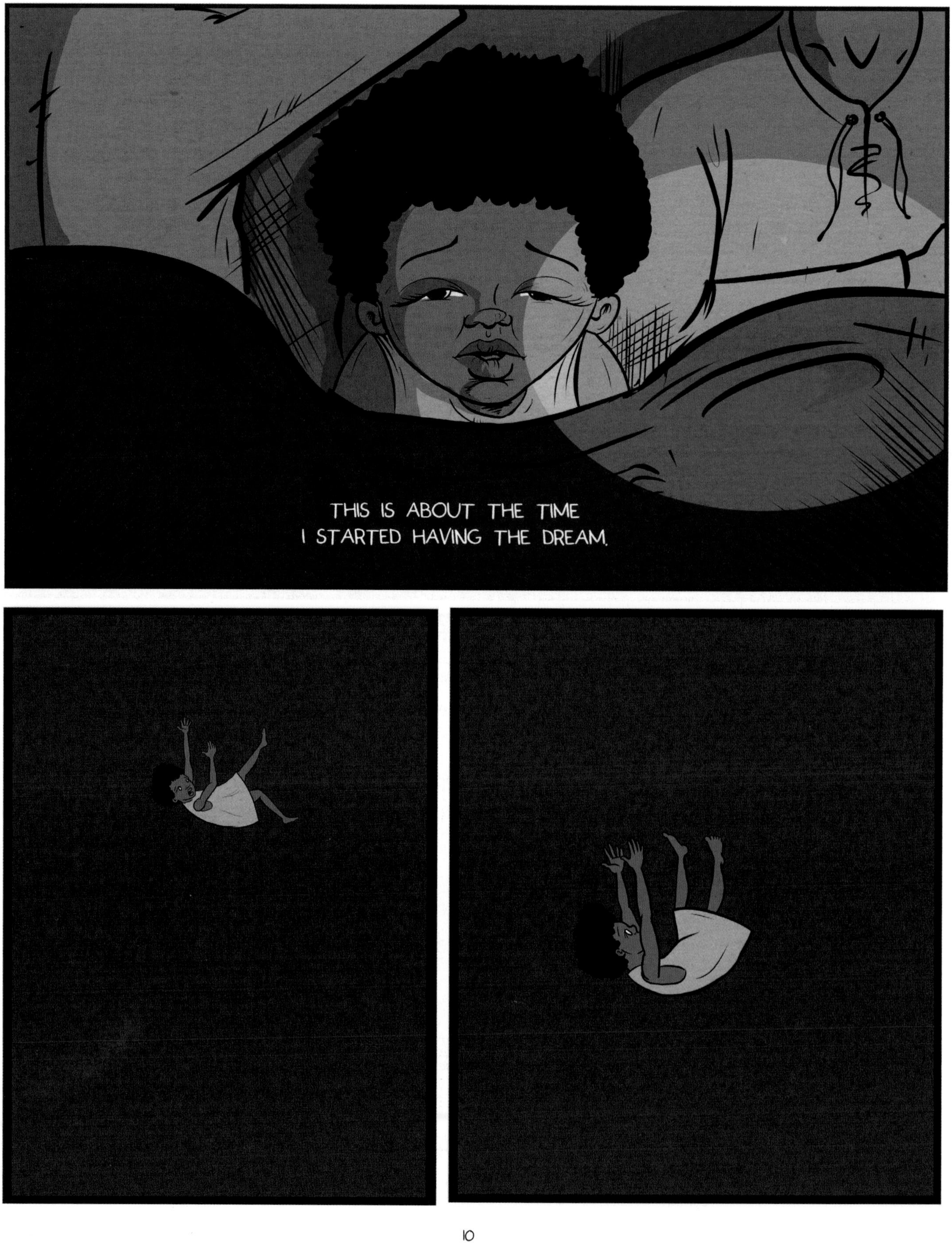
THIS IS ABOUT THE TIME
I STARTED HAVING THE DREAM.

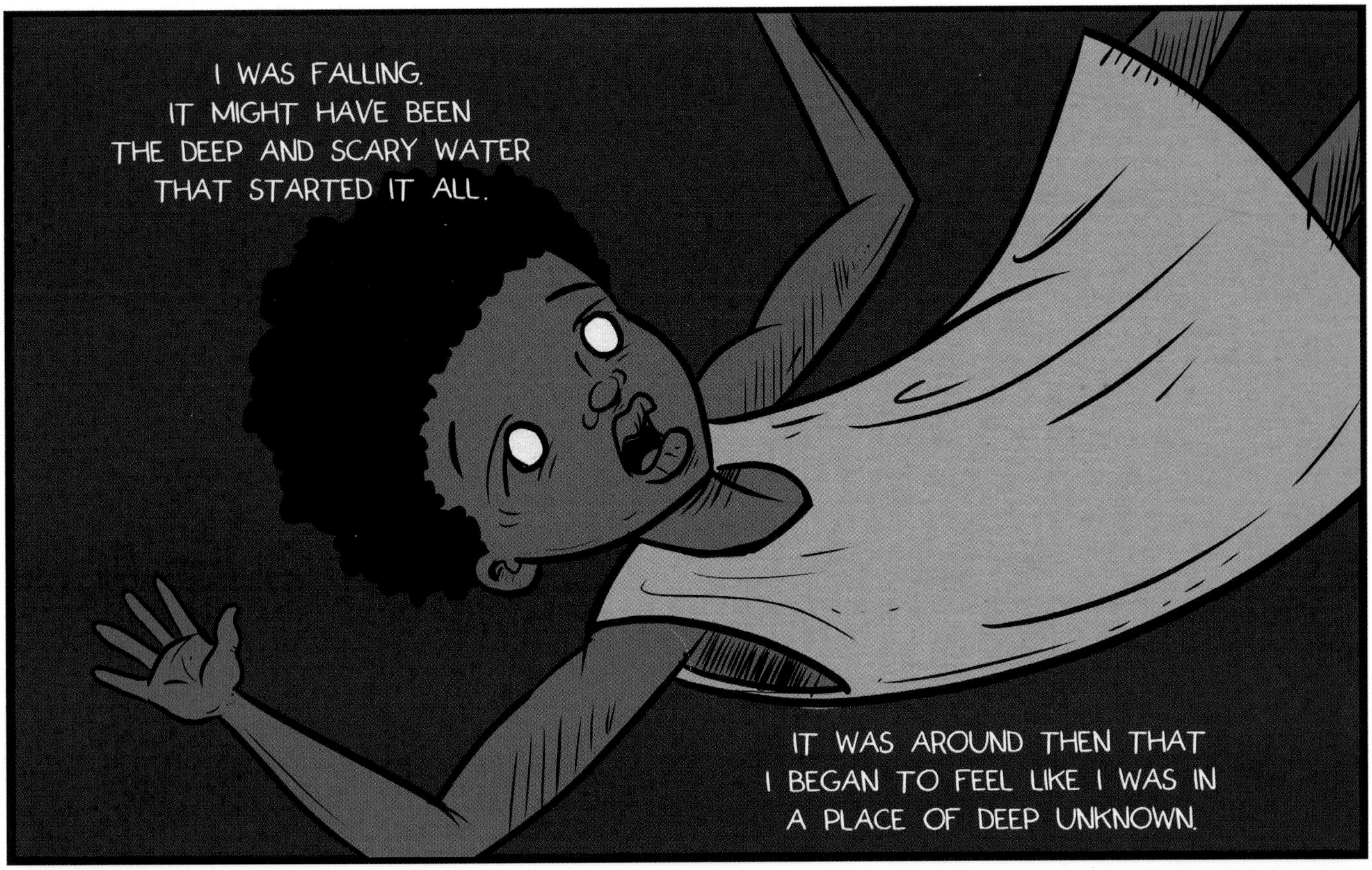
I WAS FALLING.
IT MIGHT HAVE BEEN
THE DEEP AND SCARY WATER
THAT STARTED IT ALL.
IT WAS AROUND THEN THAT
I BEGAN TO FEEL LIKE I WAS IN
A PLACE OF DEEP UNKNOWN.

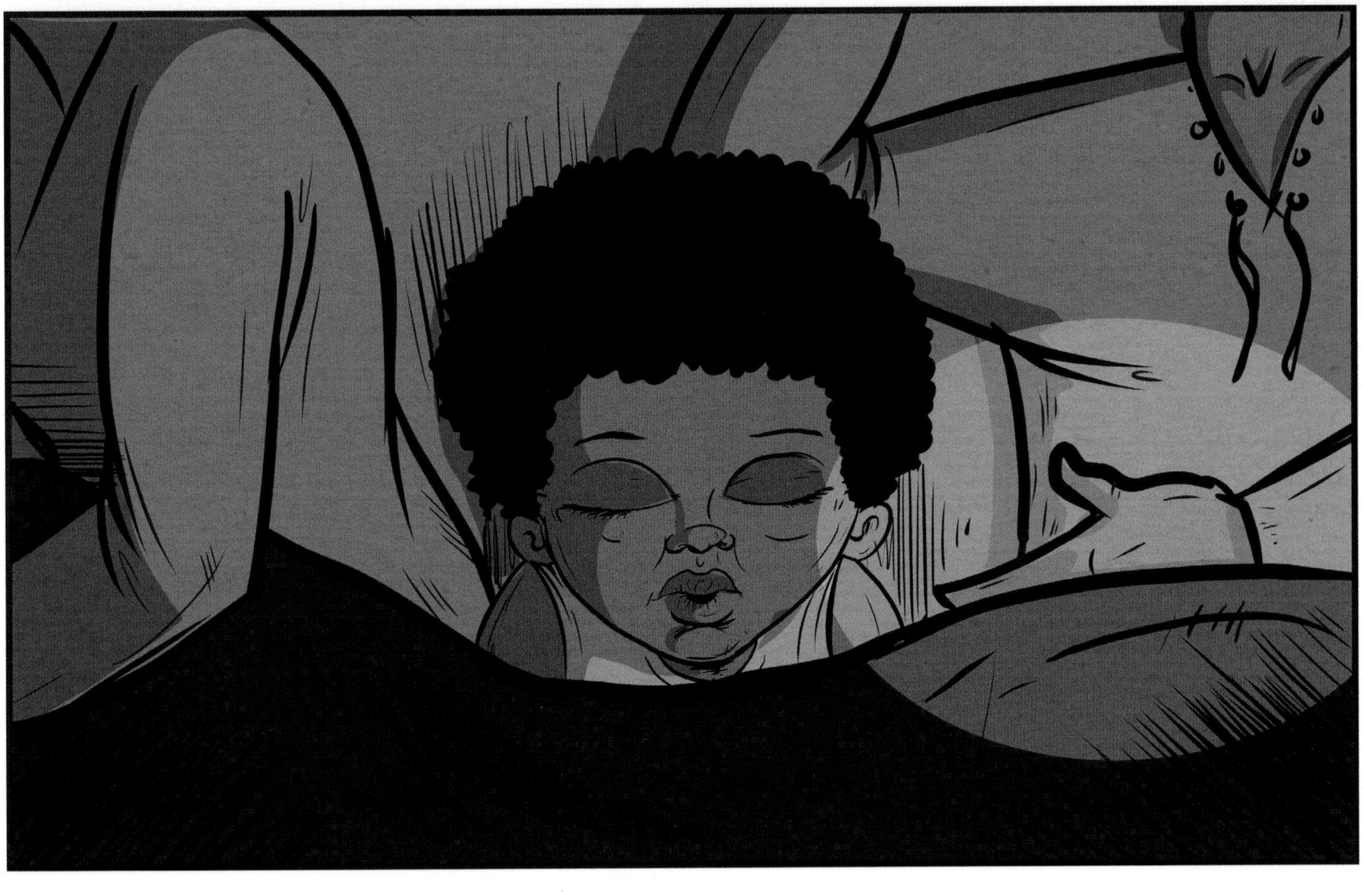

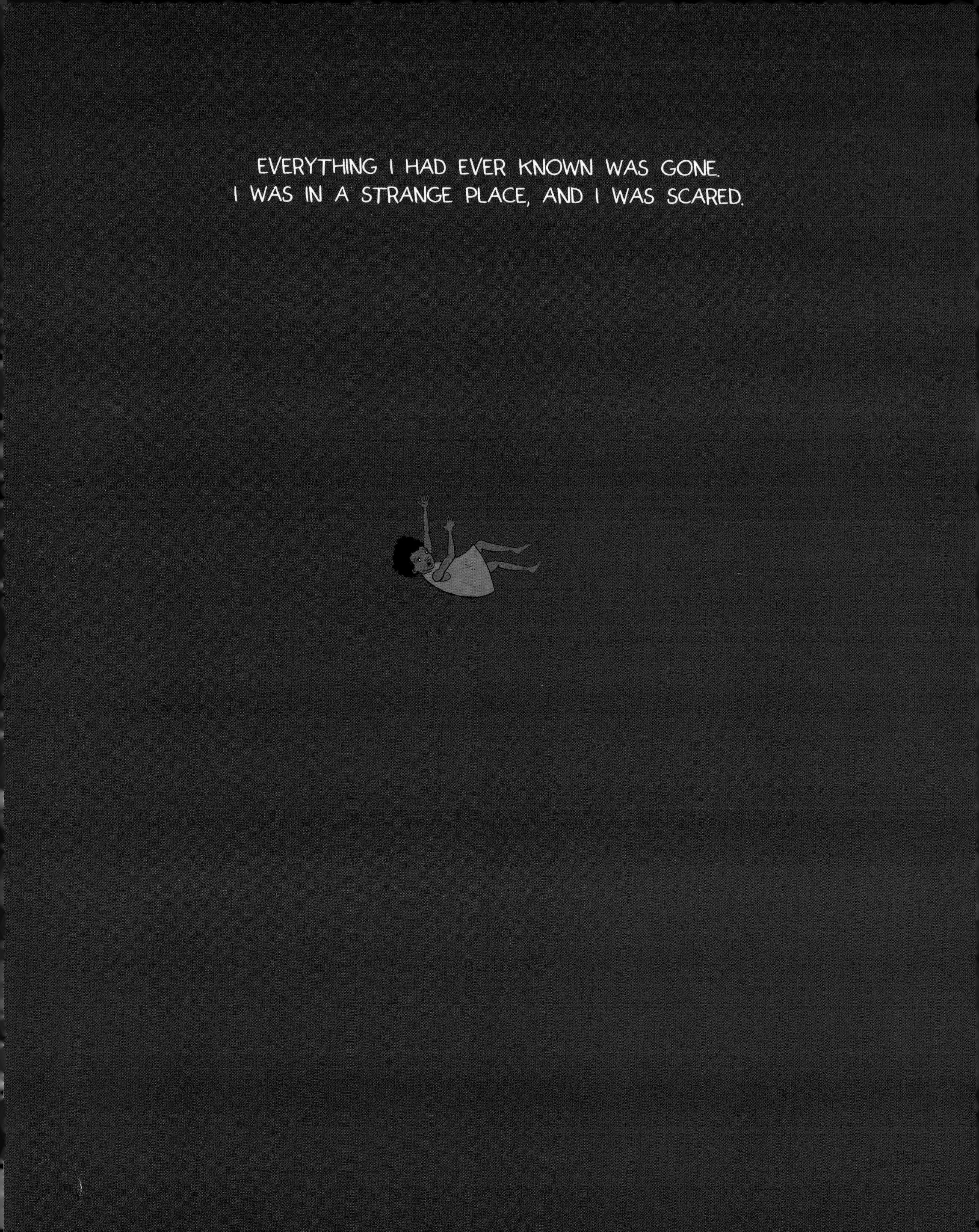
EVERYTHING I HAD EVER KNOWN WAS GONE.
I WAS IN A STRANGE PLACE, AND I WAS SCARED.

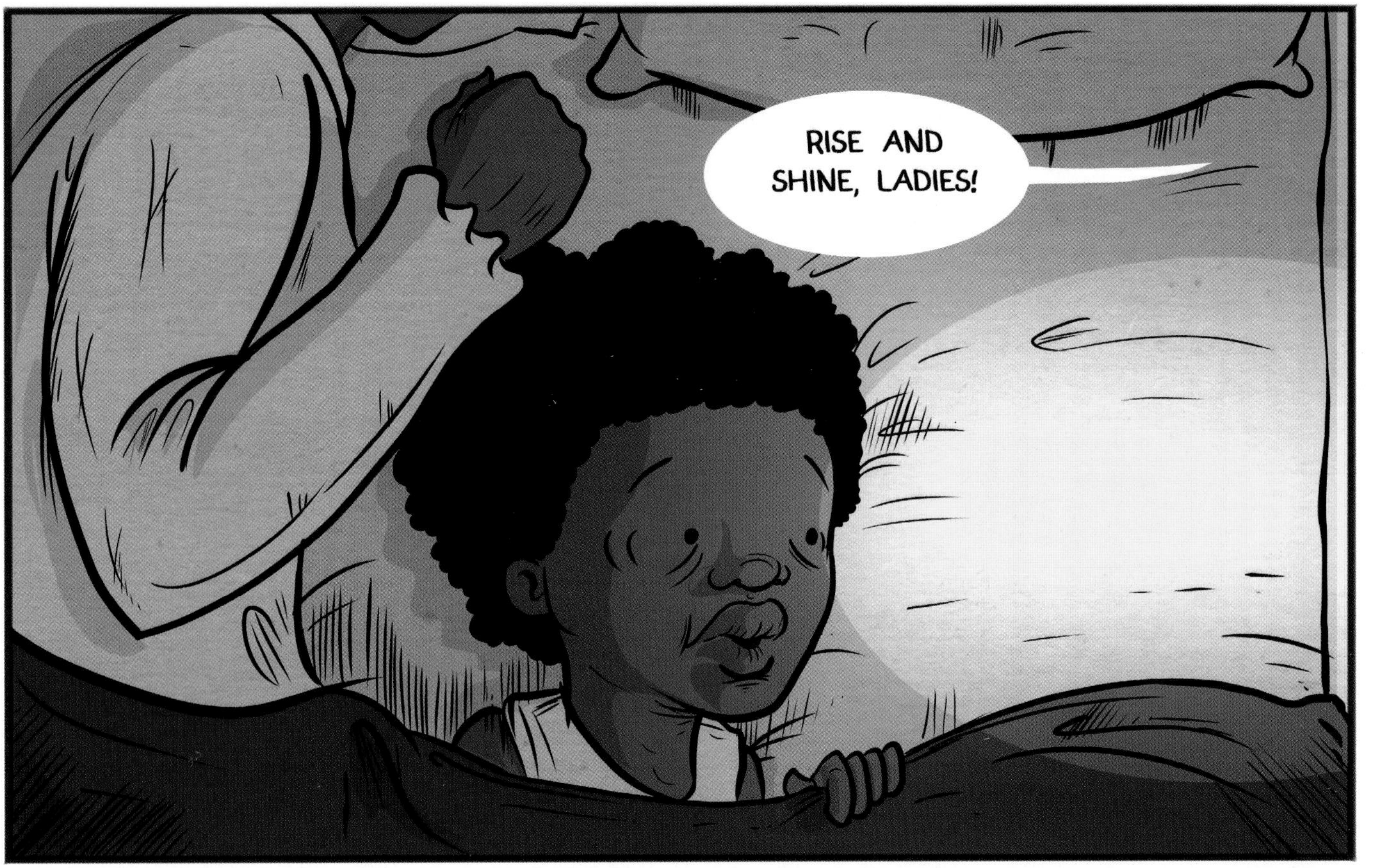
RISE AND SHINE, LADIES!

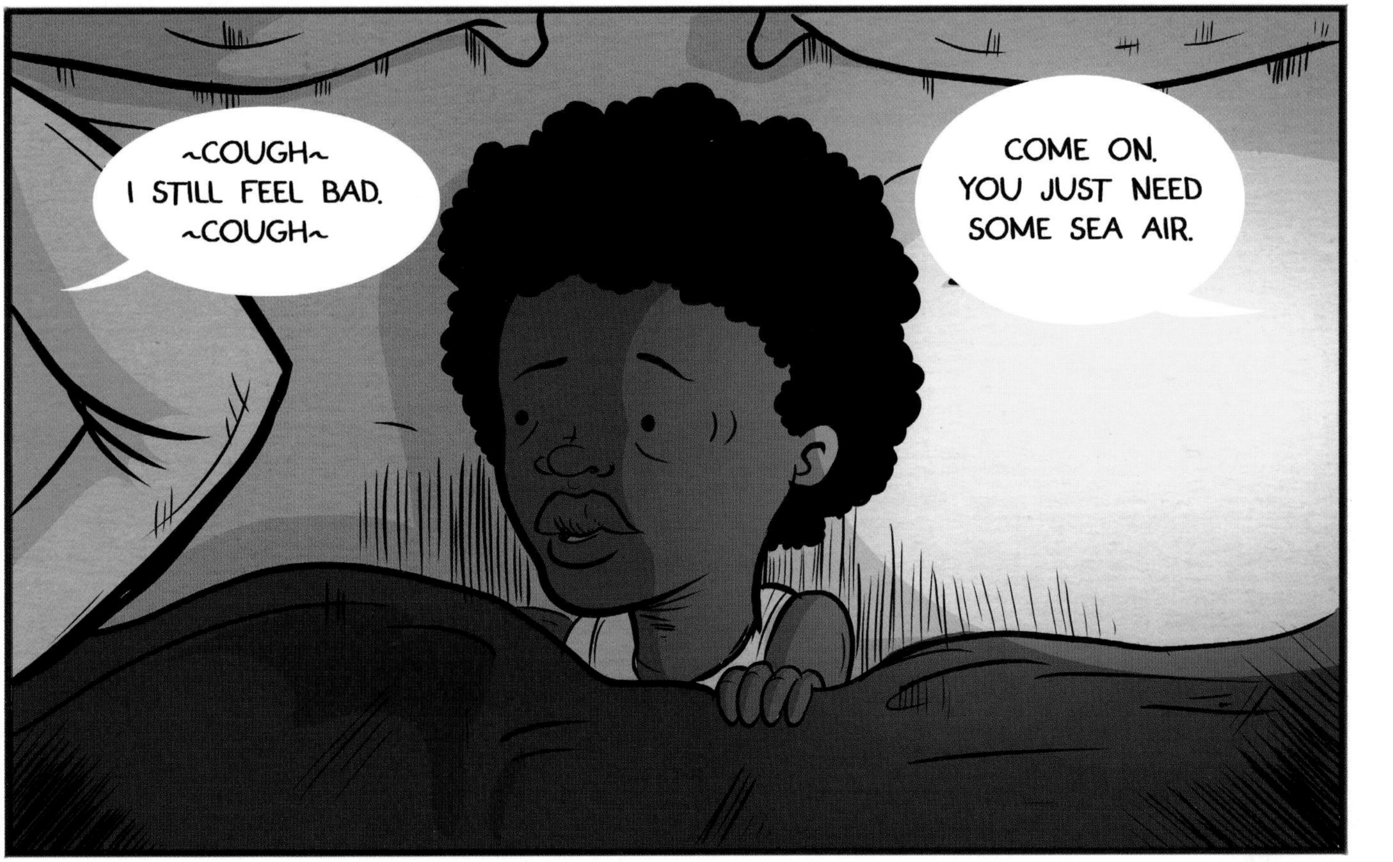
~COUGH~ I STILL FEEL BAD. ~COUGH~
COME ON. YOU JUST NEED SOME SEA AIR.

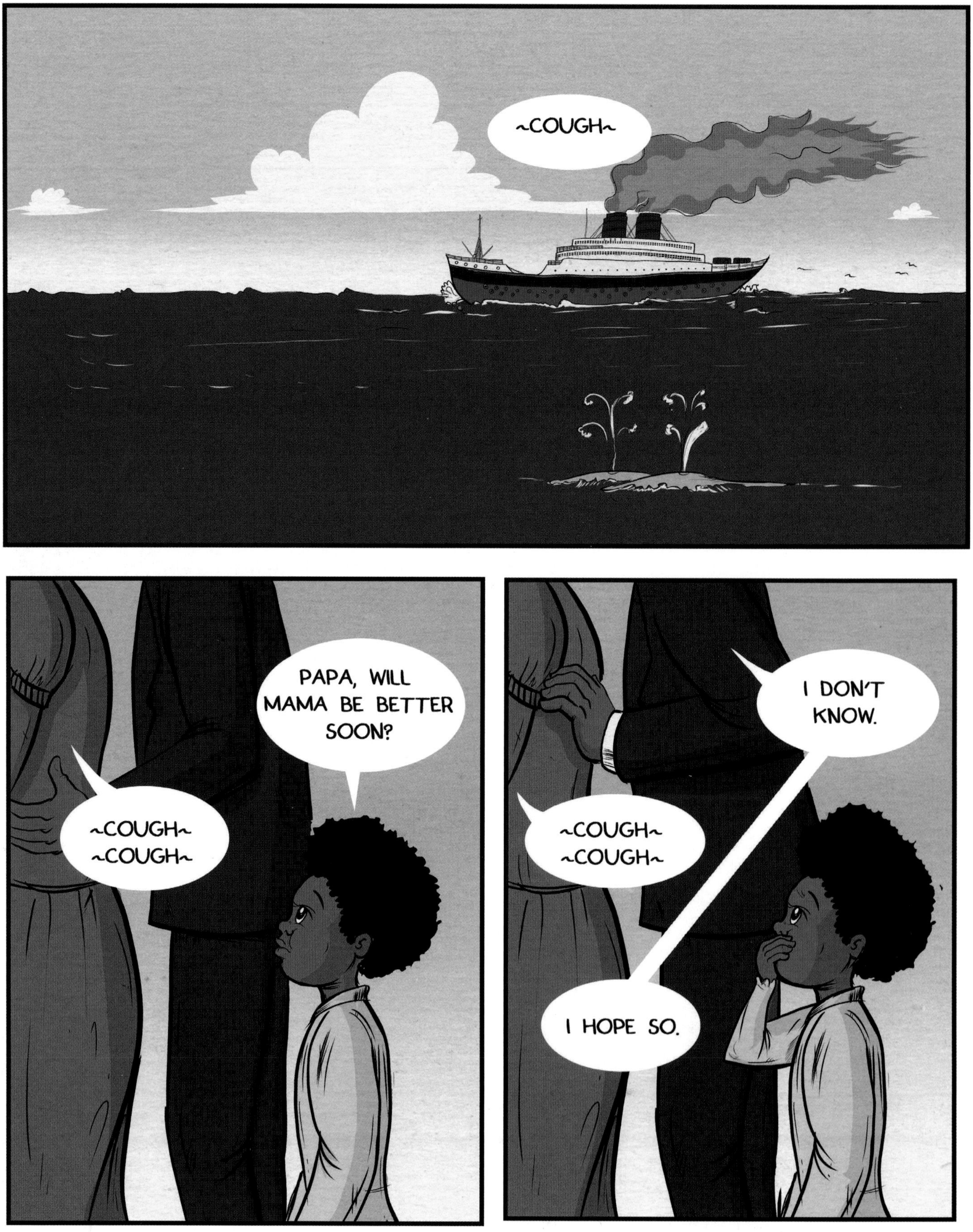
~COUGH~
PAPA, WILL MAMA BE BETTER SOON?
~COUGH~ ~COUGH~
I DON'T KNOW.
I HOPE SO.
~COUGH~ ~COUGH~

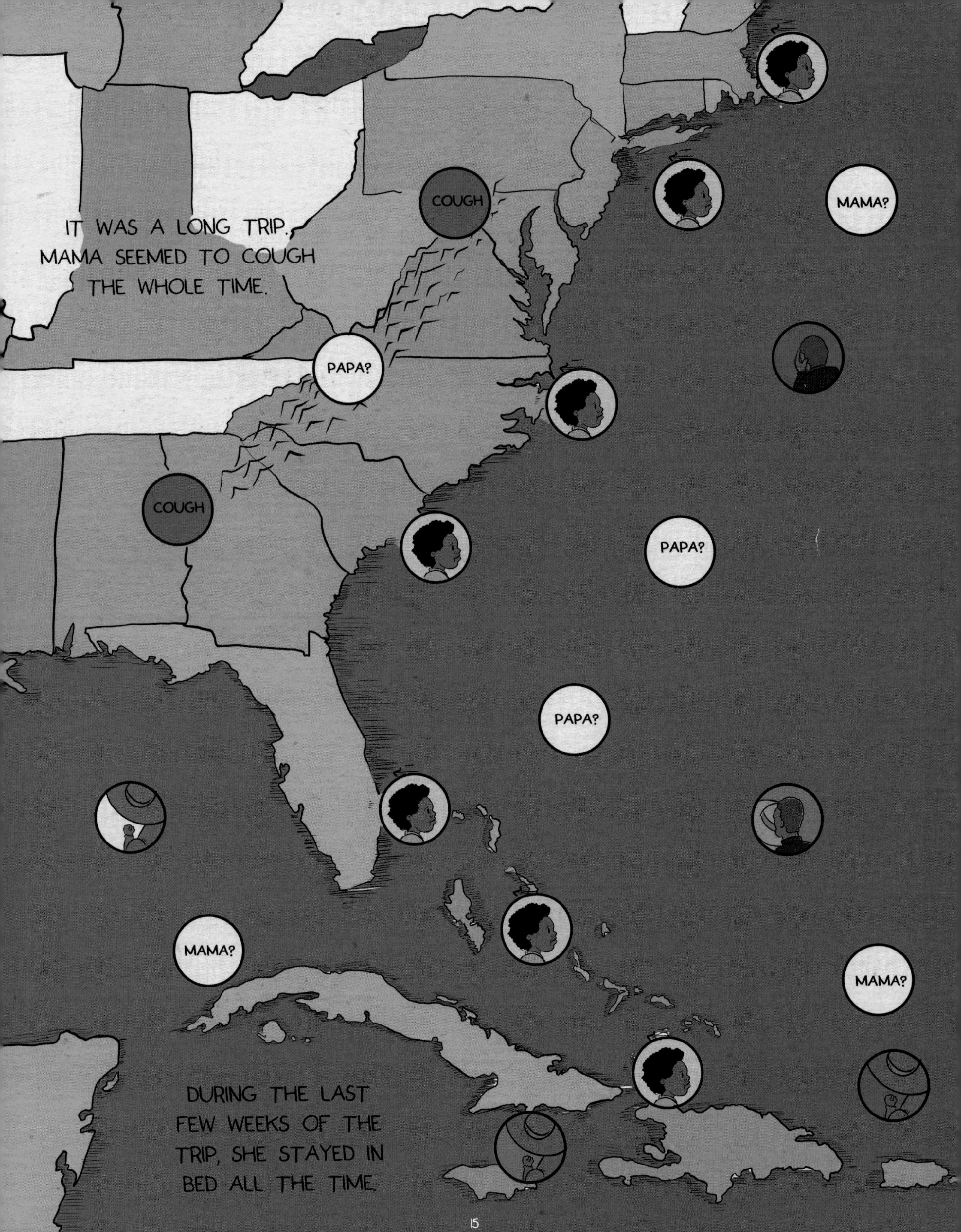
IT WAS A LONG TRIP. MAMA SEEMED TO COUGH THE WHOLE TIME.
COUGH
MAMA?
PAPA?
COUGH
PAPA?
PAPA?
MAMA?
MAMA?
DURING THE LAST FEW WEEKS OF THE TRIP, SHE STAYED IN BED ALL THE TIME.

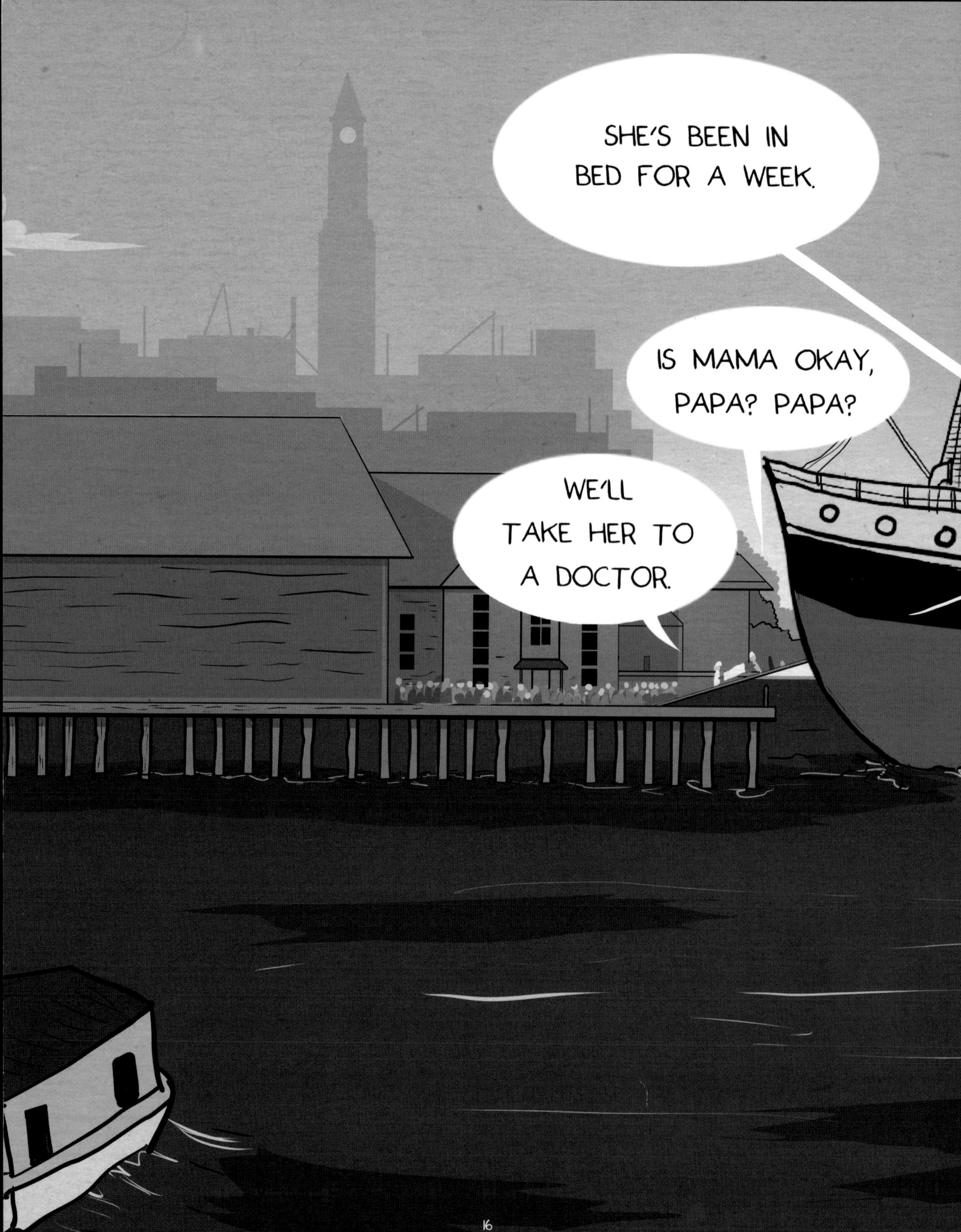
SHE'S BEEN IN BED FOR A WEEK.
IS MAMA OKAY, PAPA? PAPA?
WE'LL TAKE HER TO A DOCTOR.

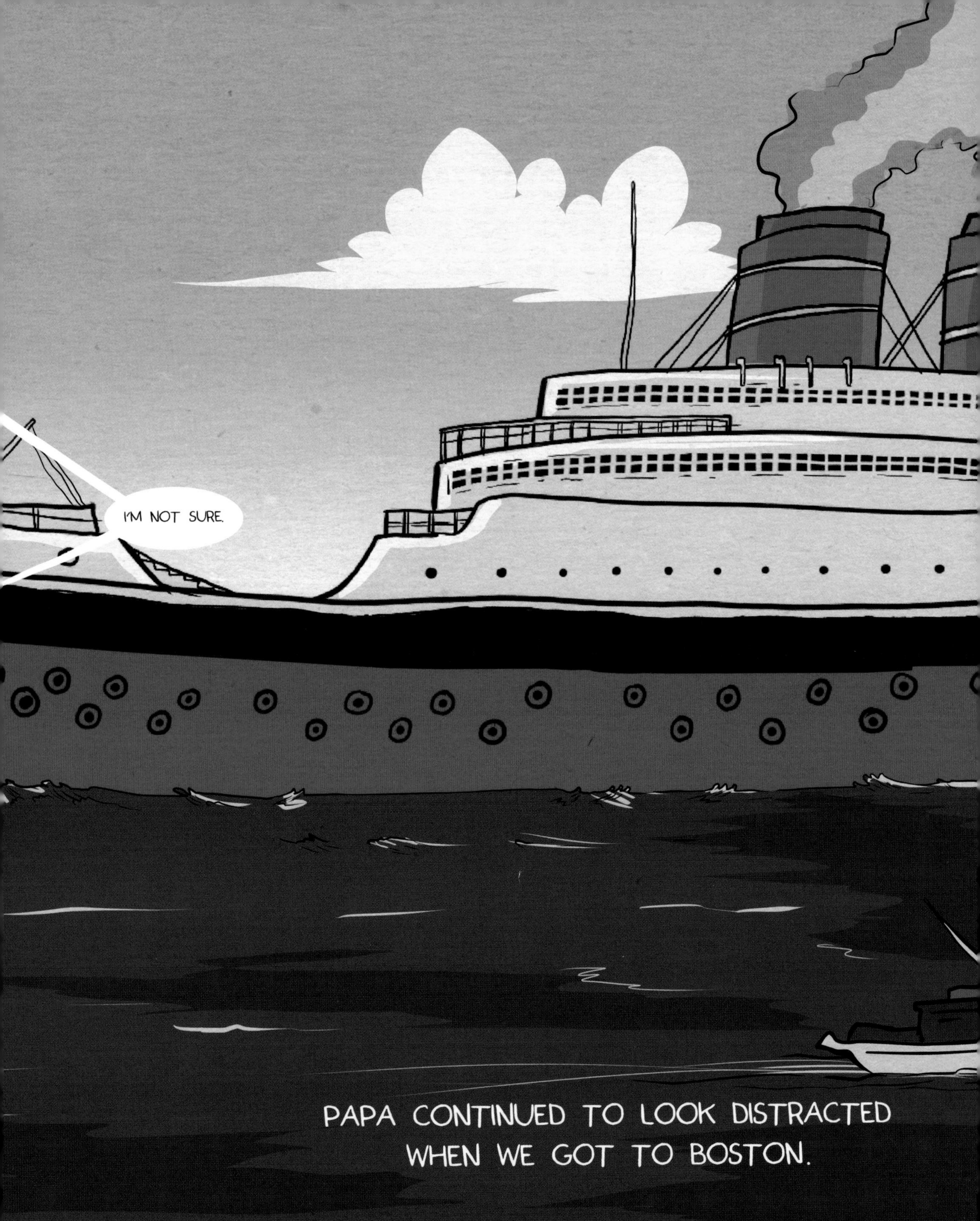
I'M NOT SURE.
PAPA CONTINUED TO LOOK DISTRACTED WHEN WE GOT TO BOSTON.

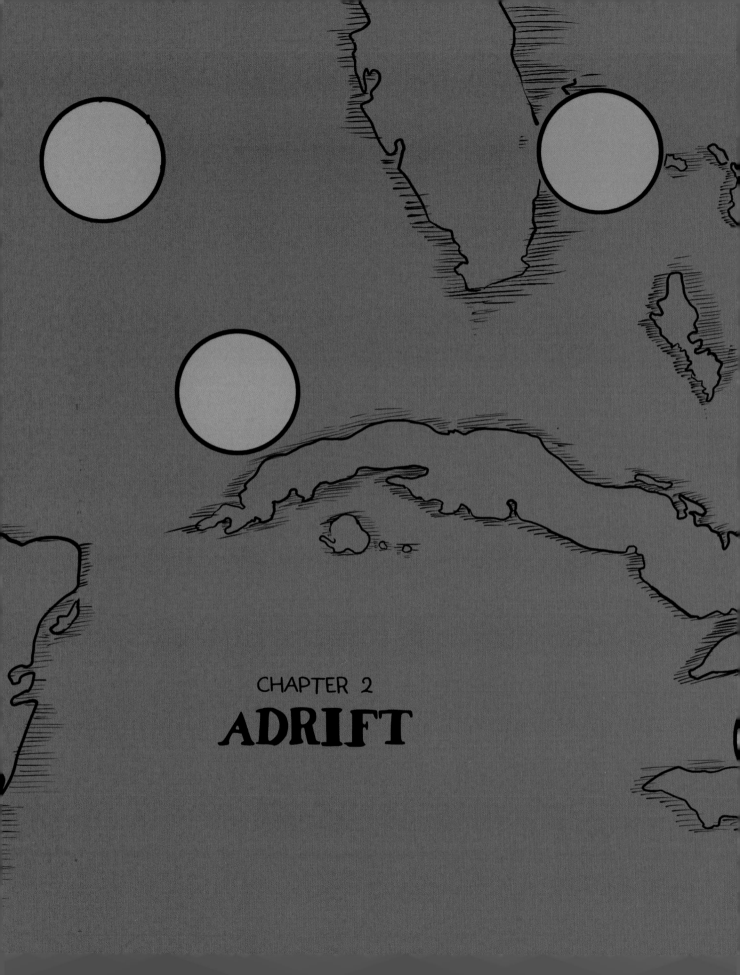

CHAPTER 2
ADRIFT

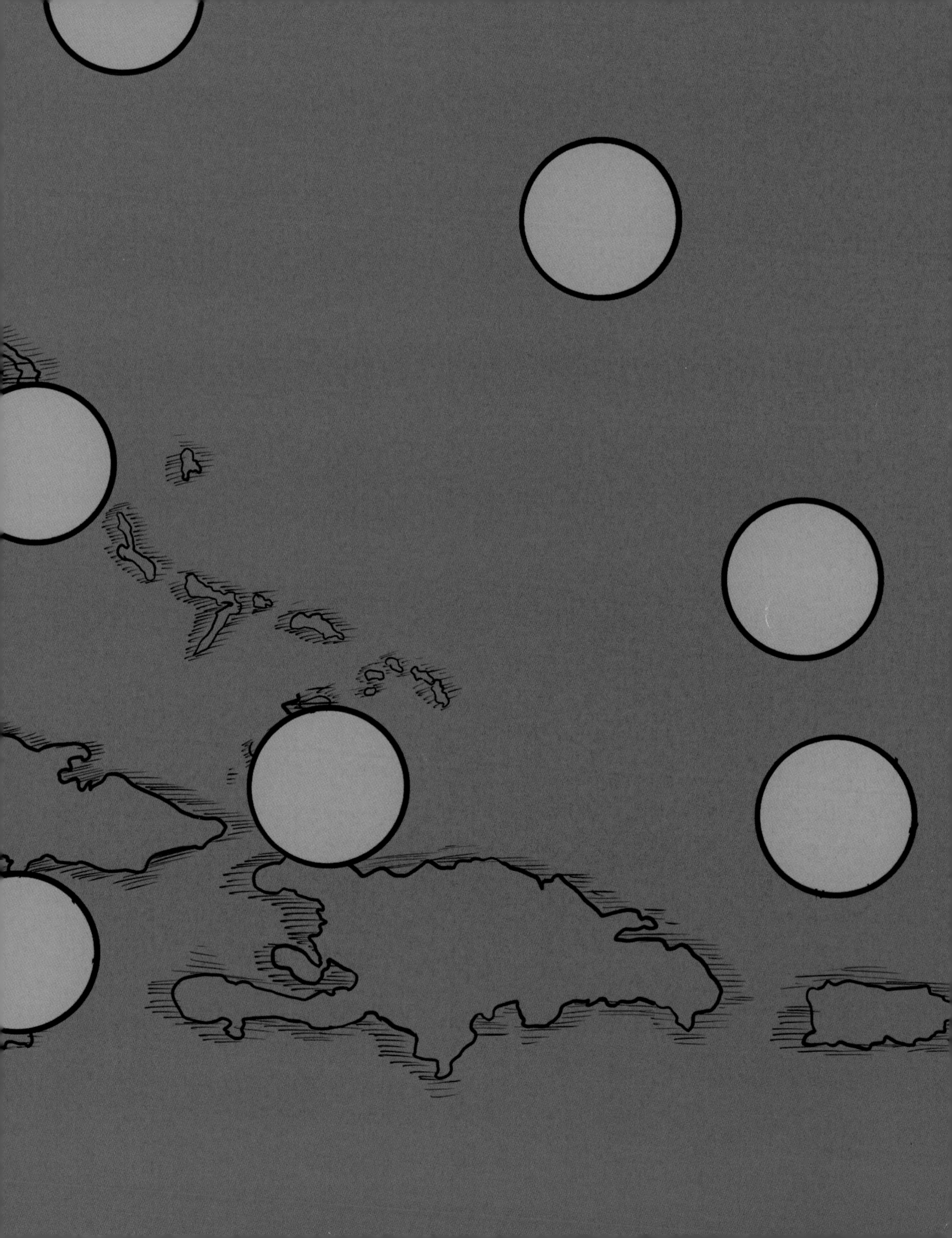

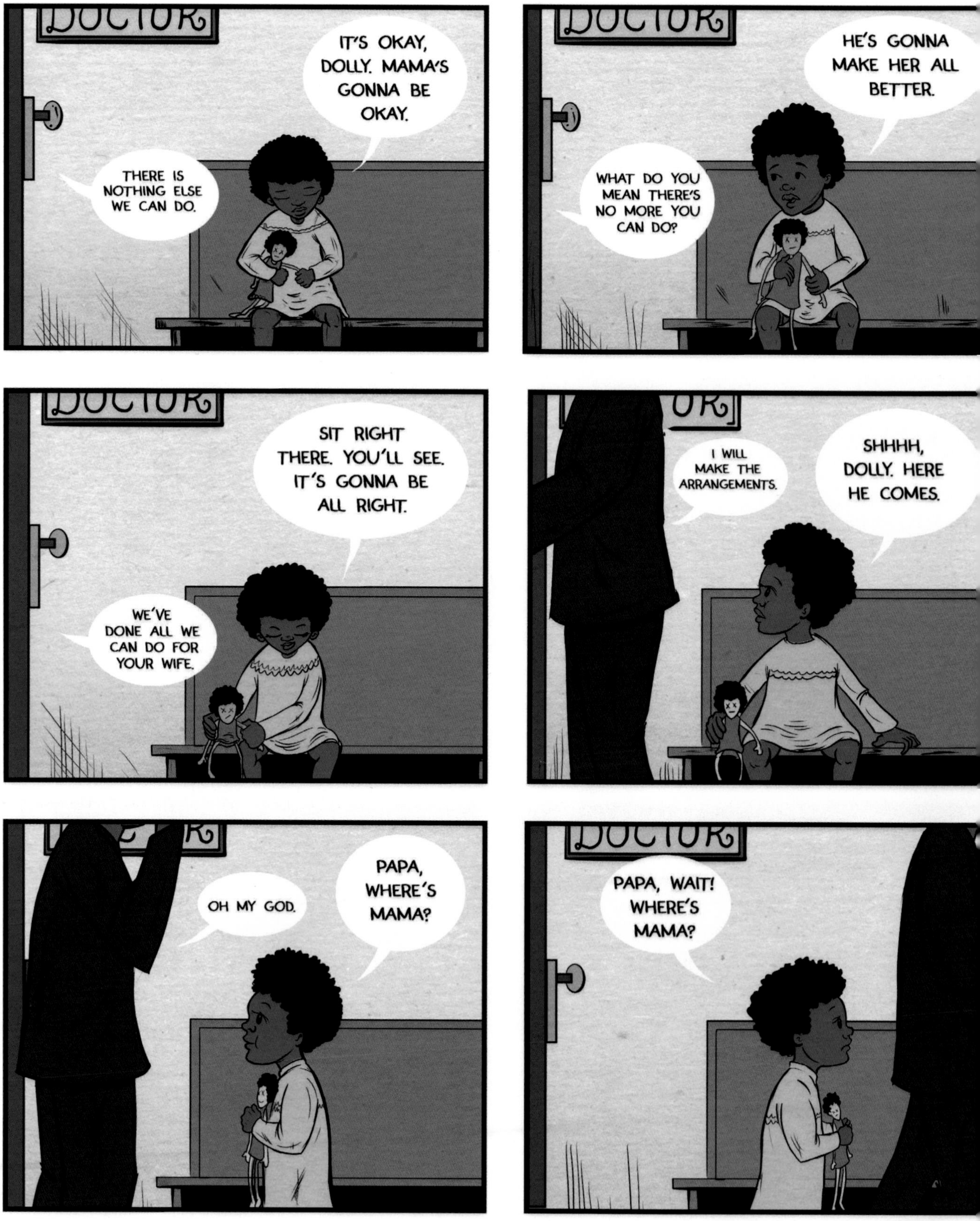
IT'S OKAY, DOLLY. MAMA'S GONNA BE OKAY.
THERE IS NOTHING ELSE WE CAN DO.
HE'S GONNA MAKE HER ALL BETTER.
WHAT DO YOU MEAN THERE'S NO MORE YOU CAN DO?
SIT RIGHT THERE. YOU'LL SEE. IT'S GONNA BE ALL RIGHT.
WE'VE DONE ALL WE CAN DO FOR YOUR WIFE.
I WILL MAKE THE ARRANGEMENTS.
SHHHH, DOLLY. HERE HE COMES.
OH MY GOD.
PAPA, WHERE'S MAMA?
PAPA, WAIT! WHERE'S MAMA?

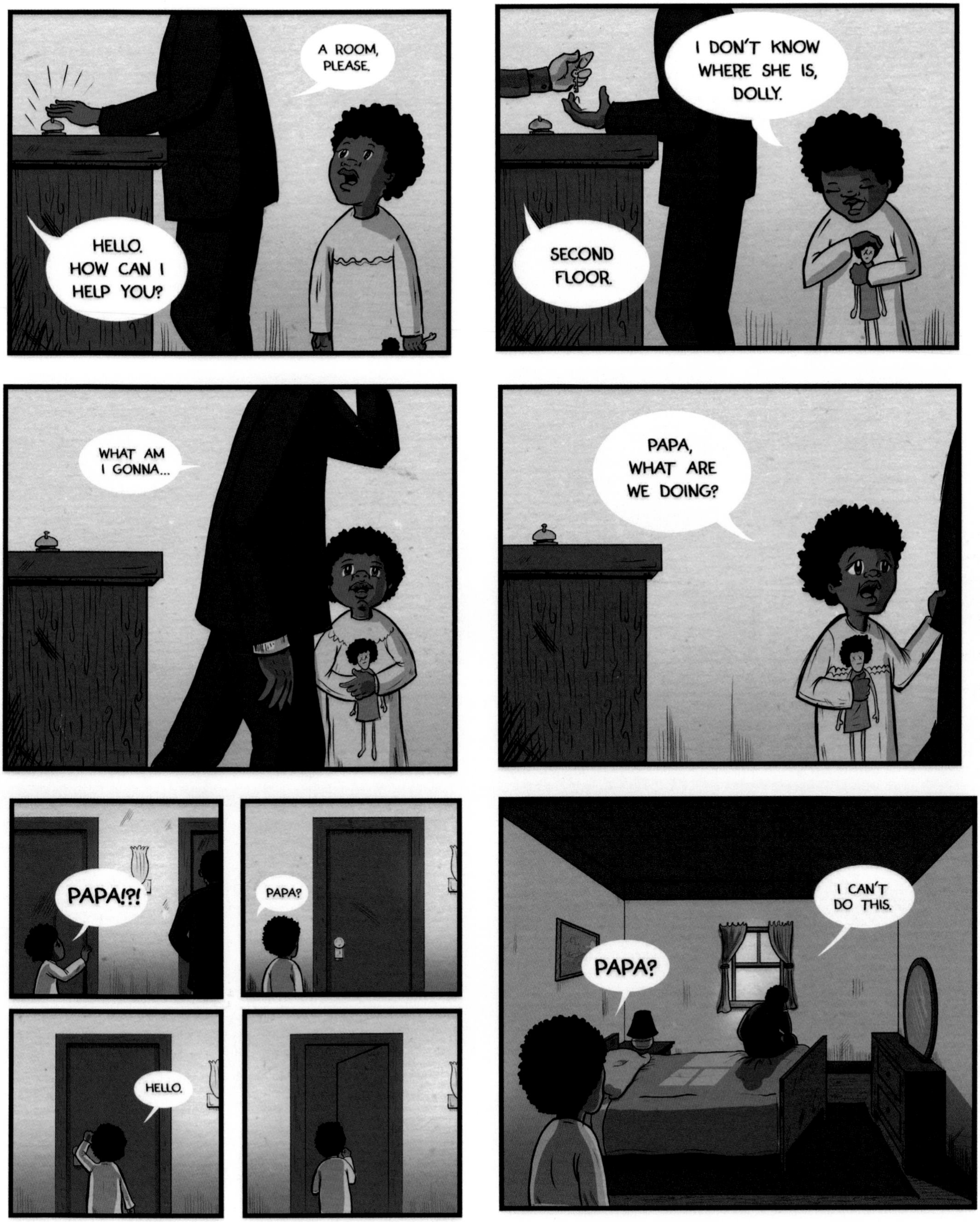
HELLO.
HOW CAN I
HELP YOU?
A ROOM,
PLEASE.
SECOND
FLOOR.
I DON'T KNOW
WHERE SHE IS,
DOLLY.
WHAT AM
I GONNA...
PAPA,
WHAT ARE
WE DOING?
PAPA!?!
PAPA?
HELLO.
PAPA?
I CAN'T
DO THIS.

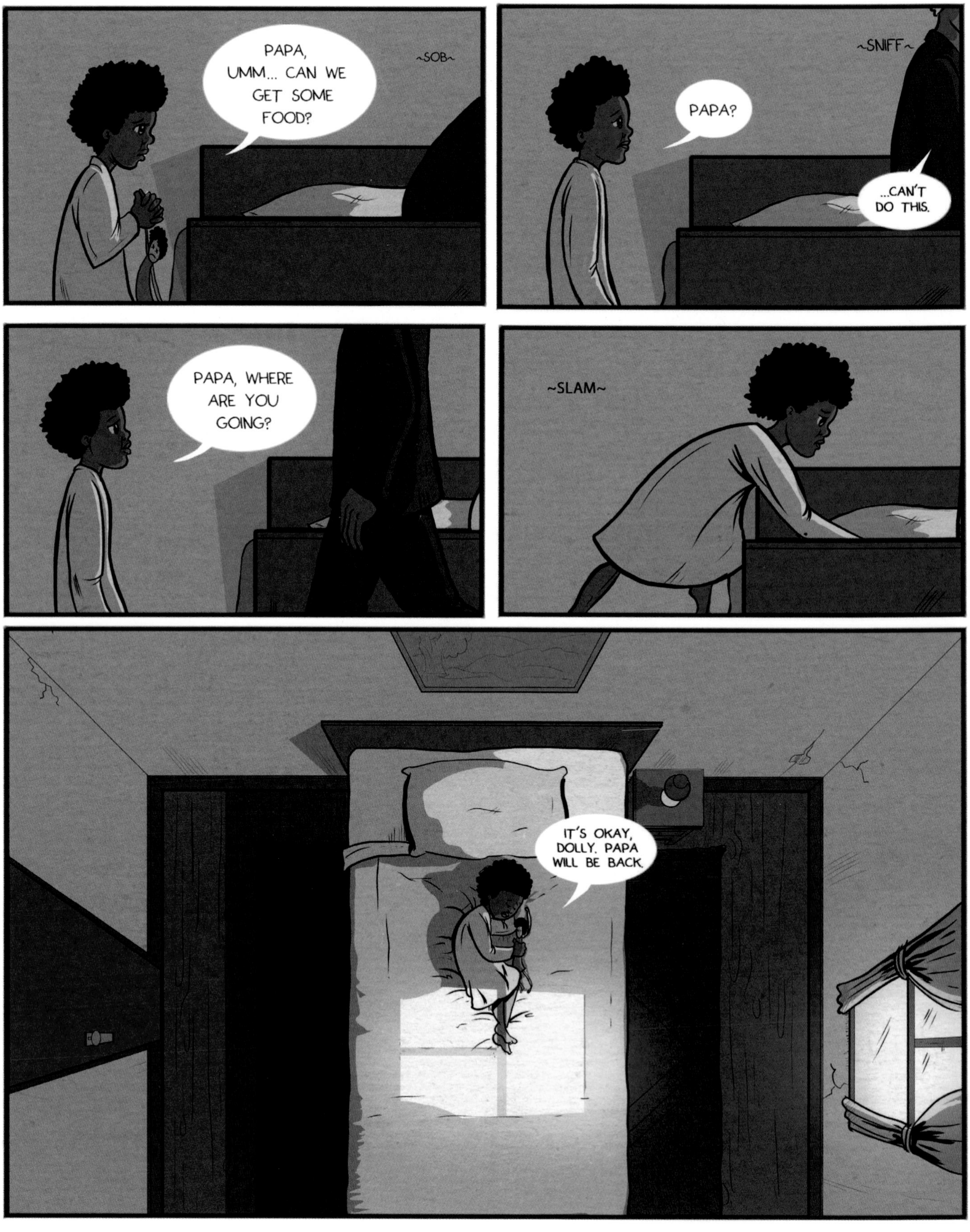

PAPA, UMM... CAN WE GET SOME FOOD?
~SOB~
~SNIFF~
PAPA?
...CAN'T DO THIS.
PAPA, WHERE ARE YOU GOING?
~SLAM~
IT'S OKAY, DOLLY. PAPA WILL BE BACK.

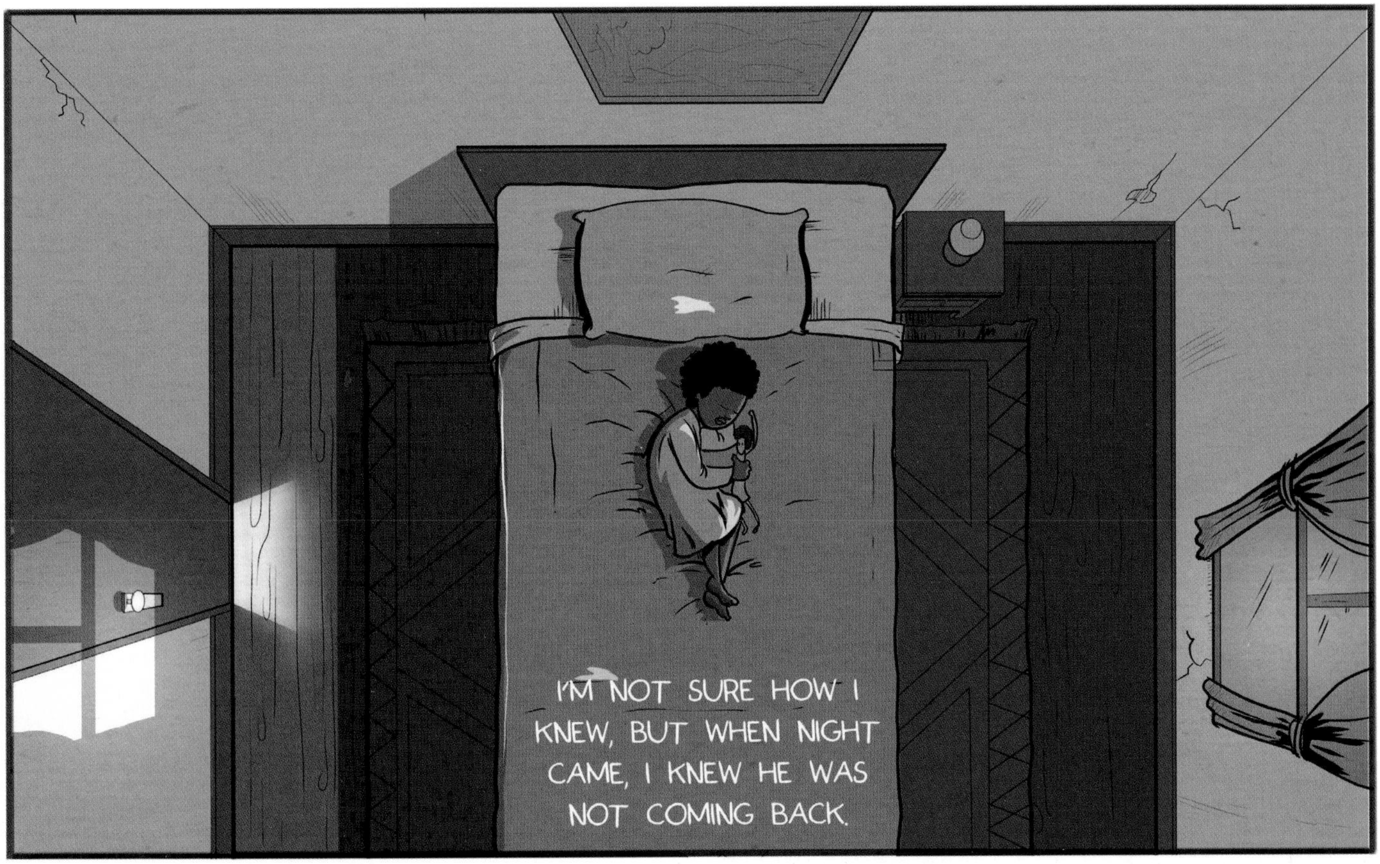
I'M NOT SURE HOW I KNEW, BUT WHEN NIGHT CAME, I KNEW HE WAS NOT COMING BACK.

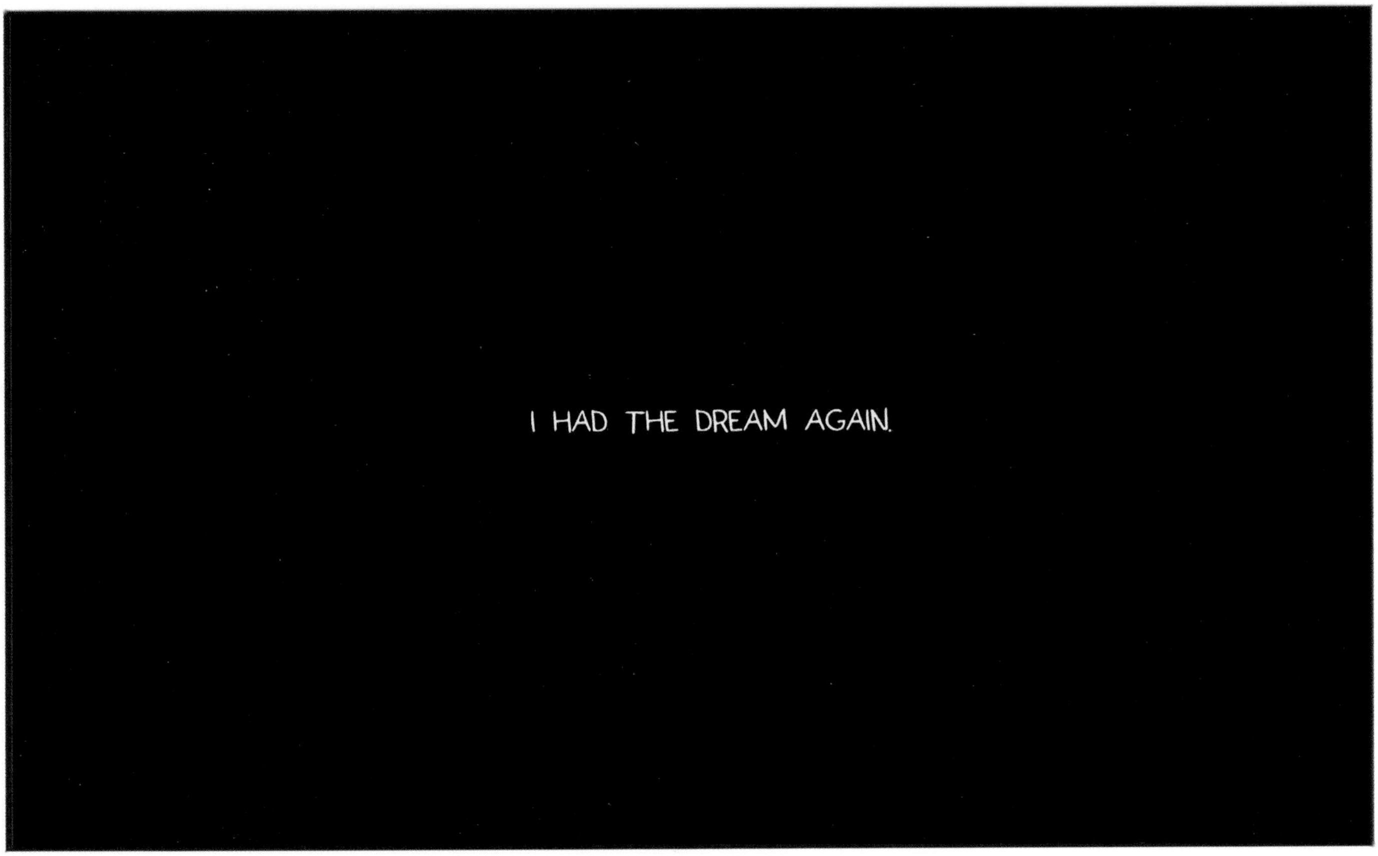
I HAD THE DREAM AGAIN.

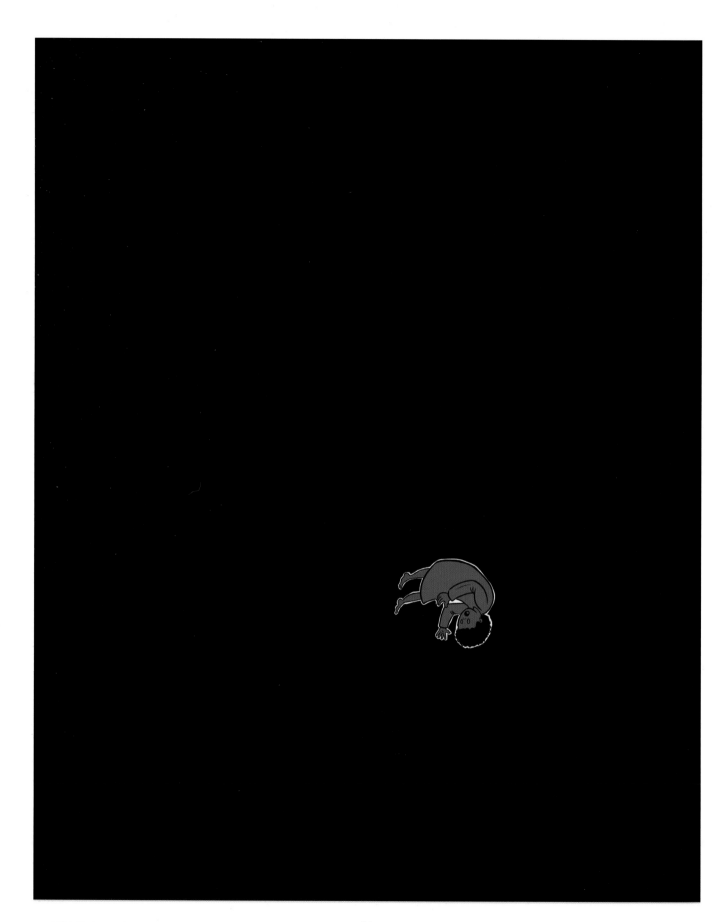

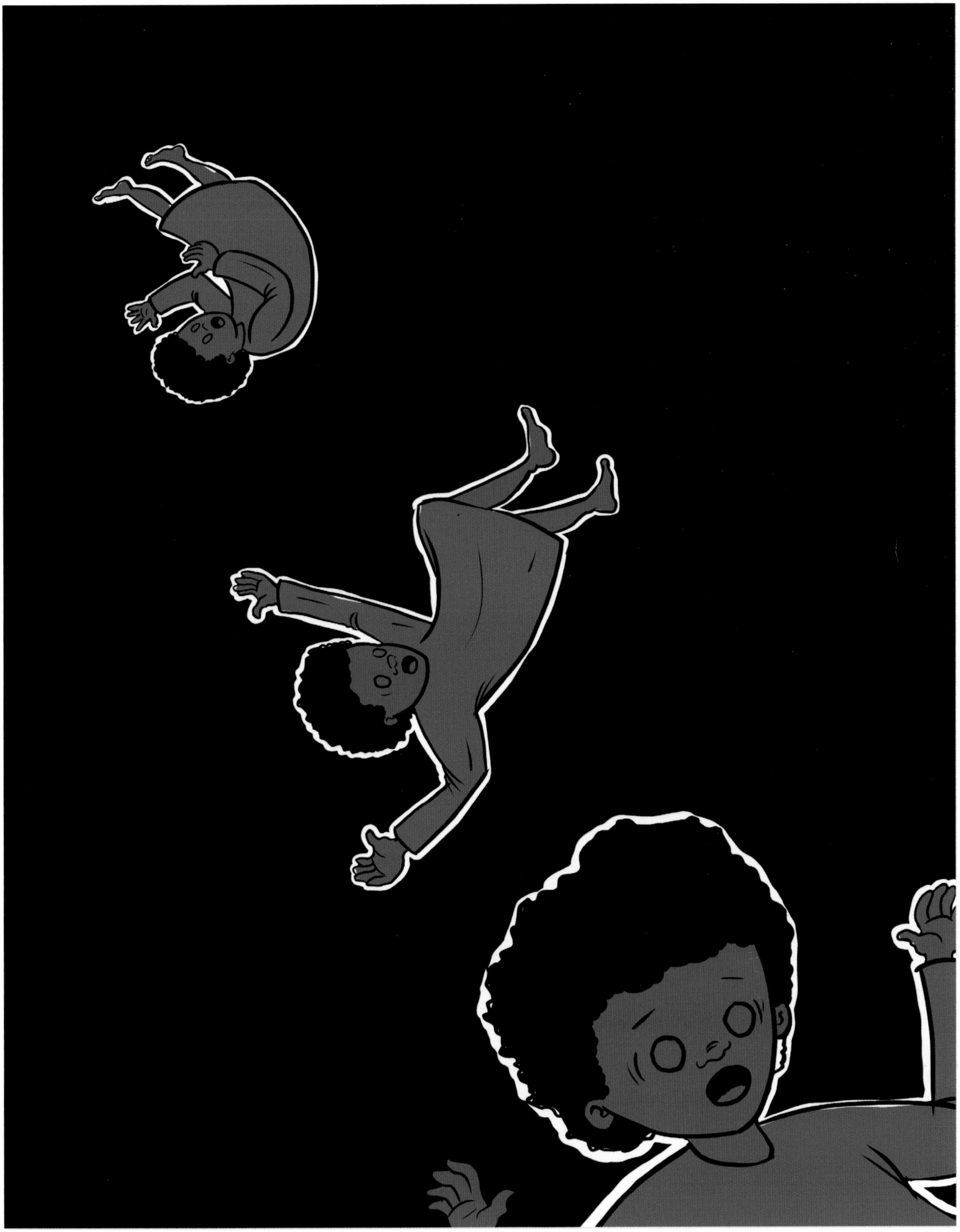

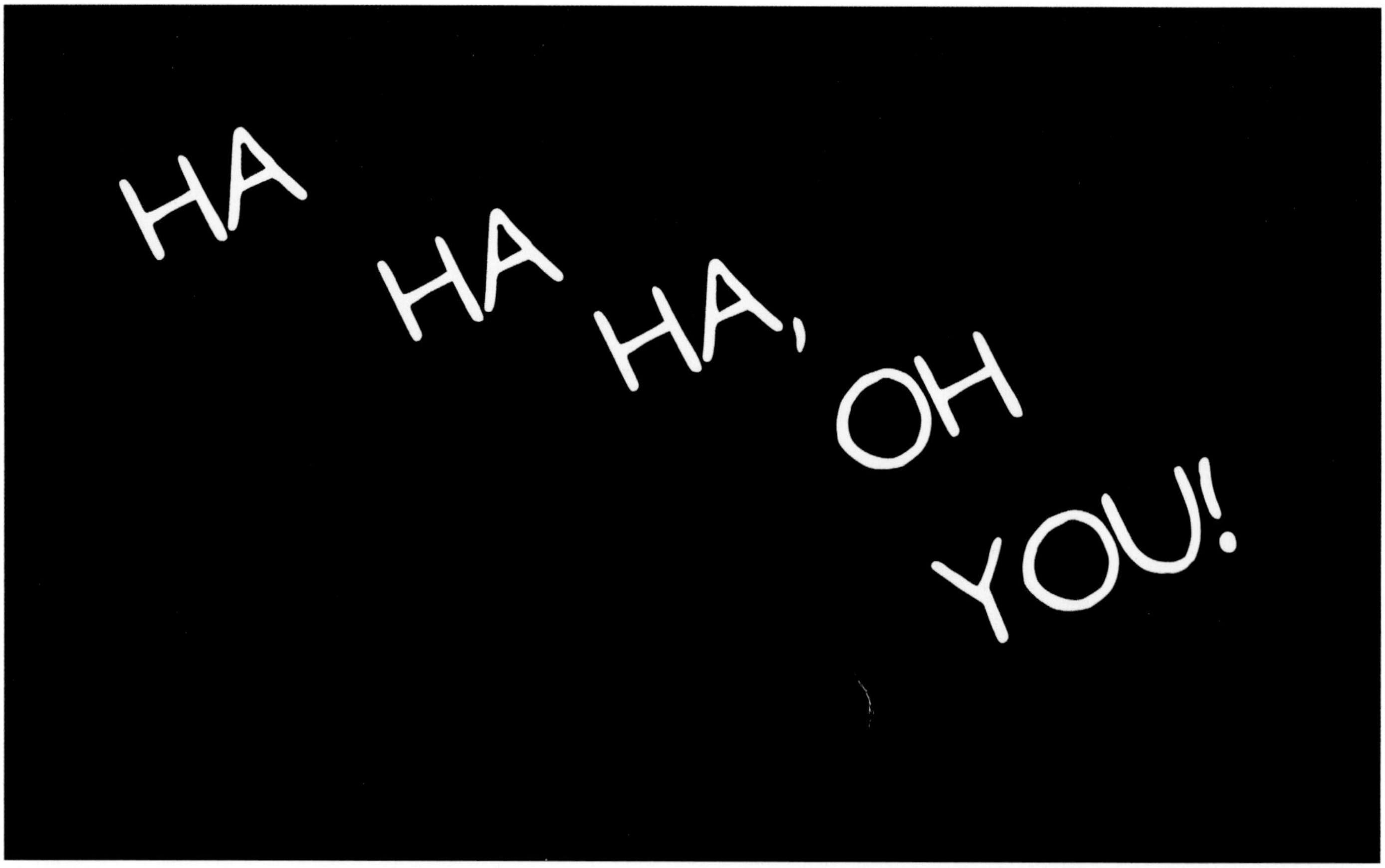
HA HA HA, OH YOU!

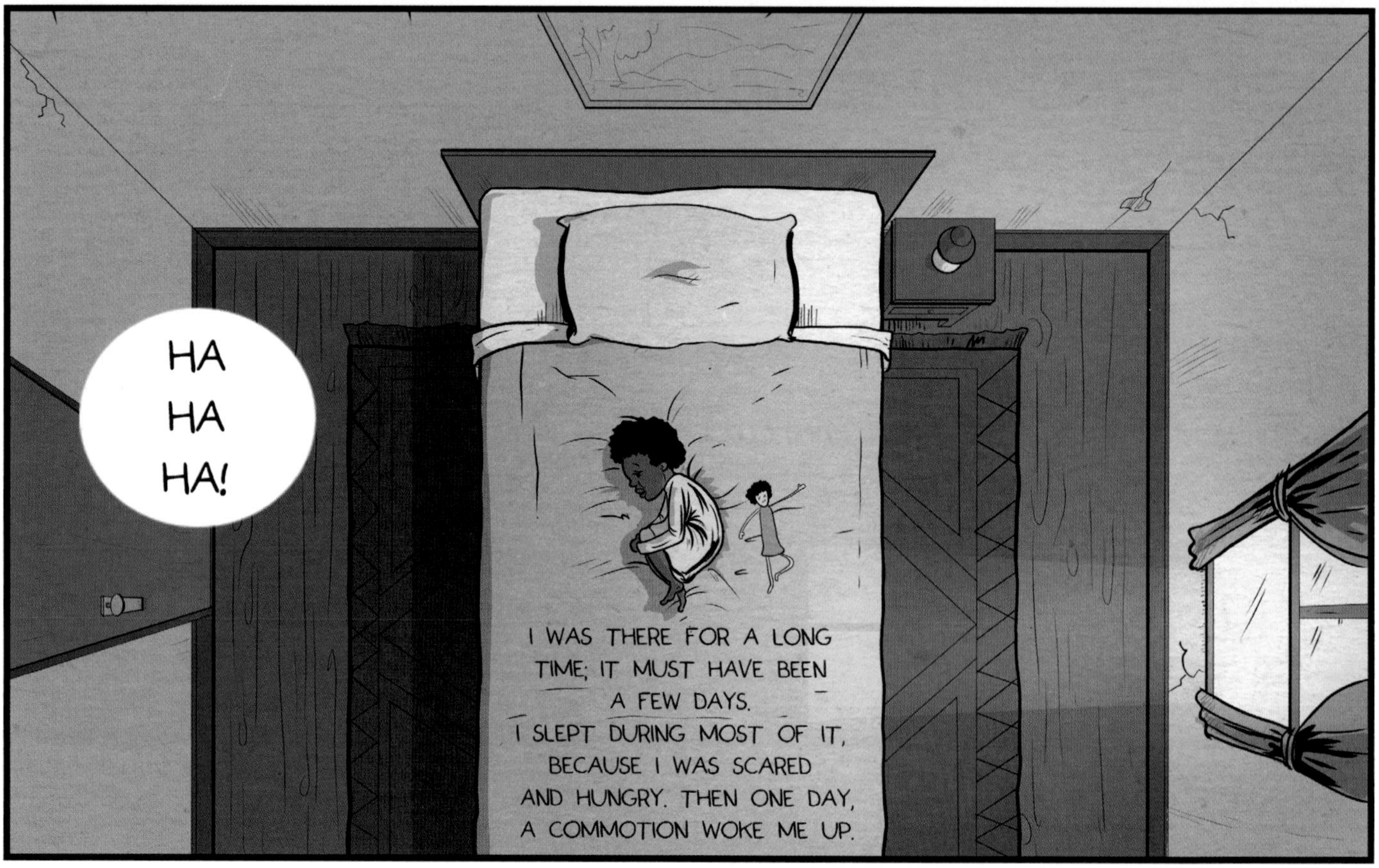
HA HA HA!
I WAS THERE FOR A LONG TIME; IT MUST HAVE BEEN A FEW DAYS.
I SLEPT DURING MOST OF IT, BECAUSE I WAS SCARED AND HUNGRY. THEN ONE DAY, A COMMOTION WOKE ME UP.

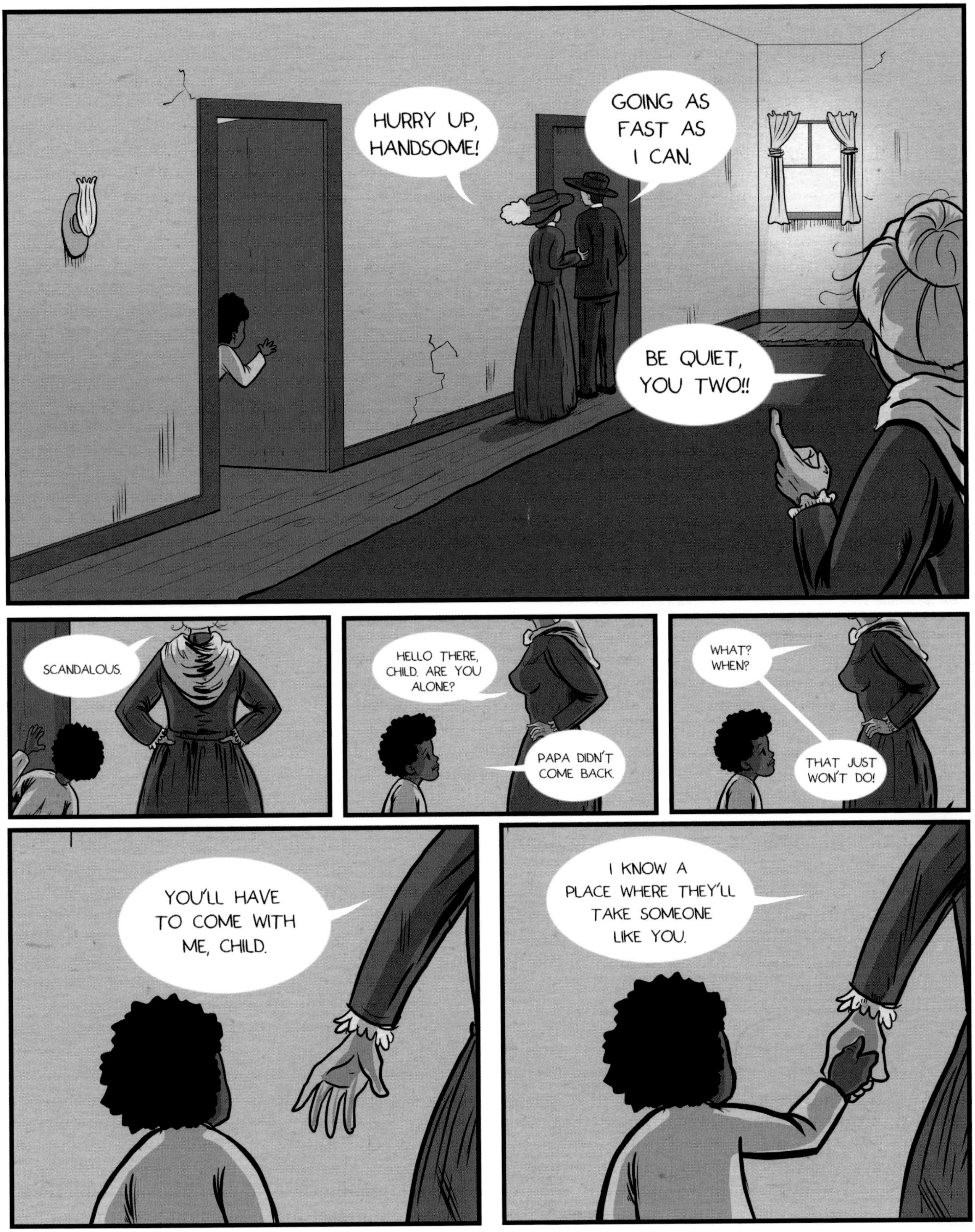
HURRY UP, HANDSOME!
GOING AS FAST AS I CAN.
BE QUIET, YOU TWO!!
SCANDALOUS.
HELLO THERE, CHILD. ARE YOU ALONE?
PAPA DIDN'T COME BACK.
WHAT? WHEN?
THAT JUST WON'T DO!
YOU'LL HAVE TO COME WITH ME, CHILD.
I KNOW A PLACE WHERE THEY'LL TAKE SOMEONE LIKE YOU.

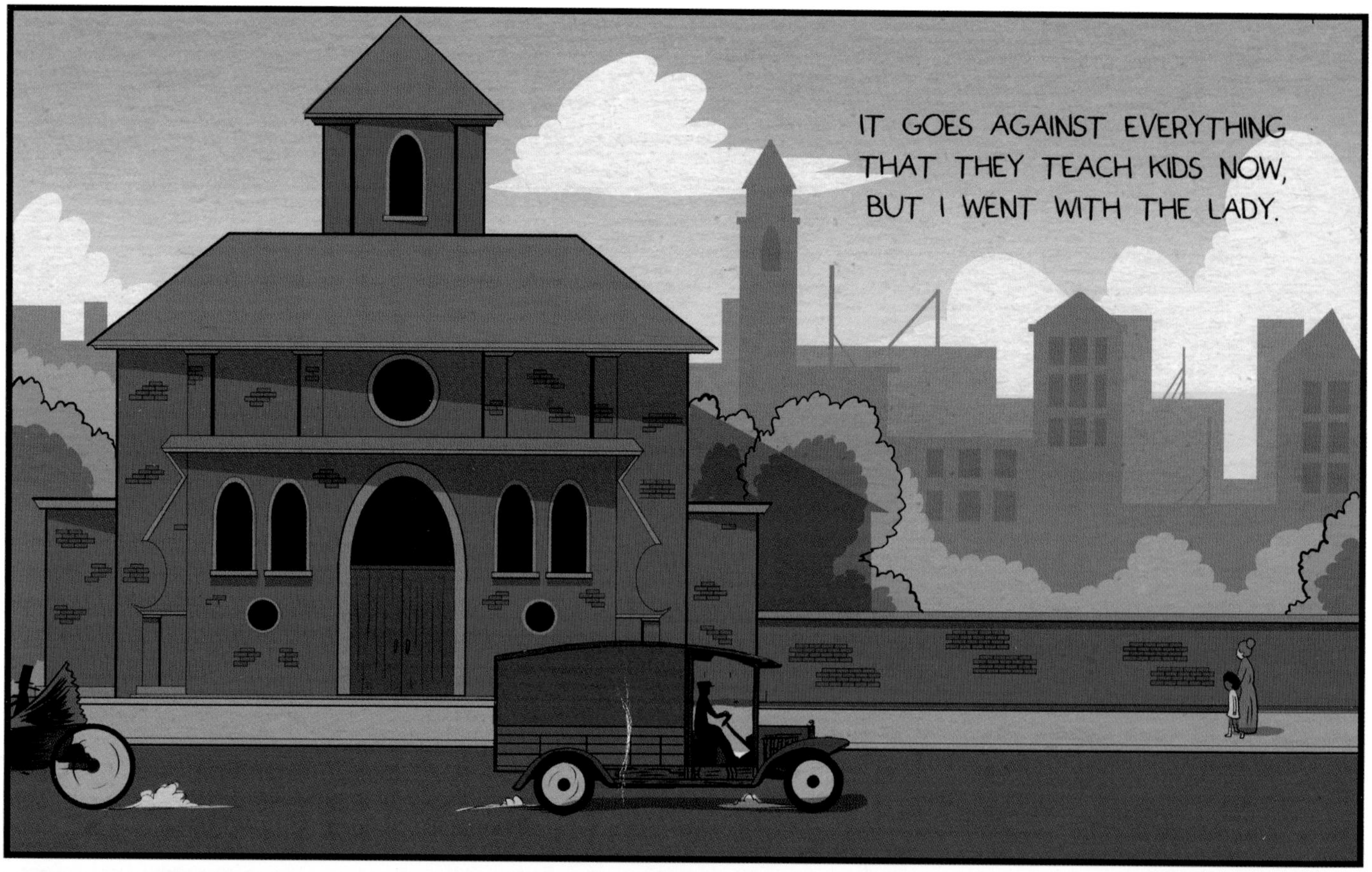
IT GOES AGAINST EVERYTHING THAT THEY TEACH KIDS NOW, BUT I WENT WITH THE LADY.

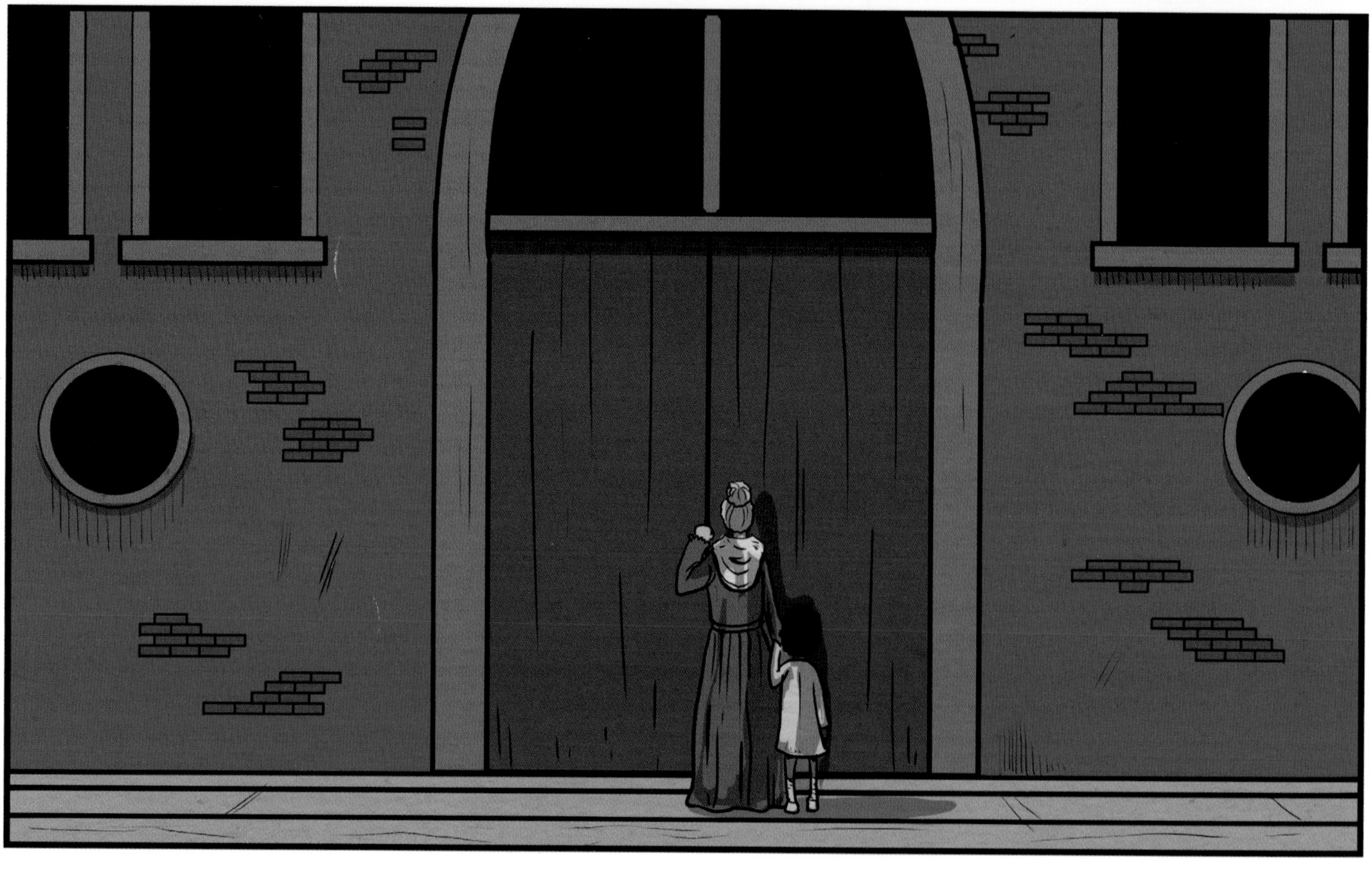

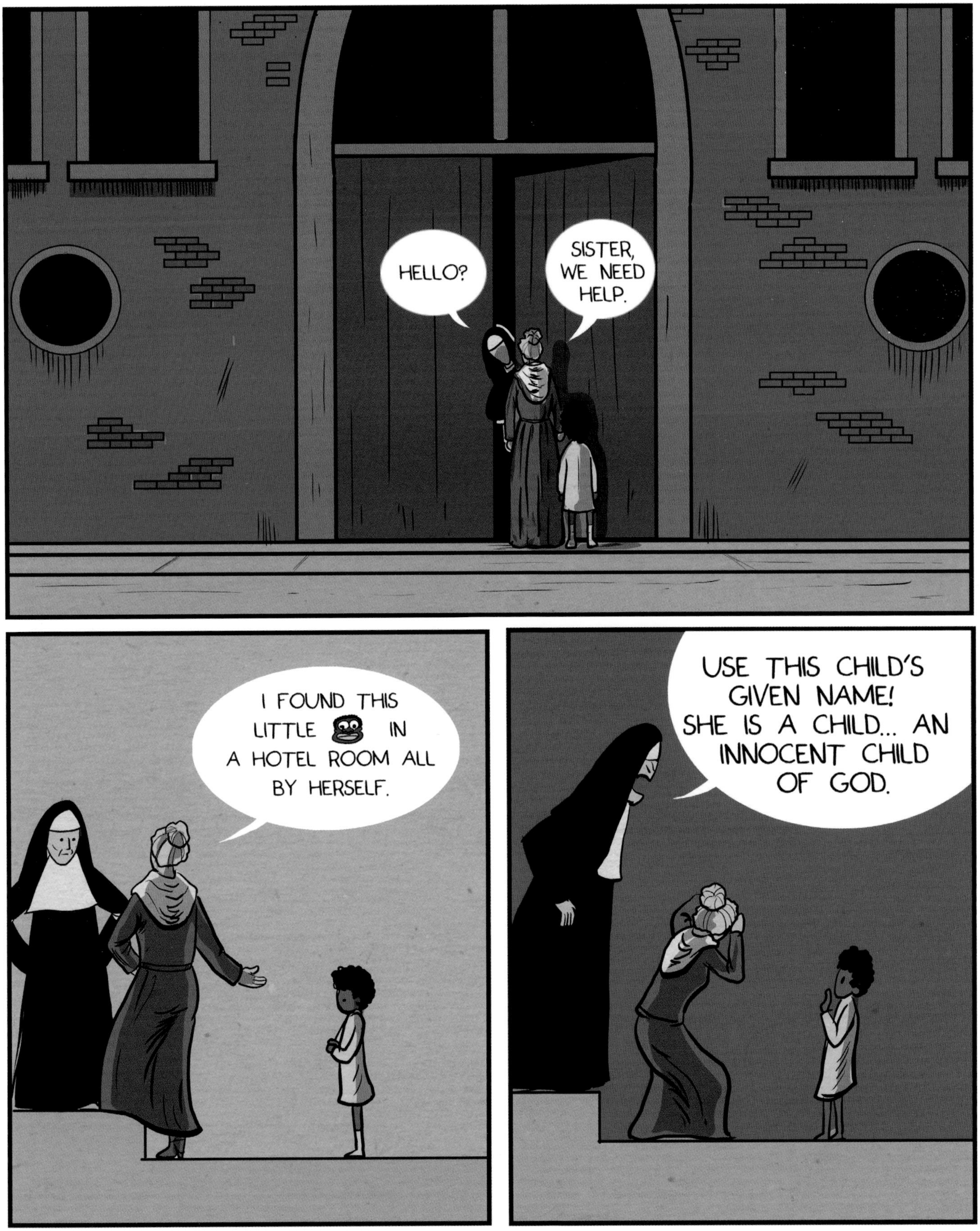
HELLO?
SISTER, WE NEED HELP.
I FOUND THIS LITTLE IN A HOTEL ROOM ALL BY HERSELF.
USE THIS CHILD'S GIVEN NAME! SHE IS A CHILD... AN INNOCENT CHILD OF GOD.

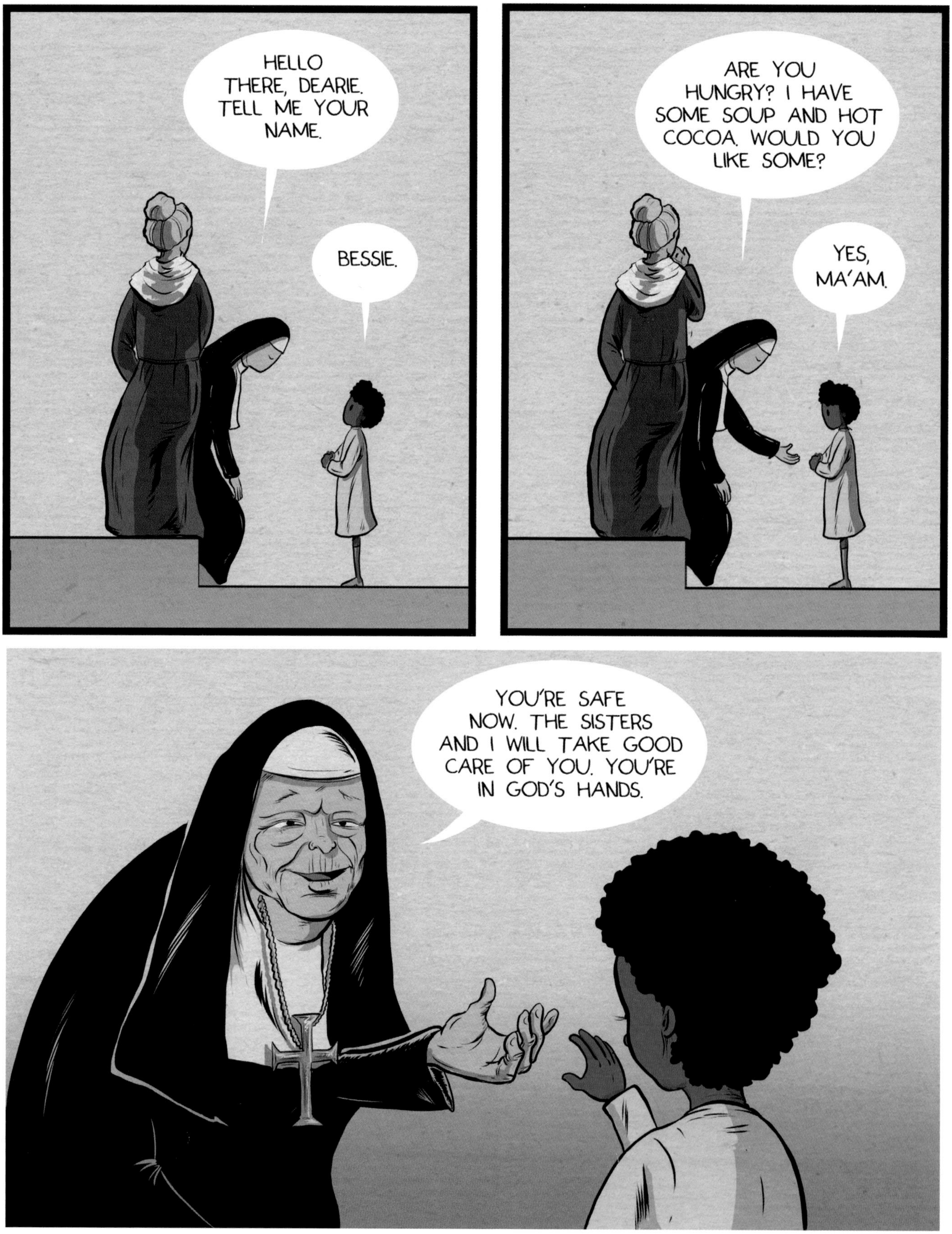
HELLO THERE, DEARIE. TELL ME YOUR NAME.
BESSIE.
ARE YOU HUNGRY? I HAVE SOME SOUP AND HOT COCOA. WOULD YOU LIKE SOME?
YES, MA'AM.
YOU'RE SAFE NOW. THE SISTERS AND I WILL TAKE GOOD CARE OF YOU. YOU'RE IN GOD'S HANDS.

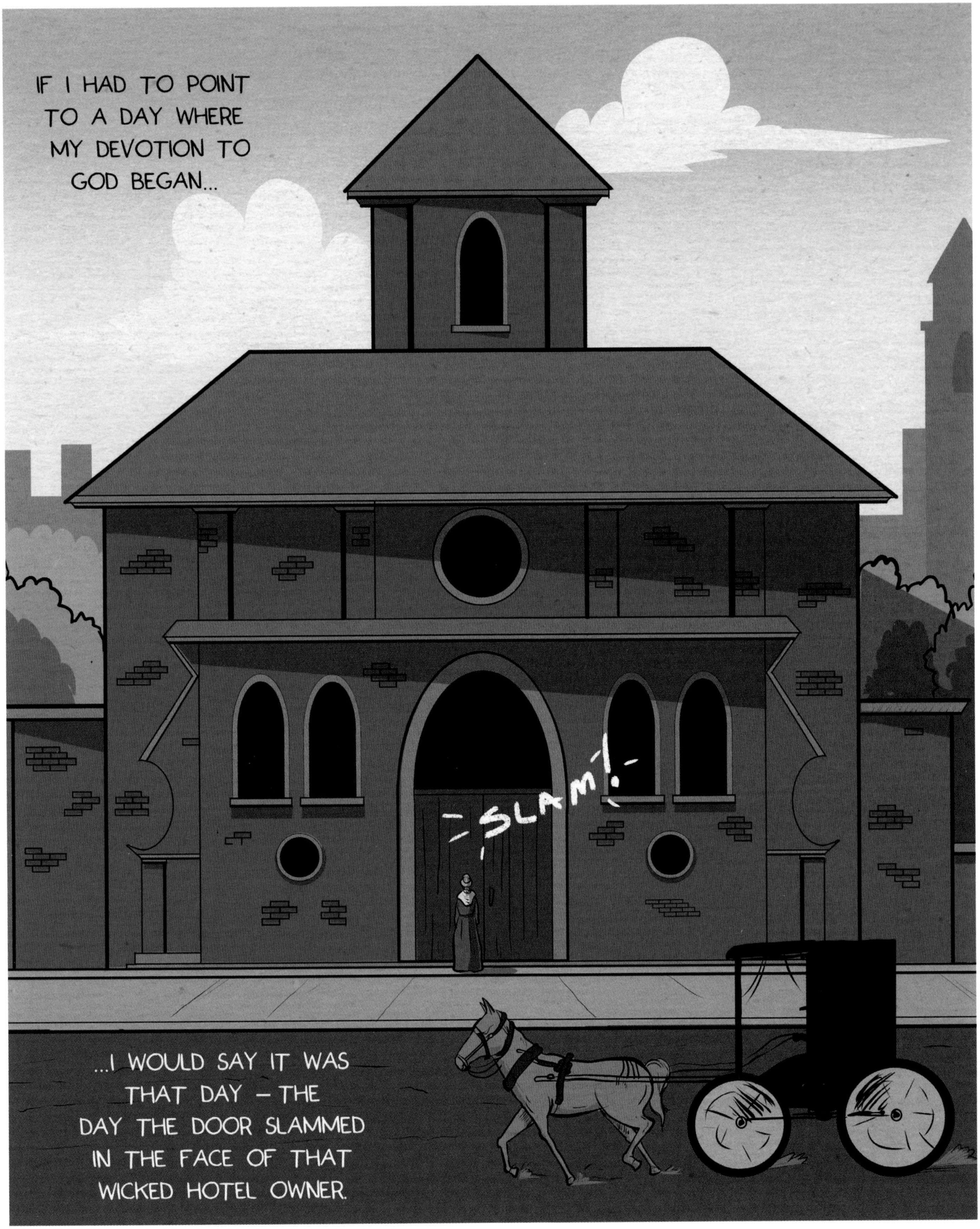
IF I HAD TO POINT TO A DAY WHERE MY DEVOTION TO GOD BEGAN...
SLAM!
...I WOULD SAY IT WAS THAT DAY – THE DAY THE DOOR SLAMMED IN THE FACE OF THAT WICKED HOTEL OWNER.

I WAS IN THE ORPHANAGE WITH THE SISTERS FOR A FEW YEARS, AND THINGS WERE GREAT. ALTHOUGH I MISSED MY MAMA AND PAPA, THE NUNS WERE KIND TO ME. THEN ONE DAY...
WELL HELLO THERE, B.B.
ARE YOU HAVING A BLESSED DAY?
OH, YES, MA'AM. I CAME IN EARLY BECAUSE I WANT TO GET A HEAD START ON THE STATE CAPITALS ASSIGNMENT.
SOMEDAY I'LL VISIT EACH AND EVERY ONE.
IT SEEMS YOU'VE BEEN HAPPY HERE THESE PAST FEW YEARS, BUT...
DO YOU EVER WONDER WHAT A NEW FAMILY WOULD BE LIKE?
OH, YES, SISTER. I DREAM ABOUT A NEW FAMILY ALL THE TIME!

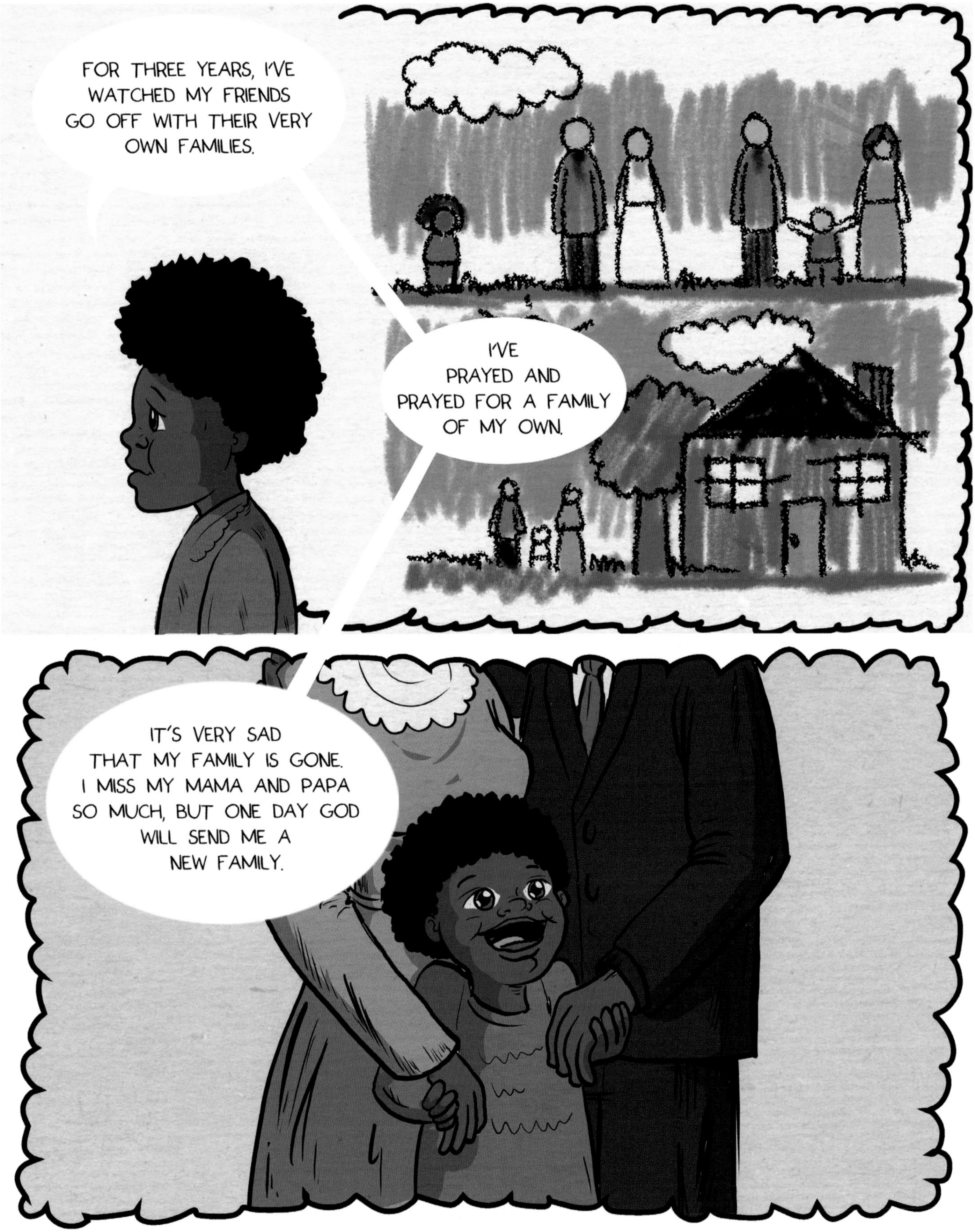
FOR THREE YEARS, I'VE WATCHED MY FRIENDS GO OFF WITH THEIR VERY OWN FAMILIES.
I'VE PRAYED AND PRAYED FOR A FAMILY OF MY OWN.
IT'S VERY SAD THAT MY FAMILY IS GONE. I MISS MY MAMA AND PAPA SO MUCH, BUT ONE DAY GOD WILL SEND ME A NEW FAMILY.

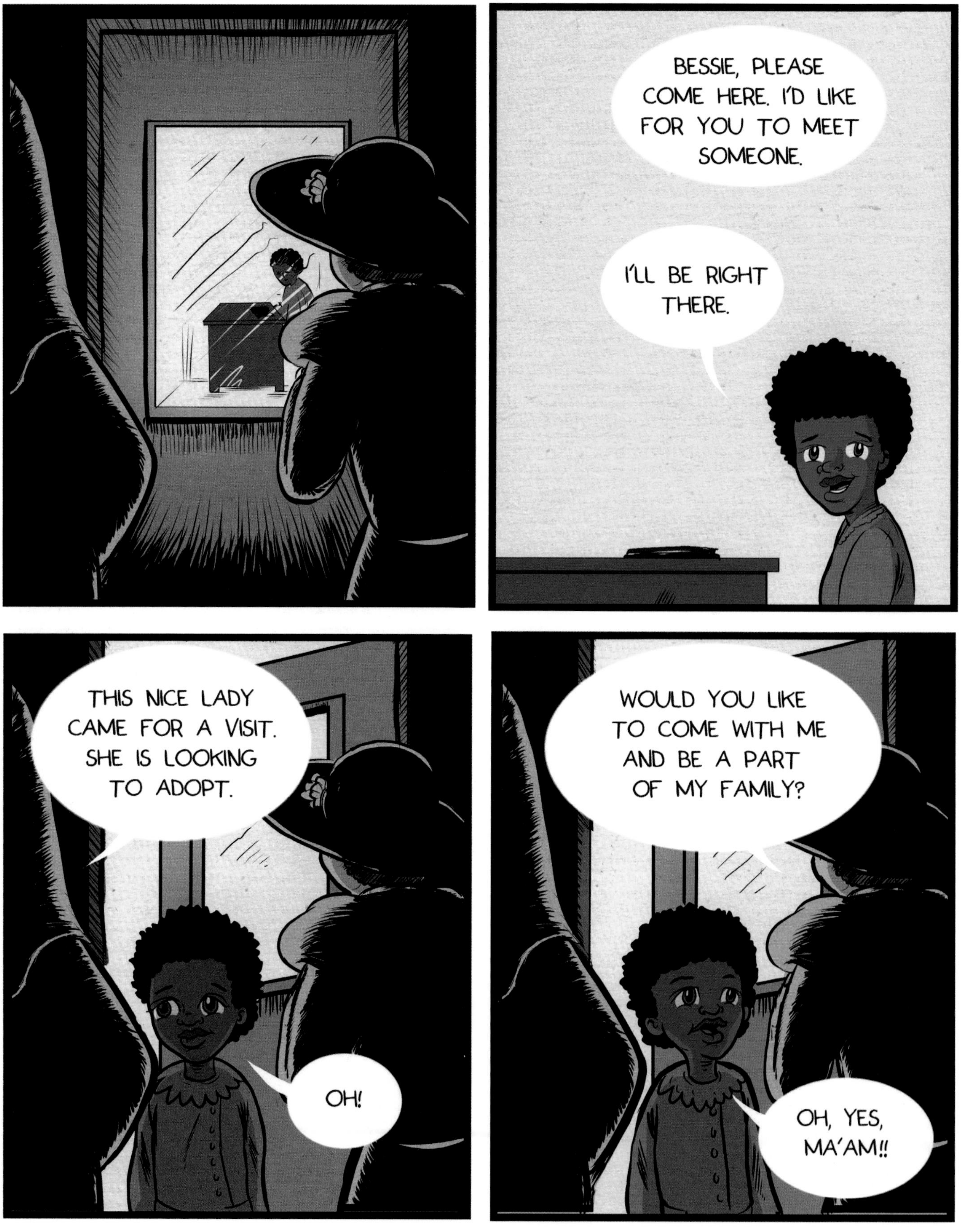
BESSIE, PLEASE COME HERE. I'D LIKE FOR YOU TO MEET SOMEONE.
I'LL BE RIGHT THERE.
THIS NICE LADY CAME FOR A VISIT. SHE IS LOOKING TO ADOPT.
OH!
WOULD YOU LIKE TO COME WITH ME AND BE A PART OF MY FAMILY?
OH, YES, MA'AM!!

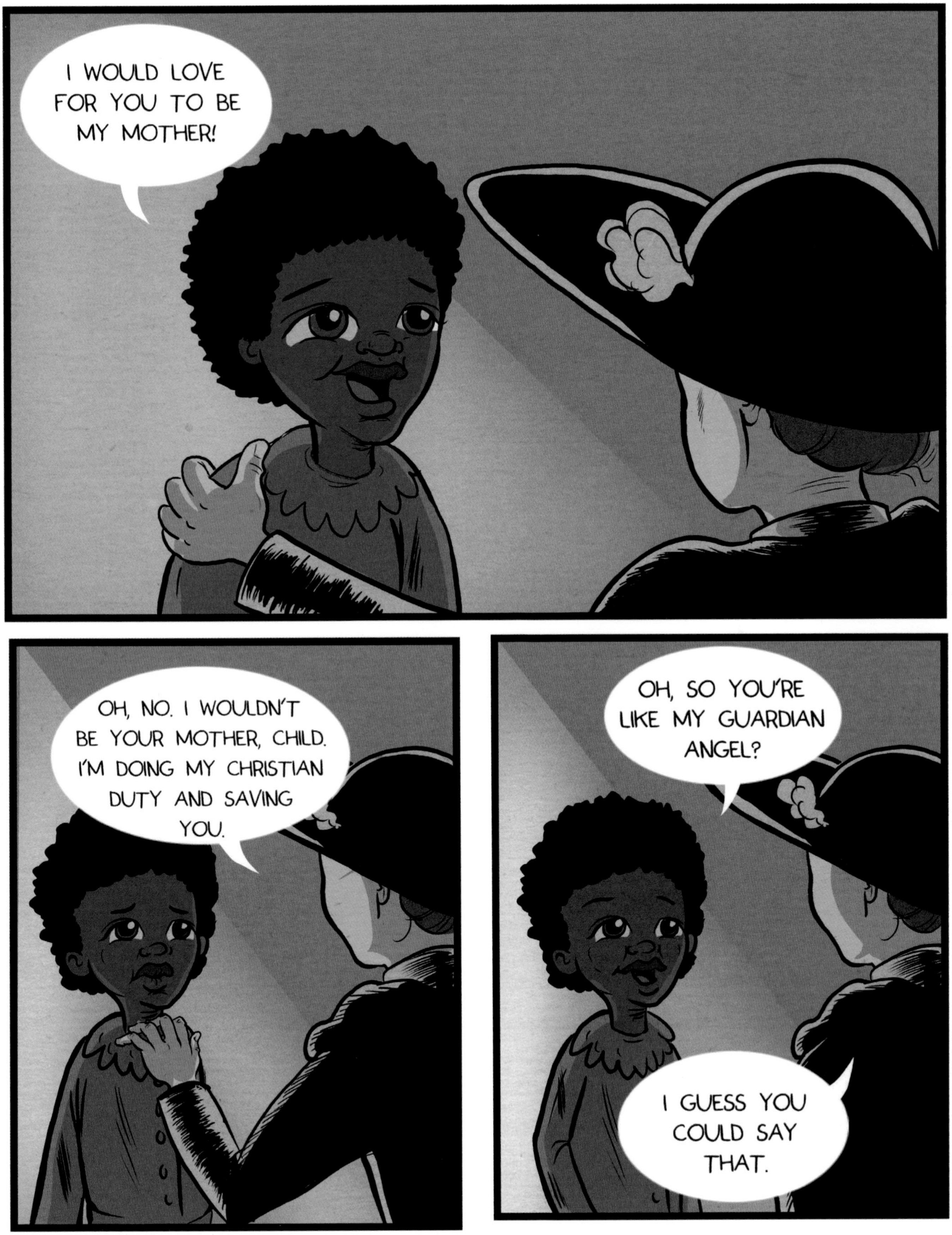
I WOULD LOVE FOR YOU TO BE MY MOTHER!
OH, NO. I WOULDN'T BE YOUR MOTHER, CHILD. I'M DOING MY CHRISTIAN DUTY AND SAVING YOU.
OH, SO YOU'RE LIKE MY GUARDIAN ANGEL?
I GUESS YOU COULD SAY THAT.

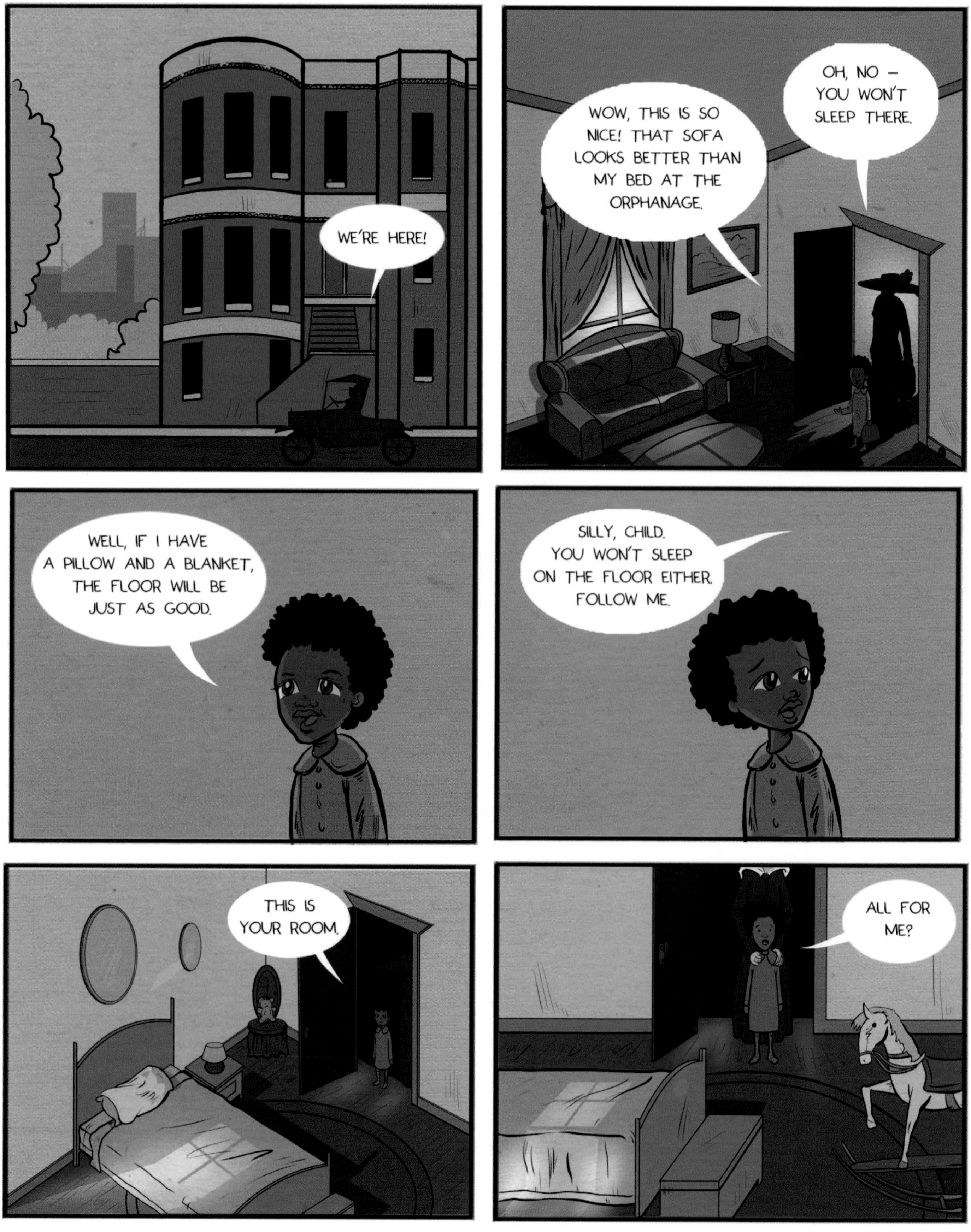
WE'RE HERE!
WOW, THIS IS SO NICE! THAT SOFA LOOKS BETTER THAN MY BED AT THE ORPHANAGE.
OH, NO – YOU WON'T SLEEP THERE.
WELL, IF I HAVE A PILLOW AND A BLANKET, THE FLOOR WILL BE JUST AS GOOD.
SILLY, CHILD. YOU WON'T SLEEP ON THE FLOOR EITHER. FOLLOW ME.
THIS IS YOUR ROOM.
ALL FOR ME?

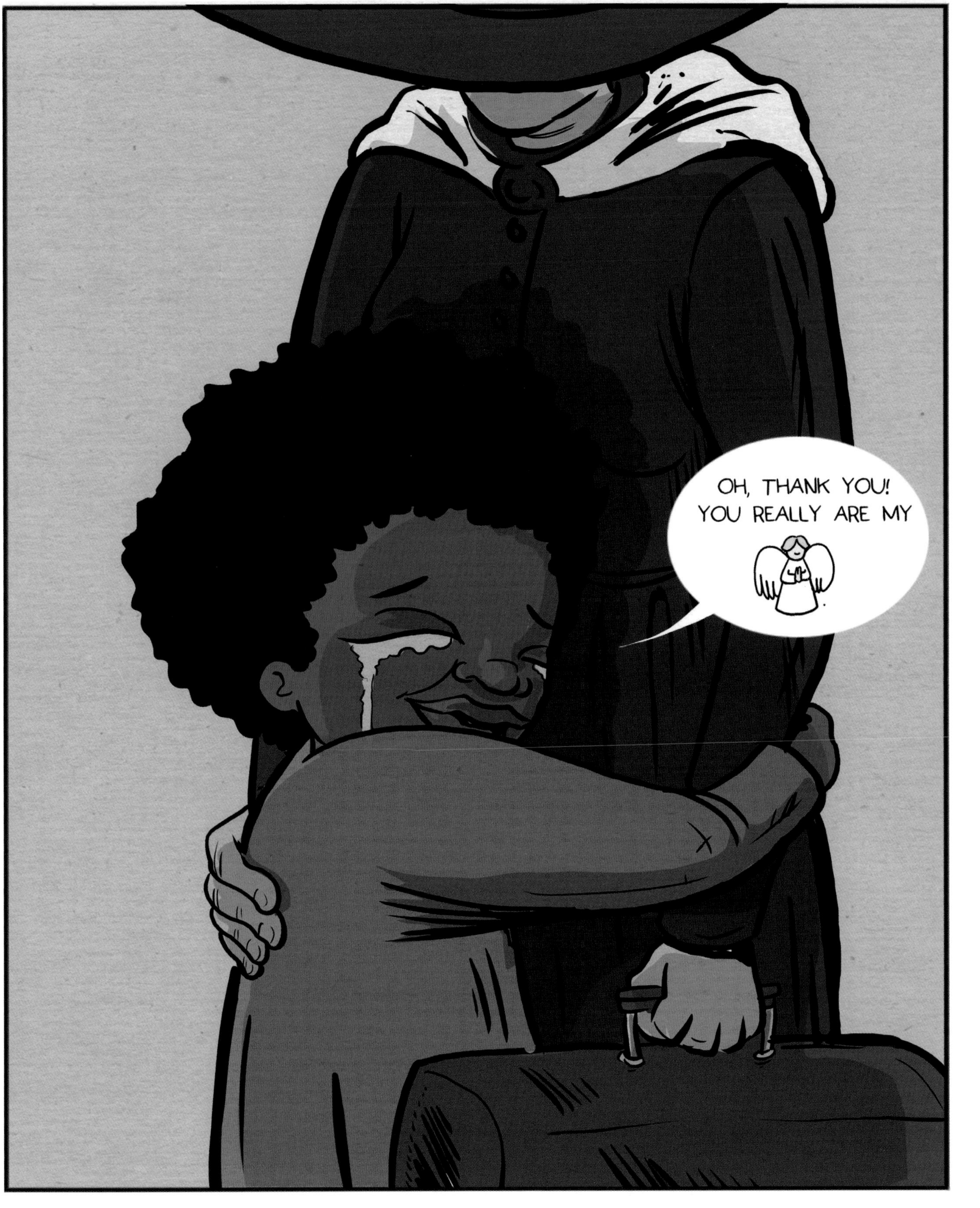
OH, THANK YOU! YOU REALLY ARE MY

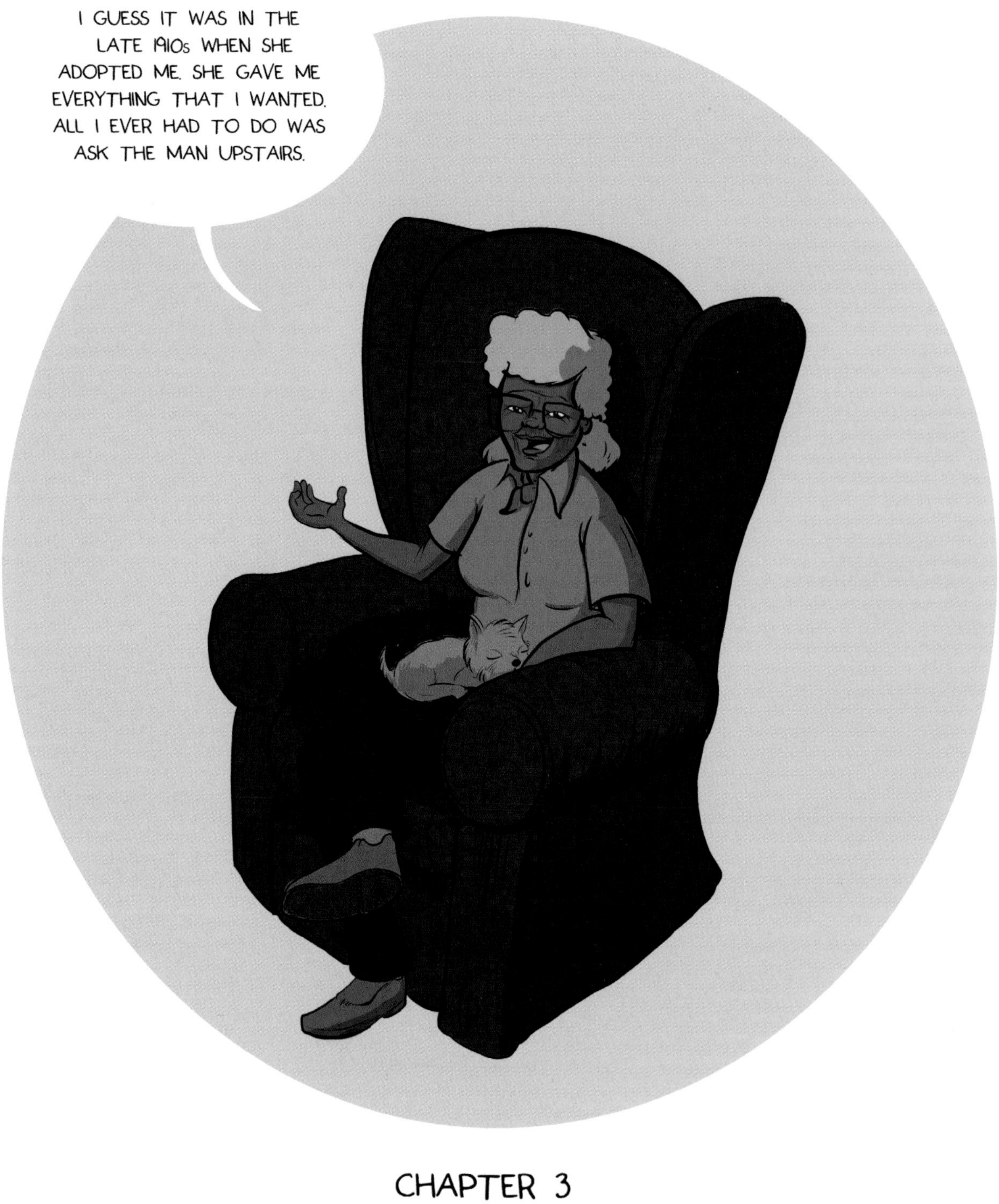
I GUESS IT WAS IN THE LATE 1910s WHEN SHE ADOPTED ME. SHE GAVE ME EVERYTHING THAT I WANTED. ALL I EVER HAD TO DO WAS ASK THE MAN UPSTAIRS.

CHAPTER 3
GIFTS

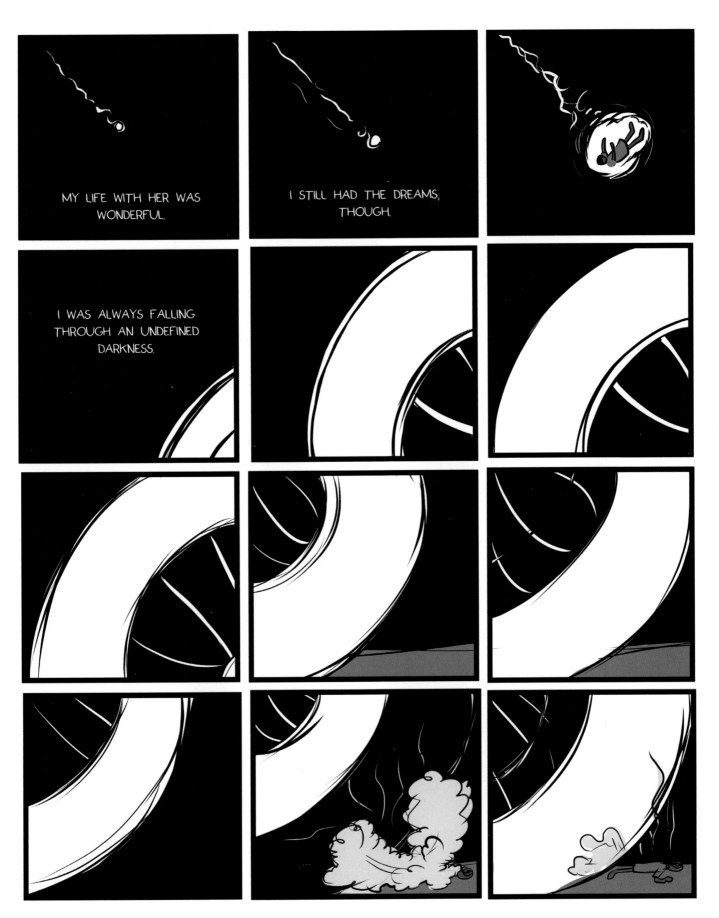

MY LIFE WITH HER WAS WONDERFUL.

I STILL HAD THE DREAMS, THOUGH.

I WAS ALWAYS FALLING THROUGH AN UNDEFINED DARKNESS.

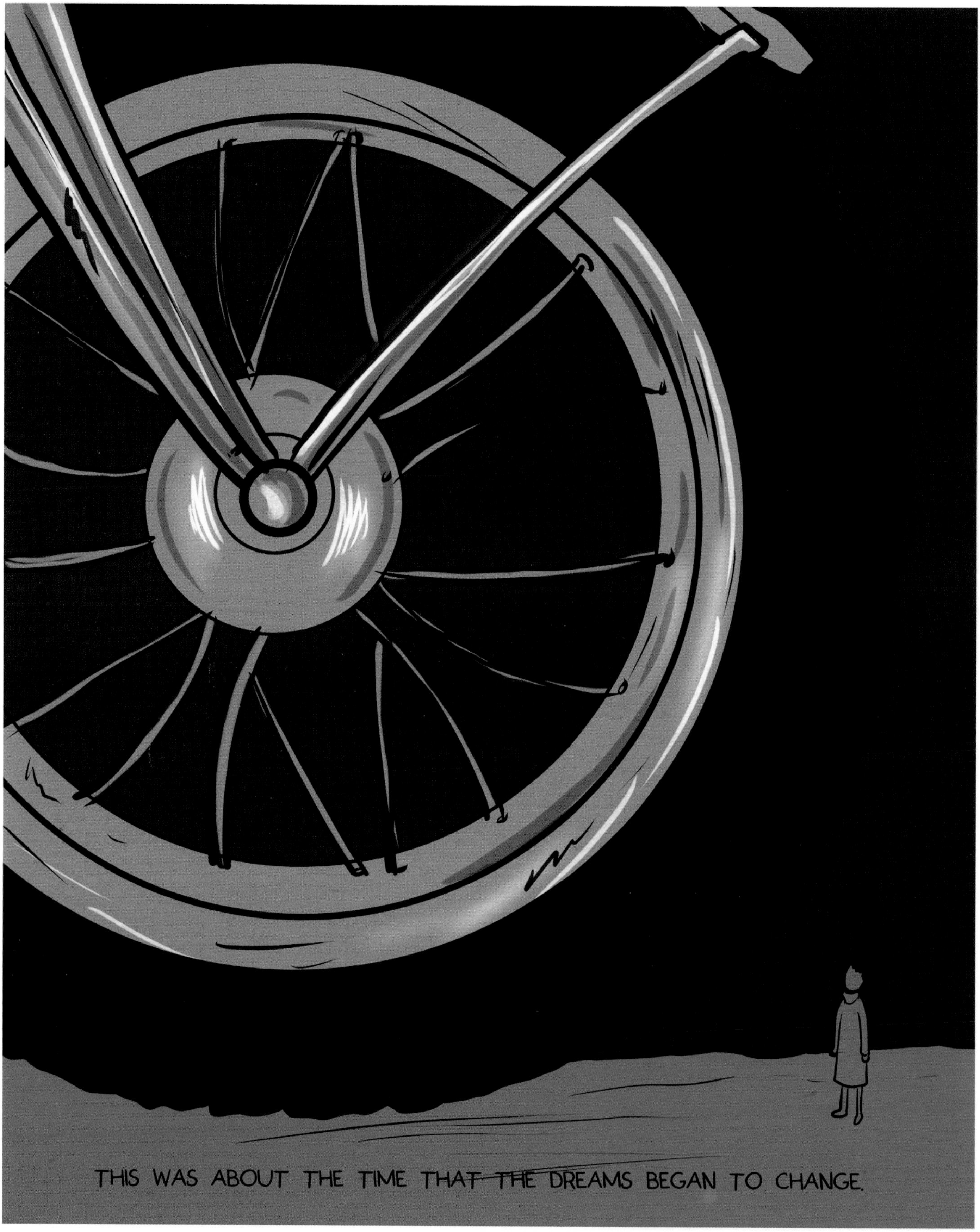
THIS WAS ABOUT THE TIME THAT THE DREAMS BEGAN TO CHANGE.

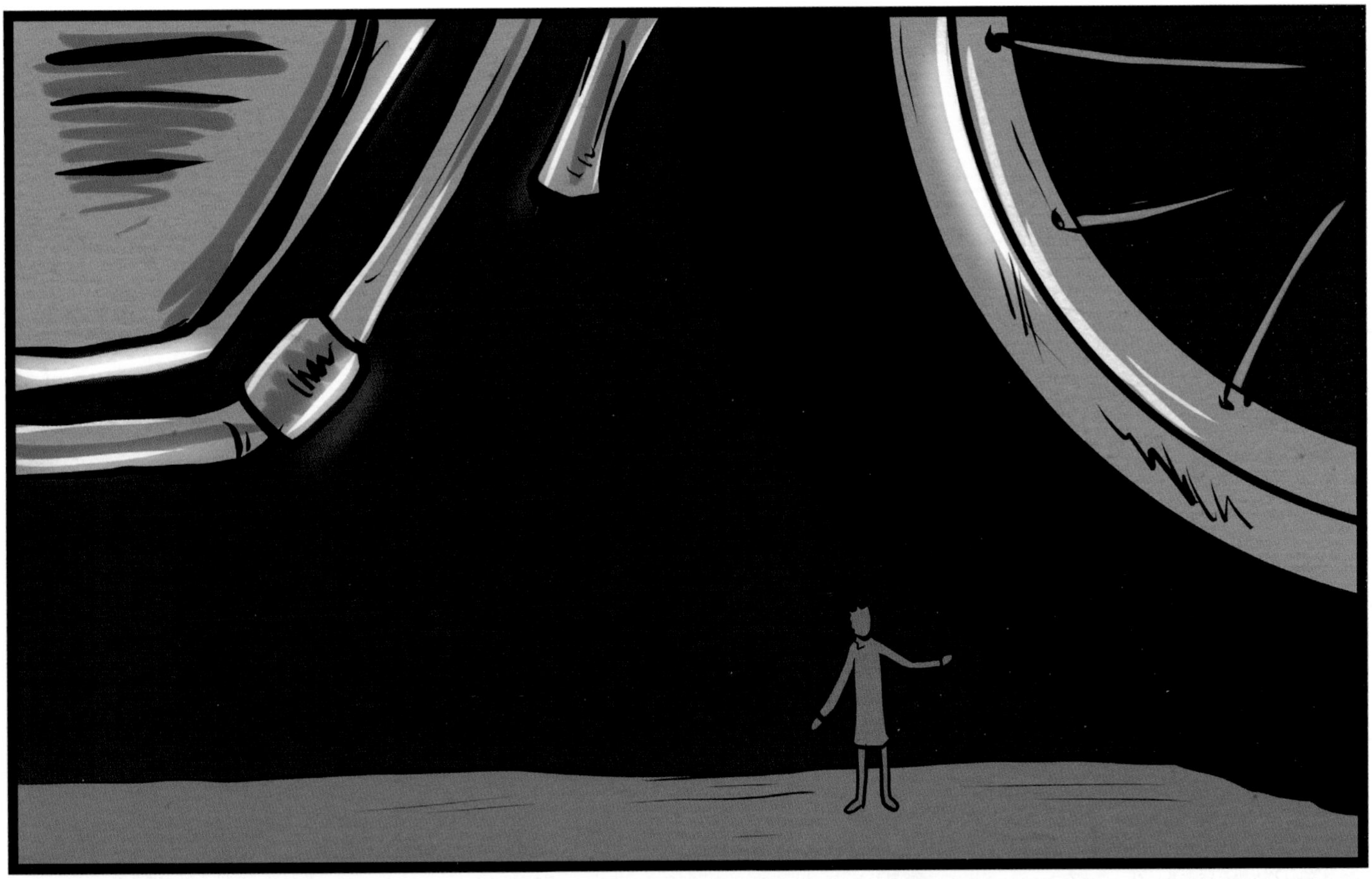

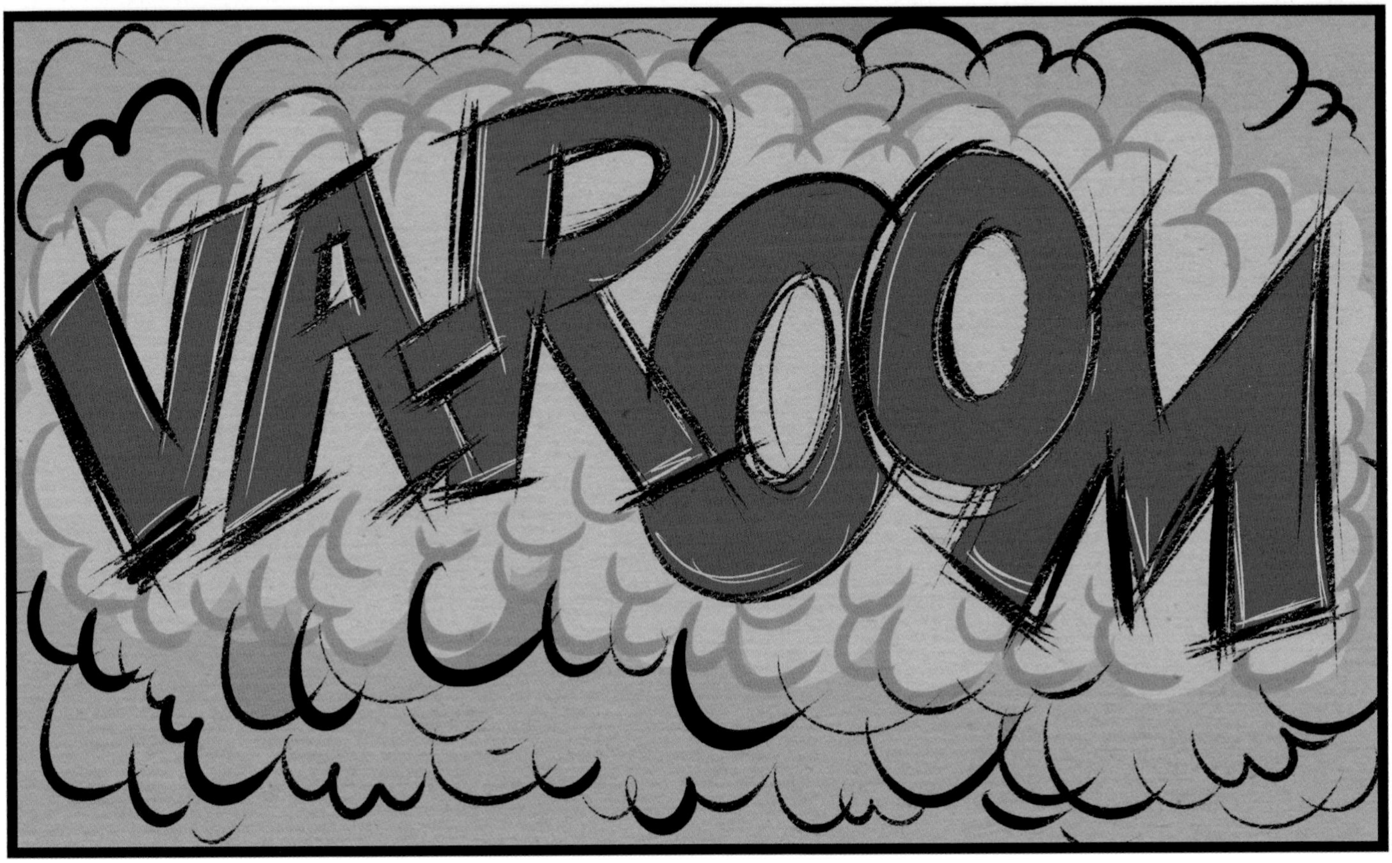
VAROOM

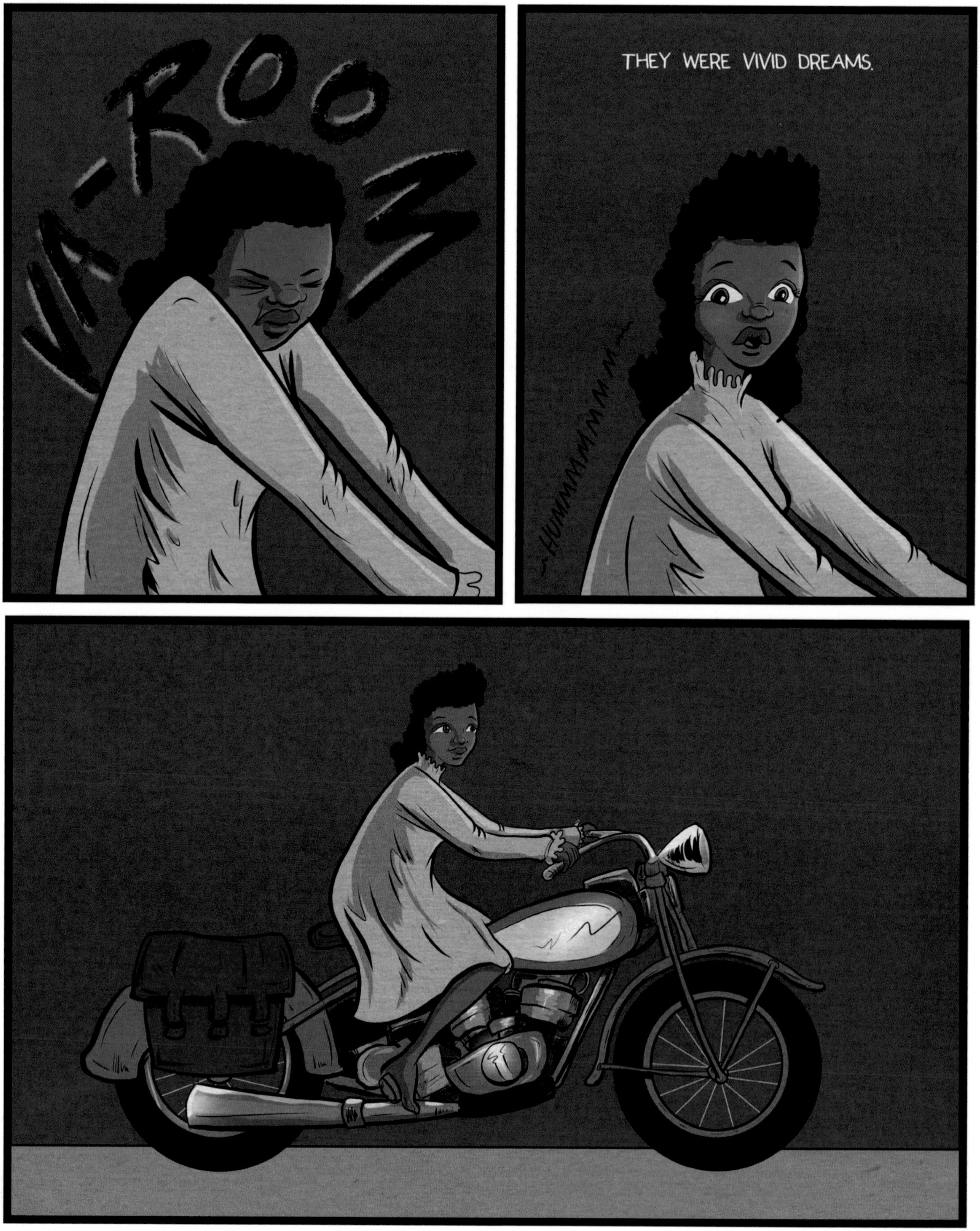
VA-ROOM
THEY WERE VIVID DREAMS.
~HUMMMMMMMM~

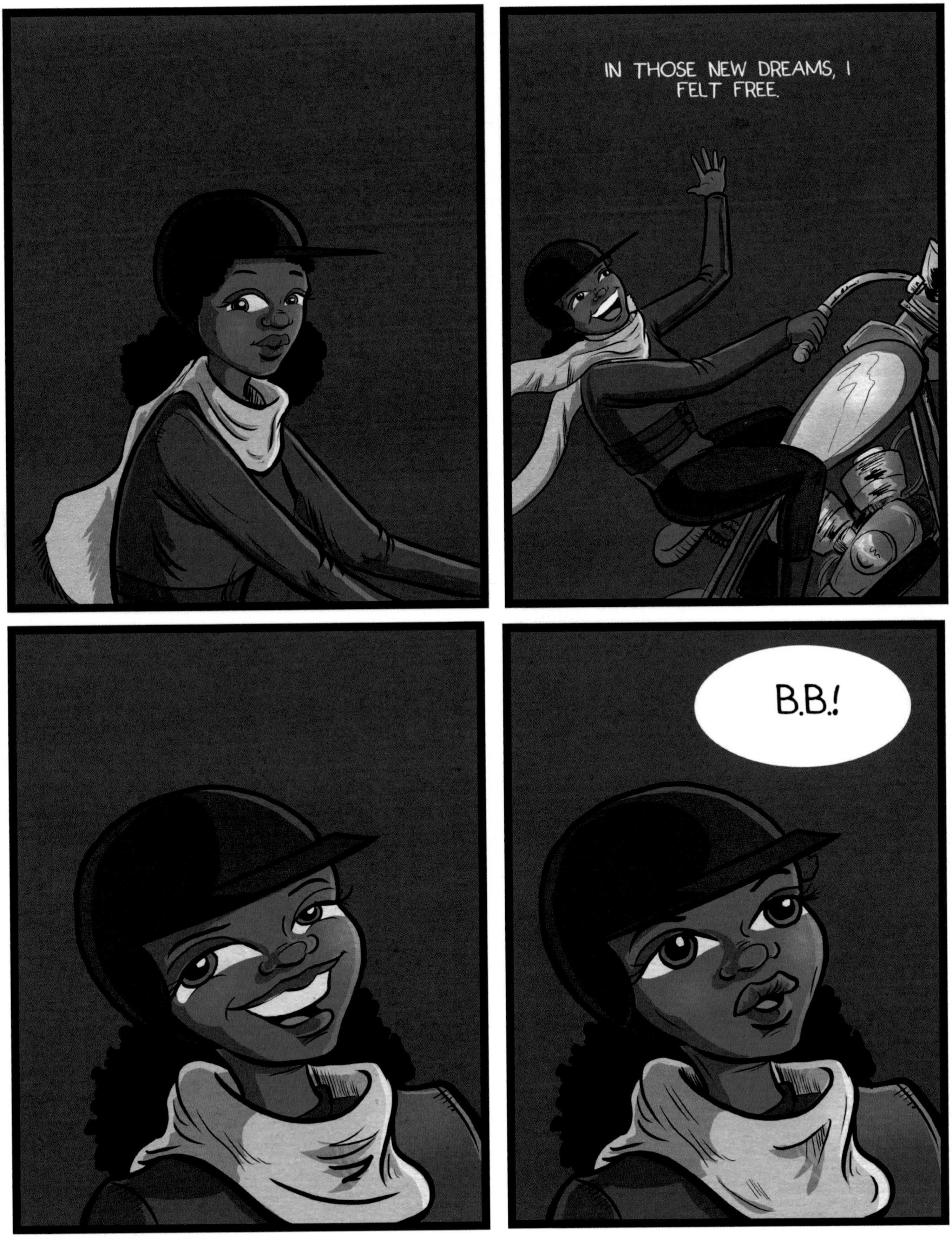
IN THOSE NEW DREAMS, I FELT FREE.
B.B.!

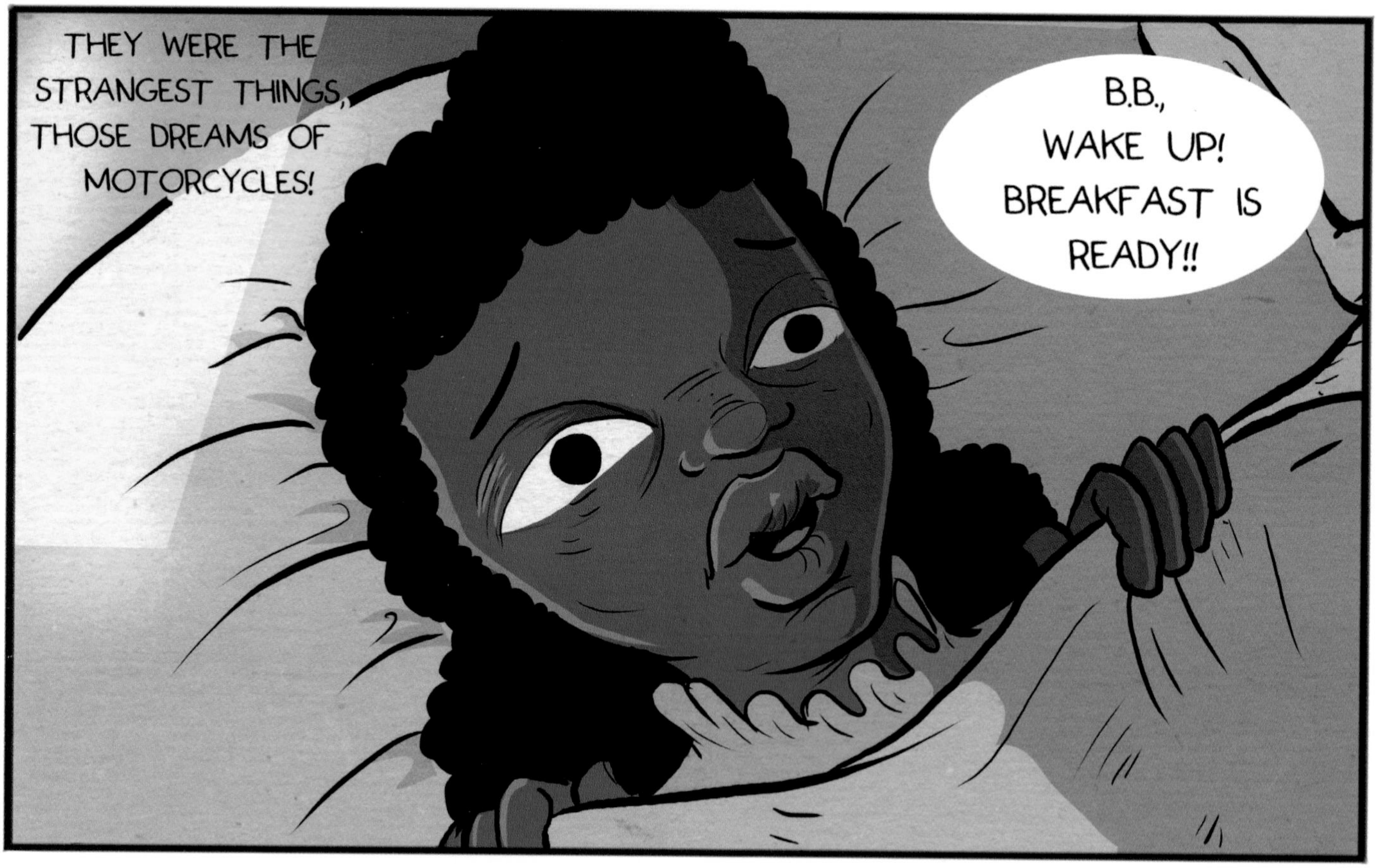
THEY WERE THE STRANGEST THINGS, THOSE DREAMS OF MOTORCYCLES!
B.B., WAKE UP! BREAKFAST IS READY!!

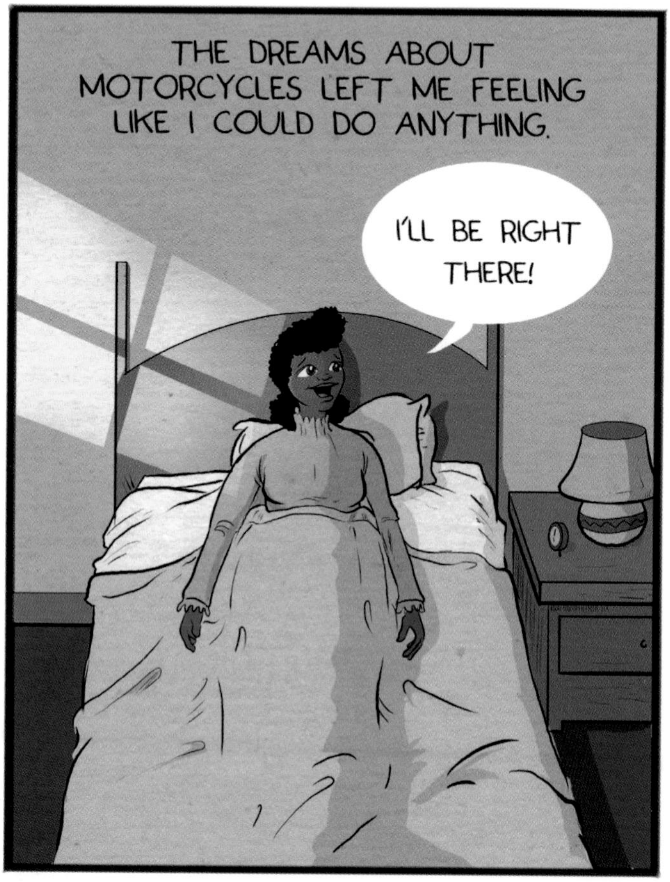
THE DREAMS ABOUT MOTORCYCLES LEFT ME FEELING LIKE I COULD DO ANYTHING.
I'LL BE RIGHT THERE!

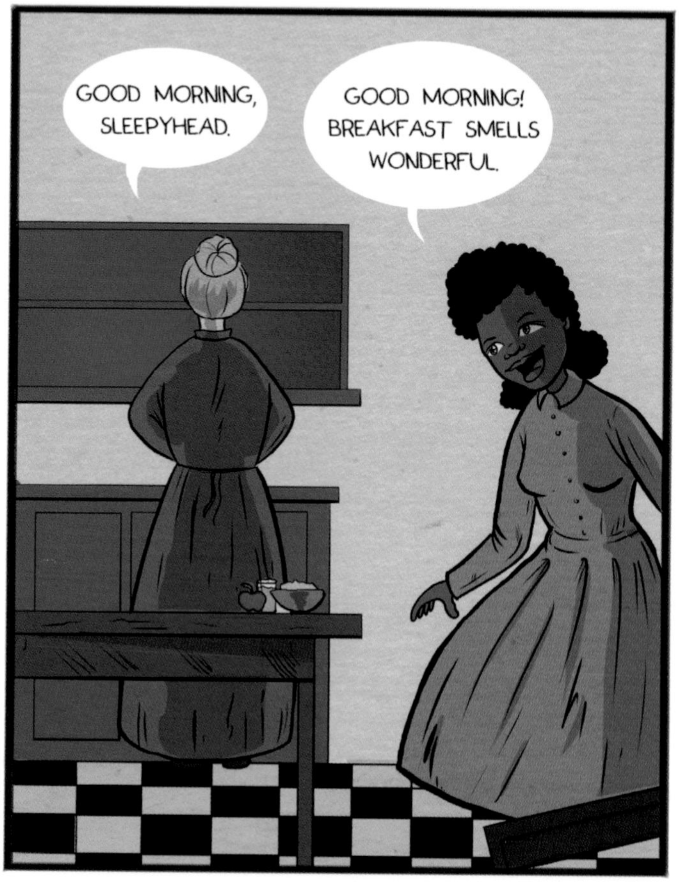
GOOD MORNING, SLEEPYHEAD.
GOOD MORNING! BREAKFAST SMELLS WONDERFUL.

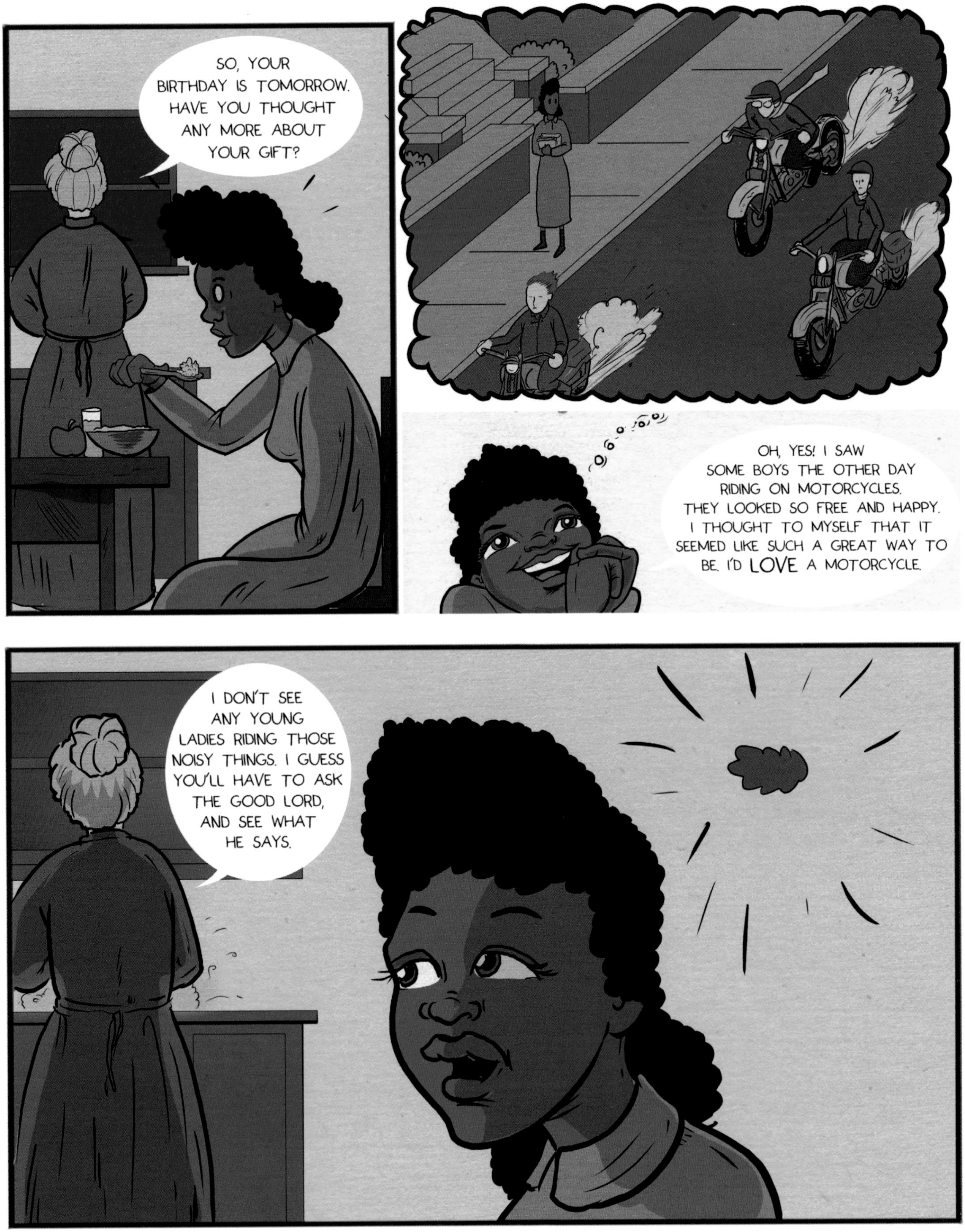
SO, YOUR BIRTHDAY IS TOMORROW. HAVE YOU THOUGHT ANY MORE ABOUT YOUR GIFT?
OH, YES! I SAW SOME BOYS THE OTHER DAY RIDING ON MOTORCYCLES. THEY LOOKED SO FREE AND HAPPY. I THOUGHT TO MYSELF THAT IT SEEMED LIKE SUCH A GREAT WAY TO BE. I'D LOVE A MOTORCYCLE.
I DON'T SEE ANY YOUNG LADIES RIDING THOSE NOISY THINGS. I GUESS YOU'LL HAVE TO ASK THE GOOD LORD, AND SEE WHAT HE SAYS.

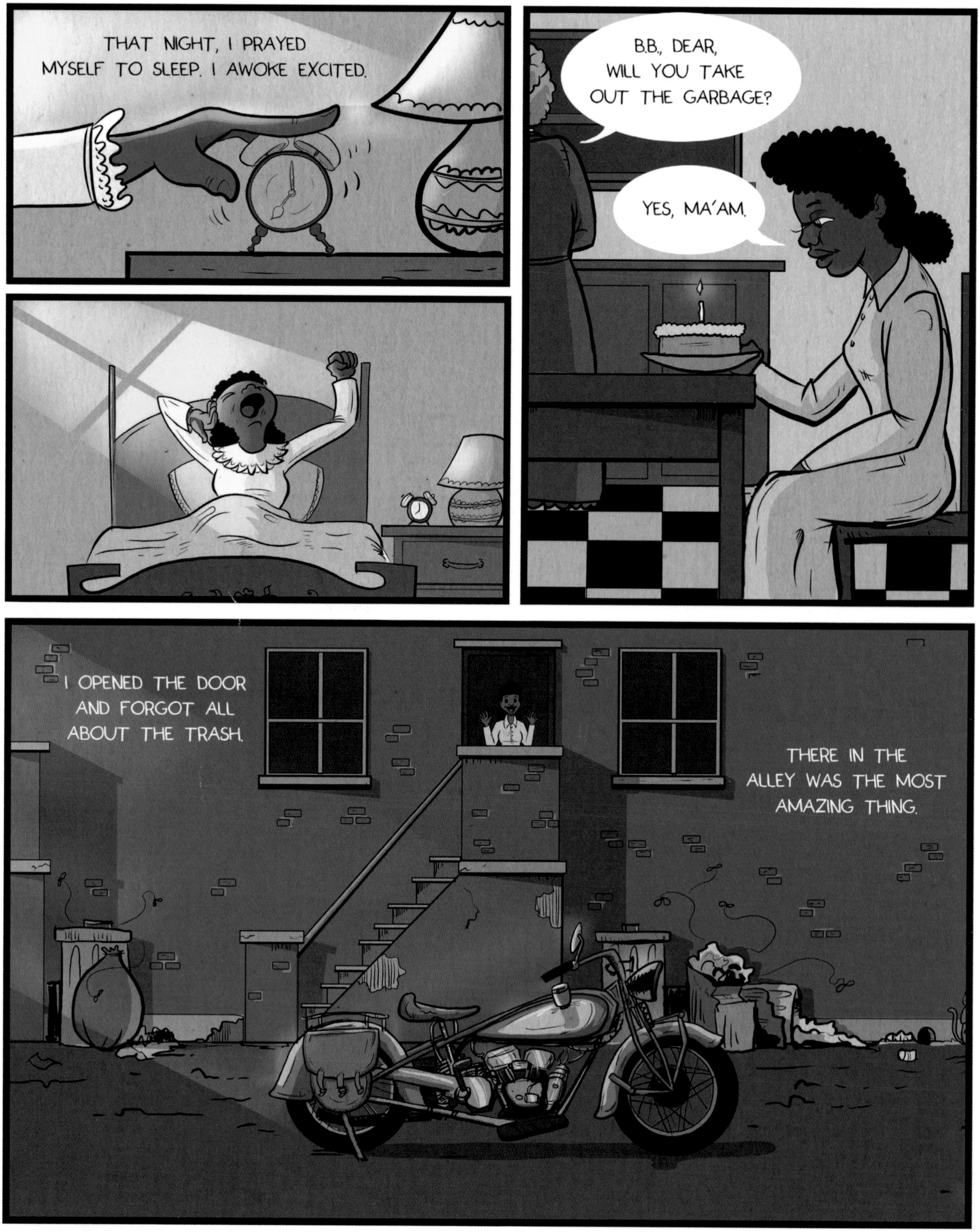
THAT NIGHT, I PRAYED MYSELF TO SLEEP. I AWOKE EXCITED.
B.B., DEAR, WILL YOU TAKE OUT THE GARBAGE?
YES, MA'AM.
I OPENED THE DOOR AND FORGOT ALL ABOUT THE TRASH.
THERE IN THE ALLEY WAS THE MOST AMAZING THING.

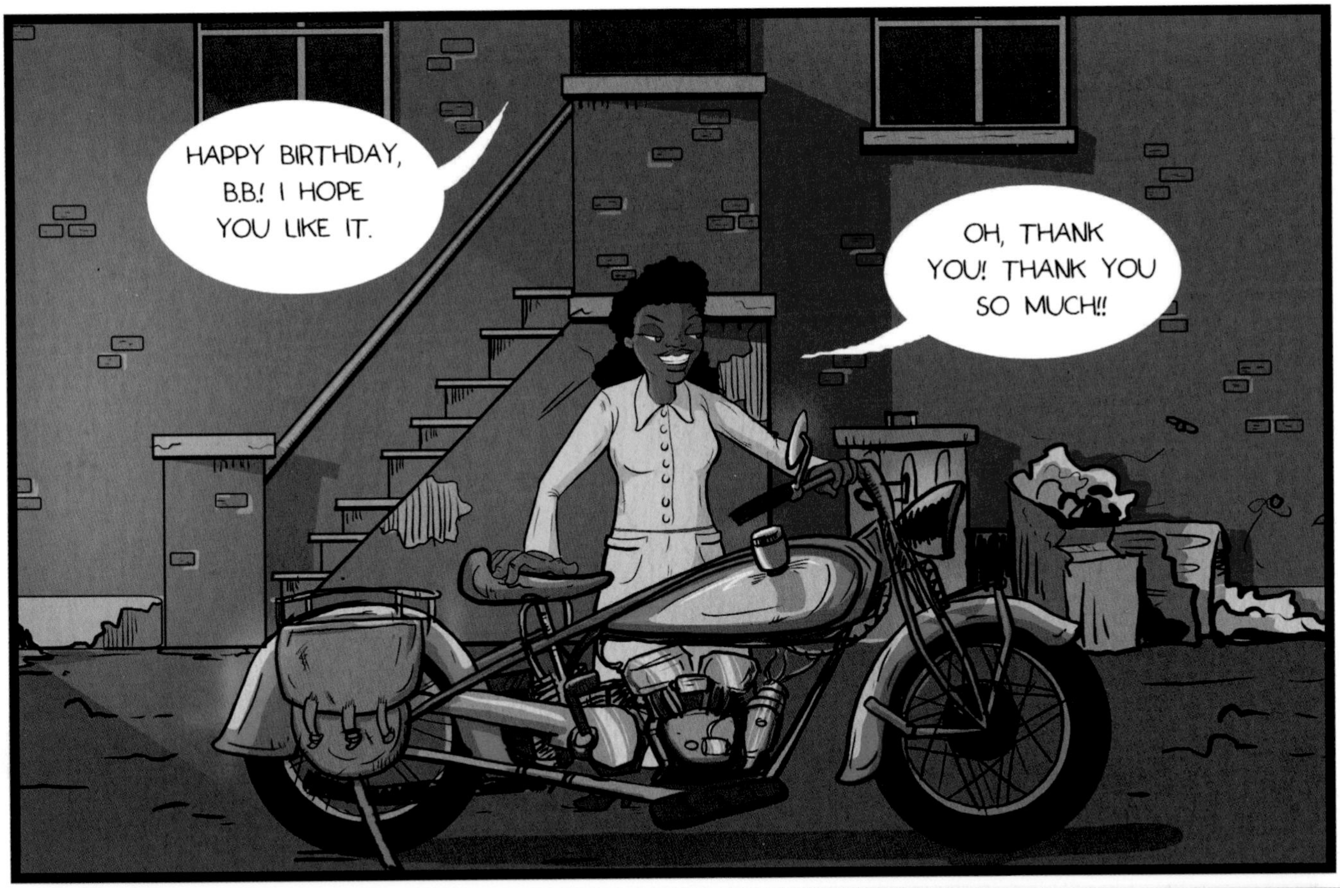
HAPPY BIRTHDAY, B.B.! I HOPE YOU LIKE IT.
OH, THANK YOU! THANK YOU SO MUCH!!

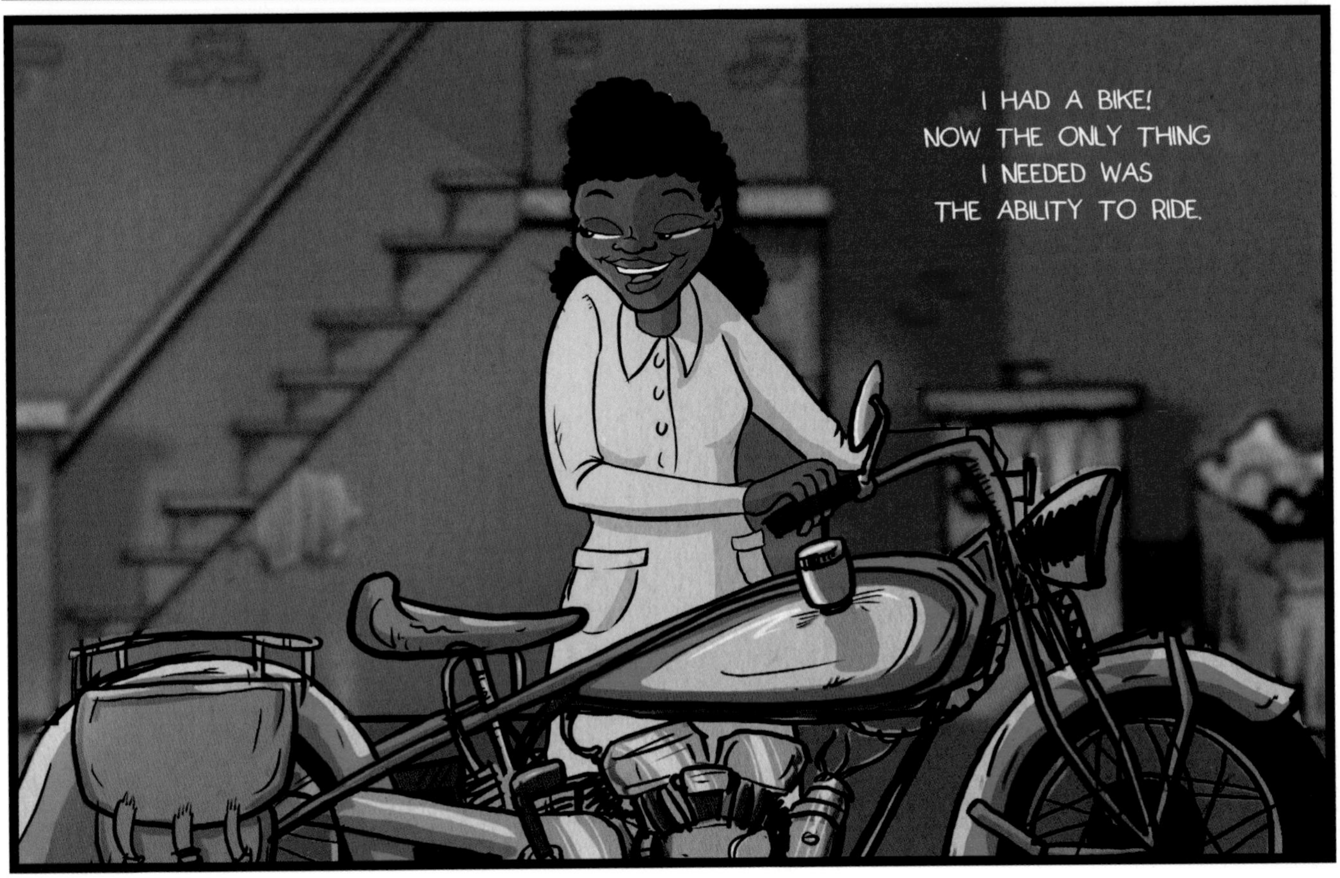
I HAD A BIKE! NOW THE ONLY THING I NEEDED WAS THE ABILITY TO RIDE.

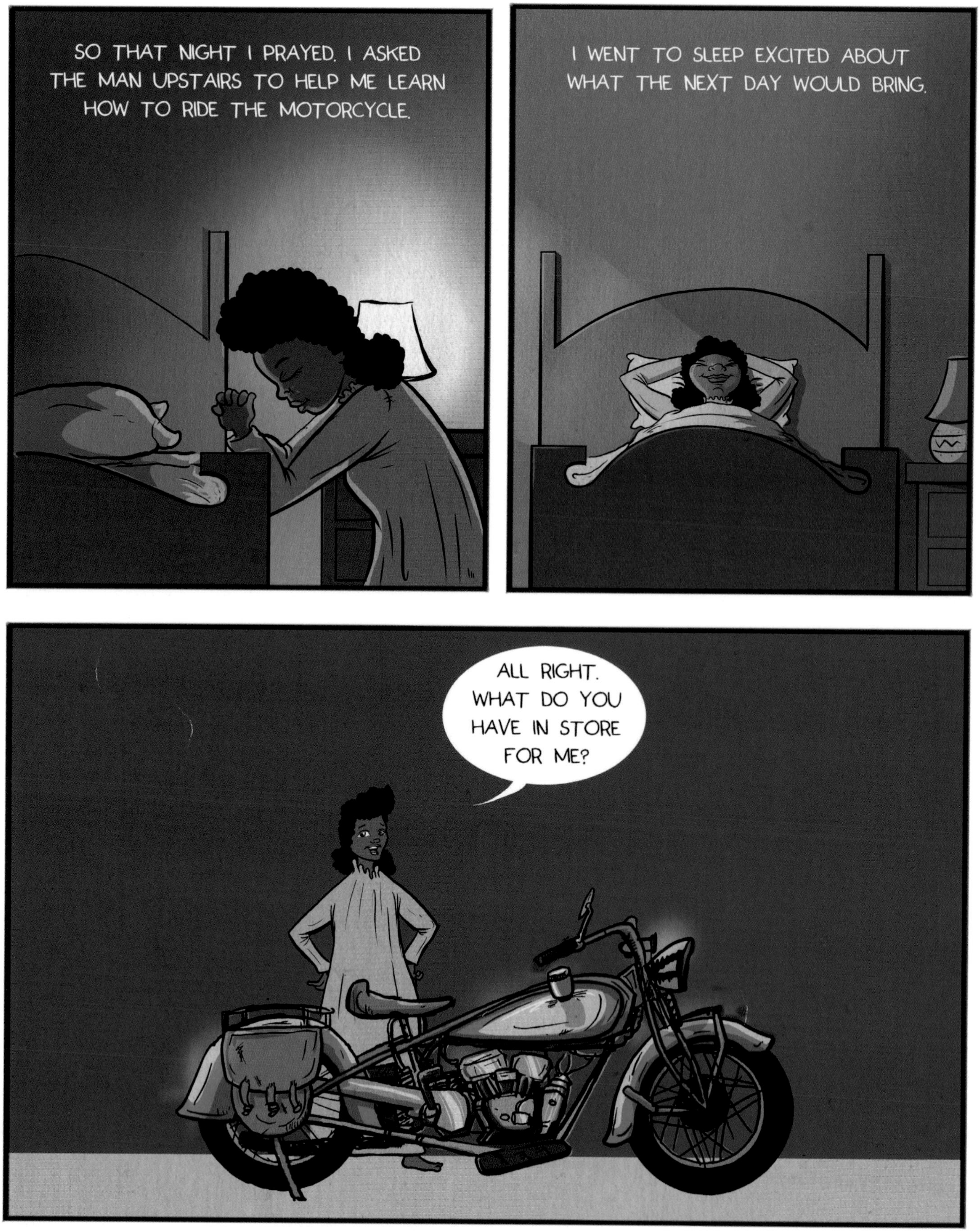
SO THAT NIGHT I PRAYED. I ASKED THE MAN UPSTAIRS TO HELP ME LEARN HOW TO RIDE THE MOTORCYCLE.
I WENT TO SLEEP EXCITED ABOUT WHAT THE NEXT DAY WOULD BRING.
ALL RIGHT. WHAT DO YOU HAVE IN STORE FOR ME?

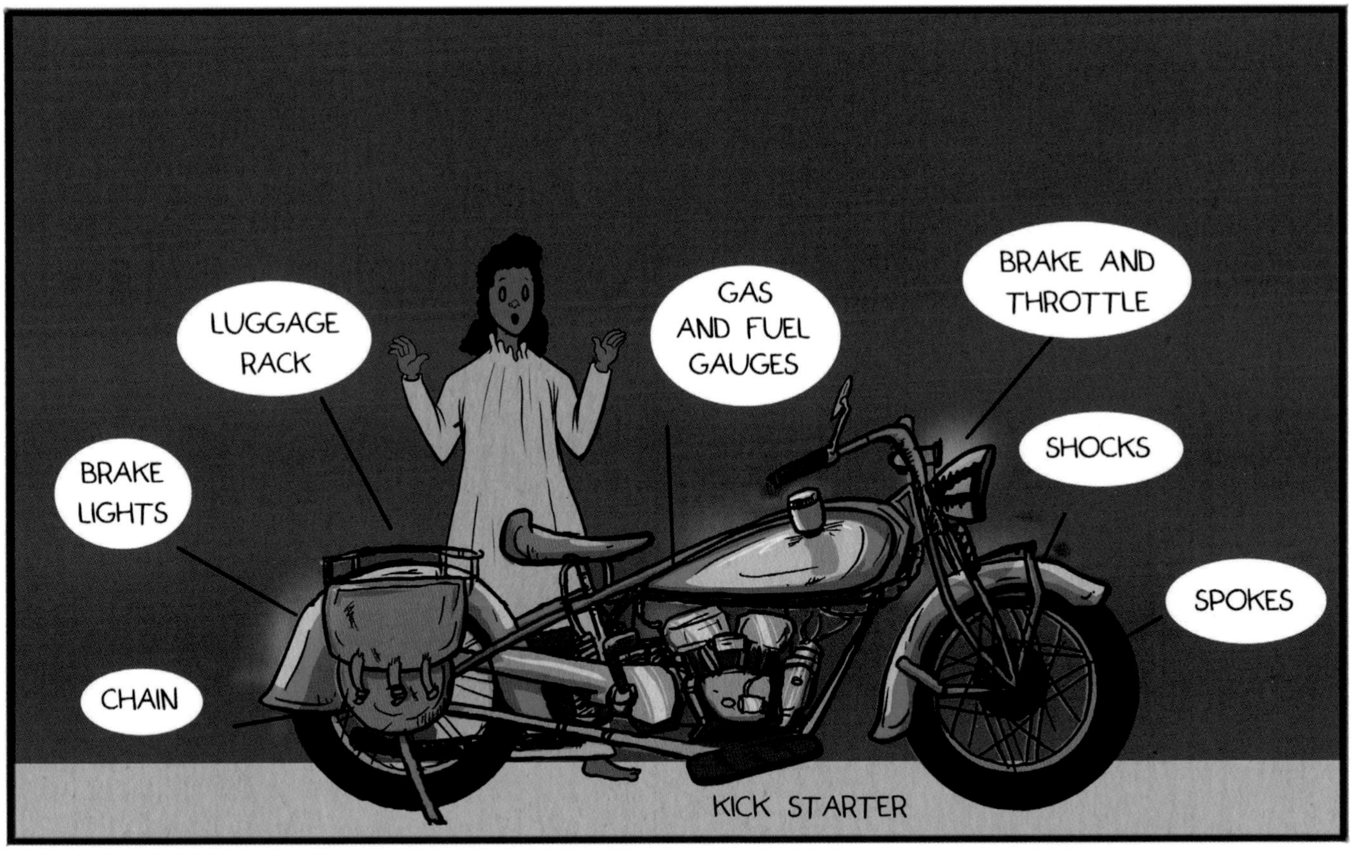
LUGGAGE RACK
GAS AND FUEL GAUGES
BRAKE AND THROTTLE
BRAKE LIGHTS
SHOCKS
SPOKES
CHAIN
KICK STARTER

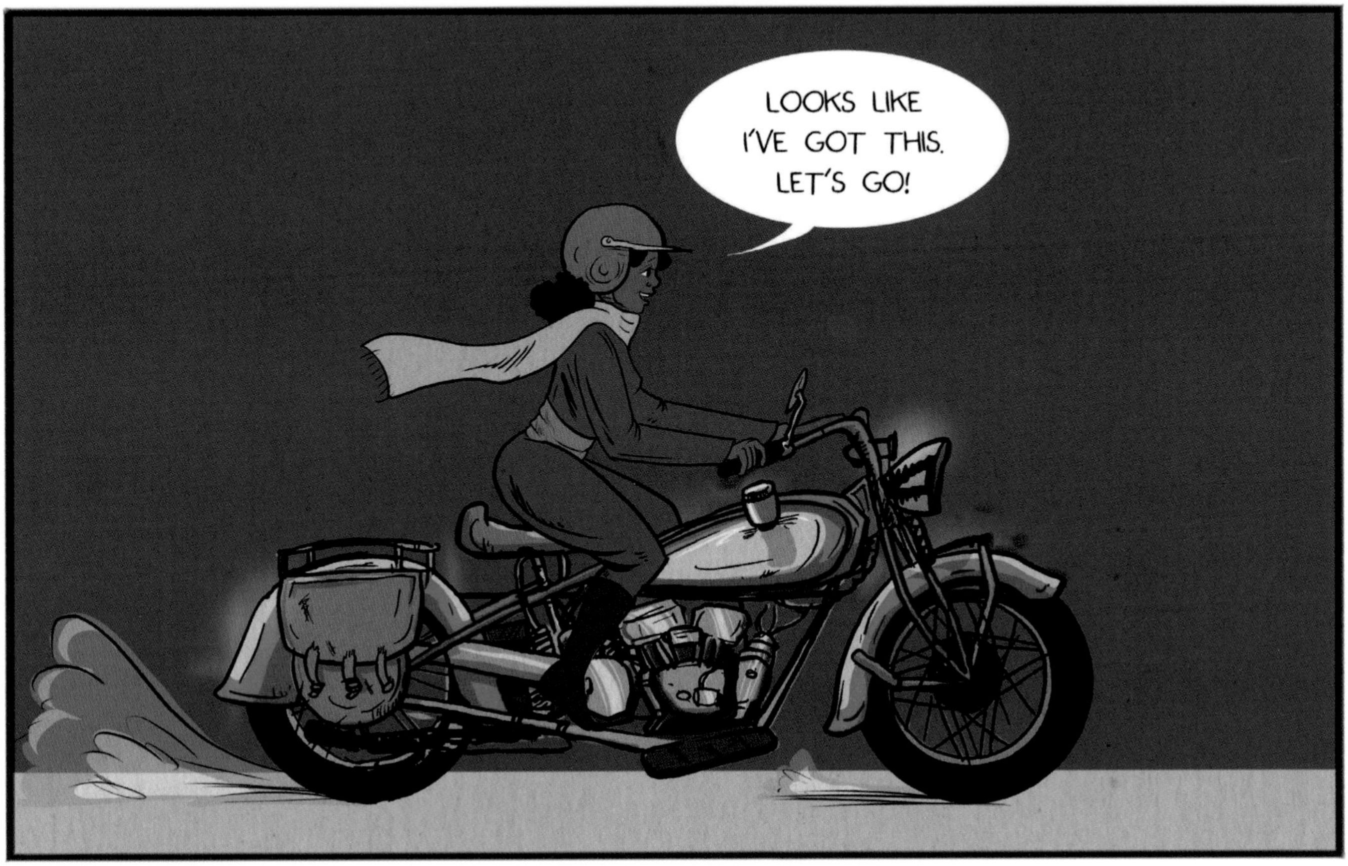
LOOKS LIKE I'VE GOT THIS. LET'S GO!

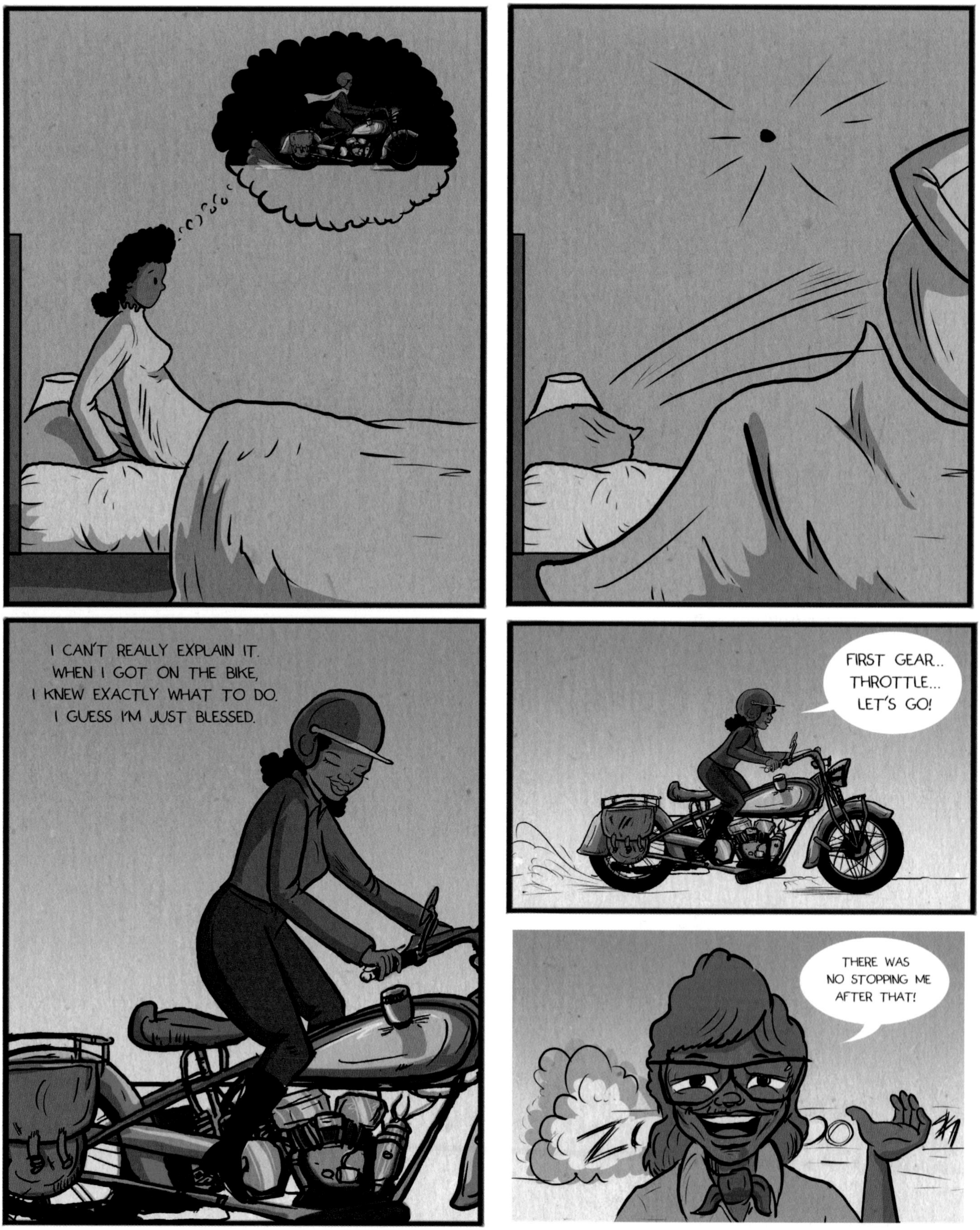
I CAN'T REALLY EXPLAIN IT. WHEN I GOT ON THE BIKE, I KNEW EXACTLY WHAT TO DO. I GUESS I'M JUST BLESSED.
FIRST GEAR.. THROTTLE... LET'S GO!
THERE WAS NO STOPPING ME AFTER THAT!
ZOOM

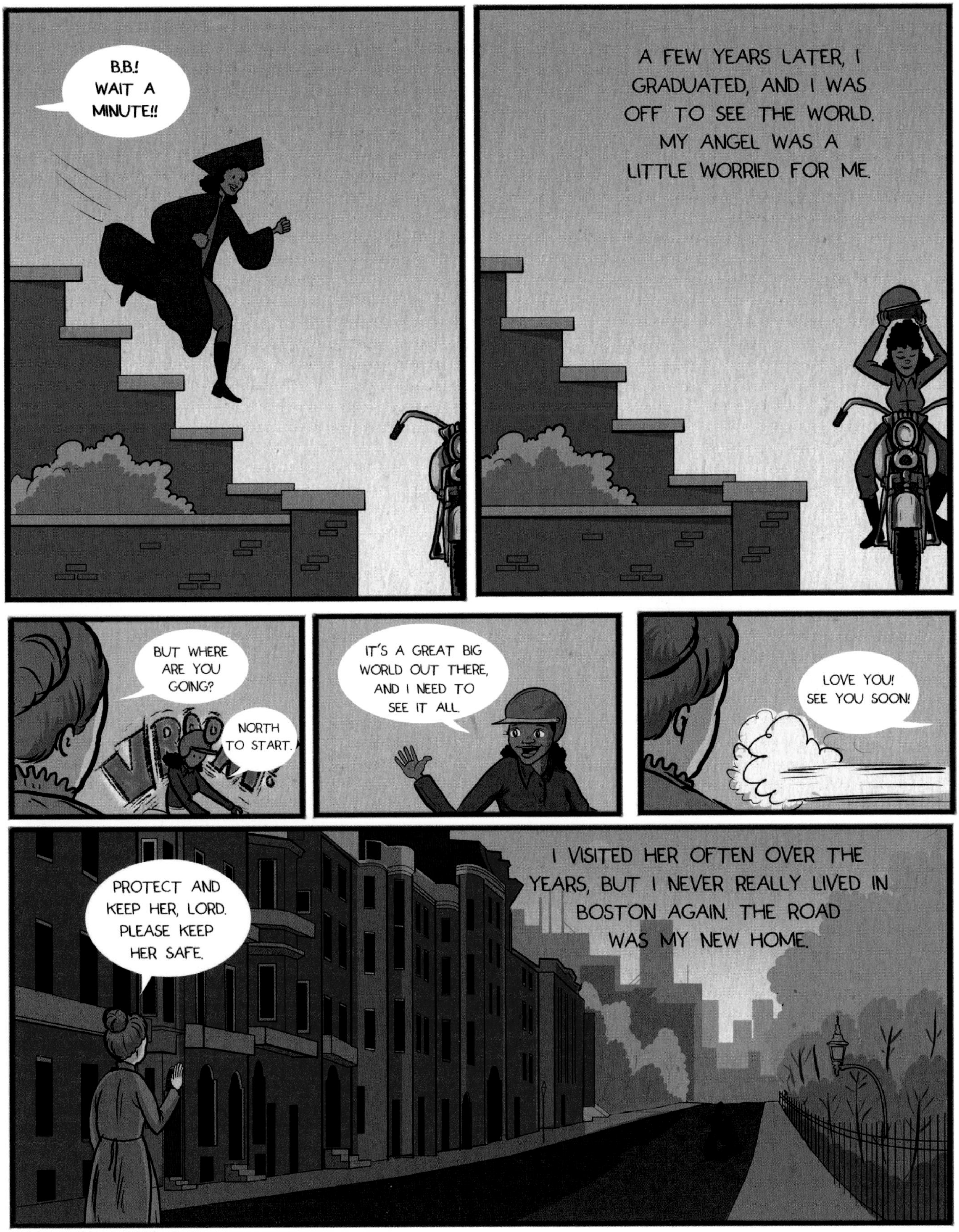
B.B.! WAIT A MINUTE!!
A FEW YEARS LATER, I GRADUATED, AND I WAS OFF TO SEE THE WORLD. MY ANGEL WAS A LITTLE WORRIED FOR ME.
BUT WHERE ARE YOU GOING?
NORTH TO START.
IT'S A GREAT BIG WORLD OUT THERE, AND I NEED TO SEE IT ALL.
LOVE YOU! SEE YOU SOON!
I VISITED HER OFTEN OVER THE YEARS, BUT I NEVER REALLY LIVED IN BOSTON AGAIN. THE ROAD WAS MY NEW HOME.
PROTECT AND KEEP HER, LORD. PLEASE KEEP HER SAFE.

CHAPTER 4

THE ROAD

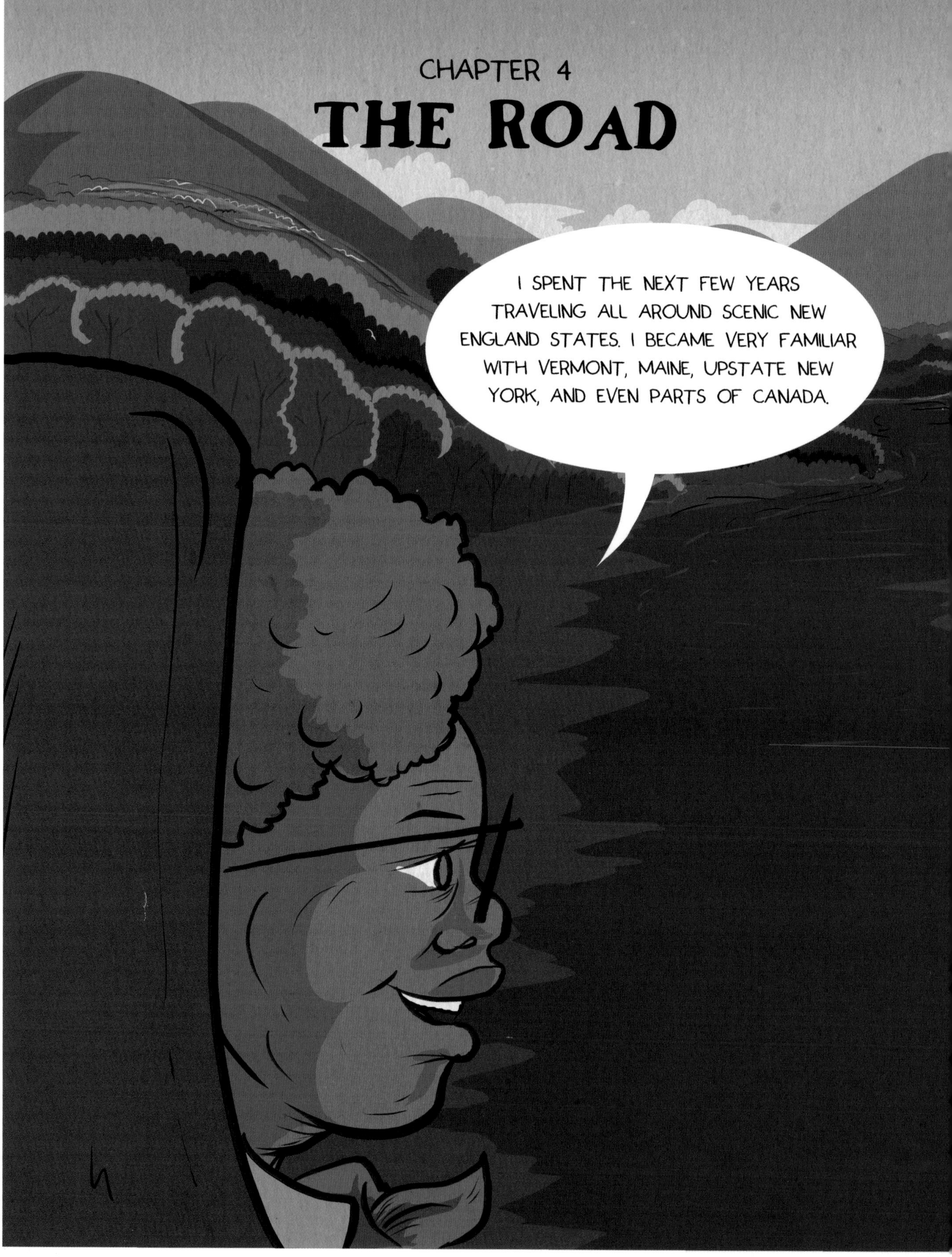

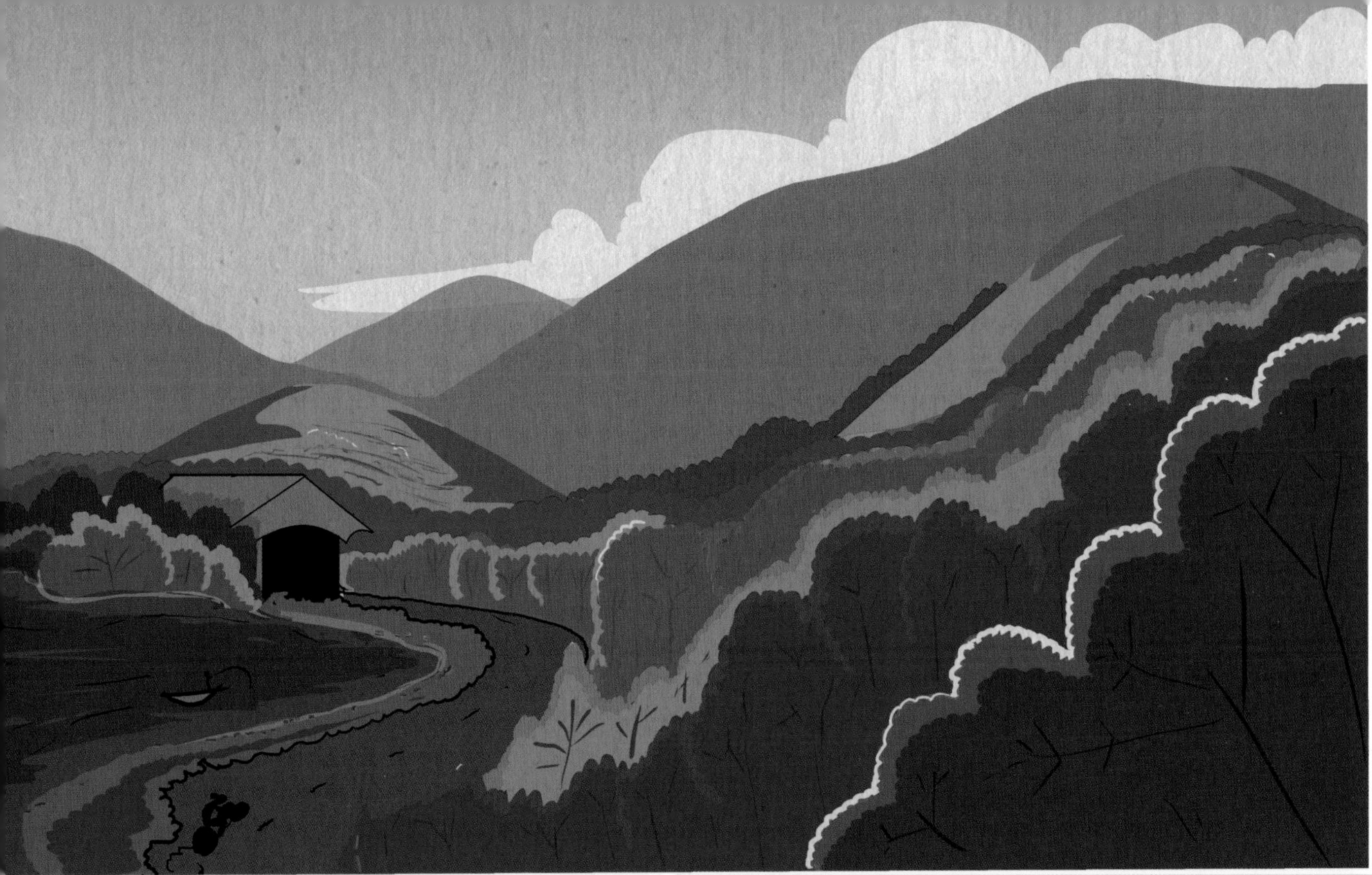

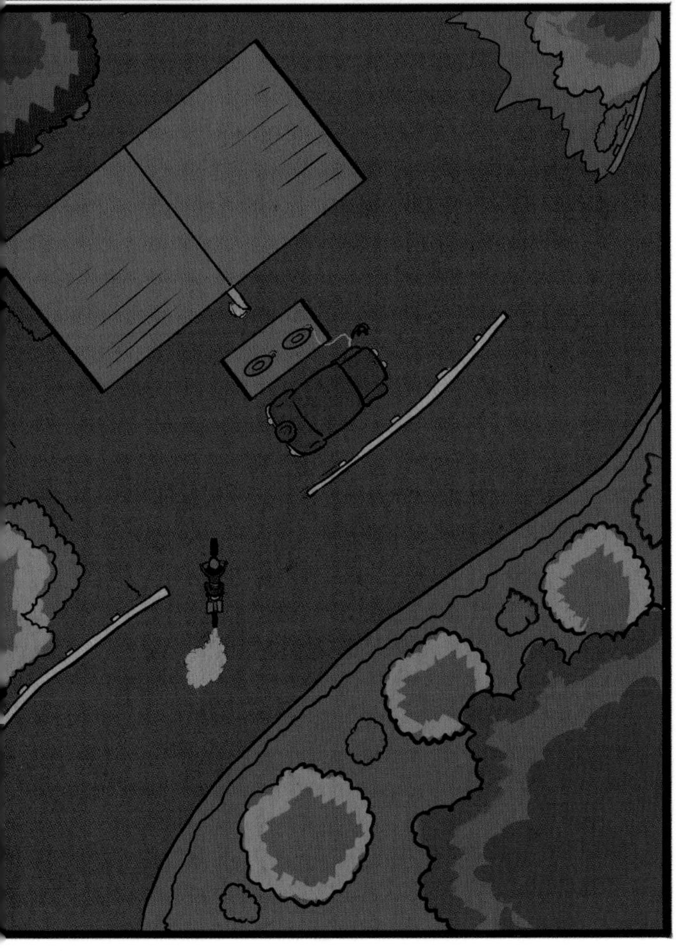

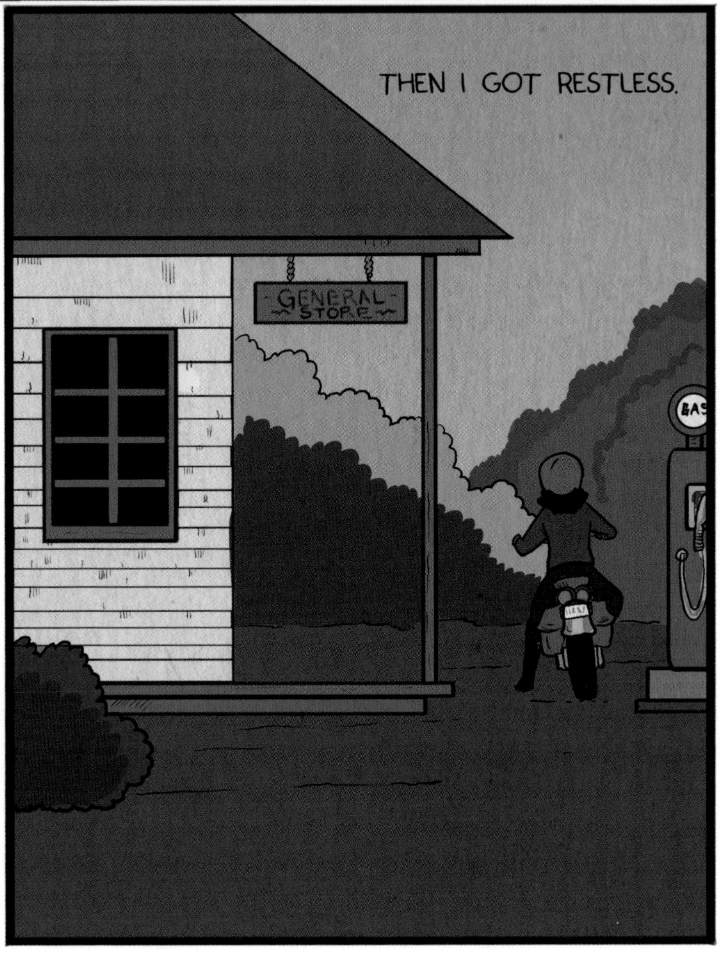
THEN I GOT RESTLESS.
GENERAL STORE
GAS

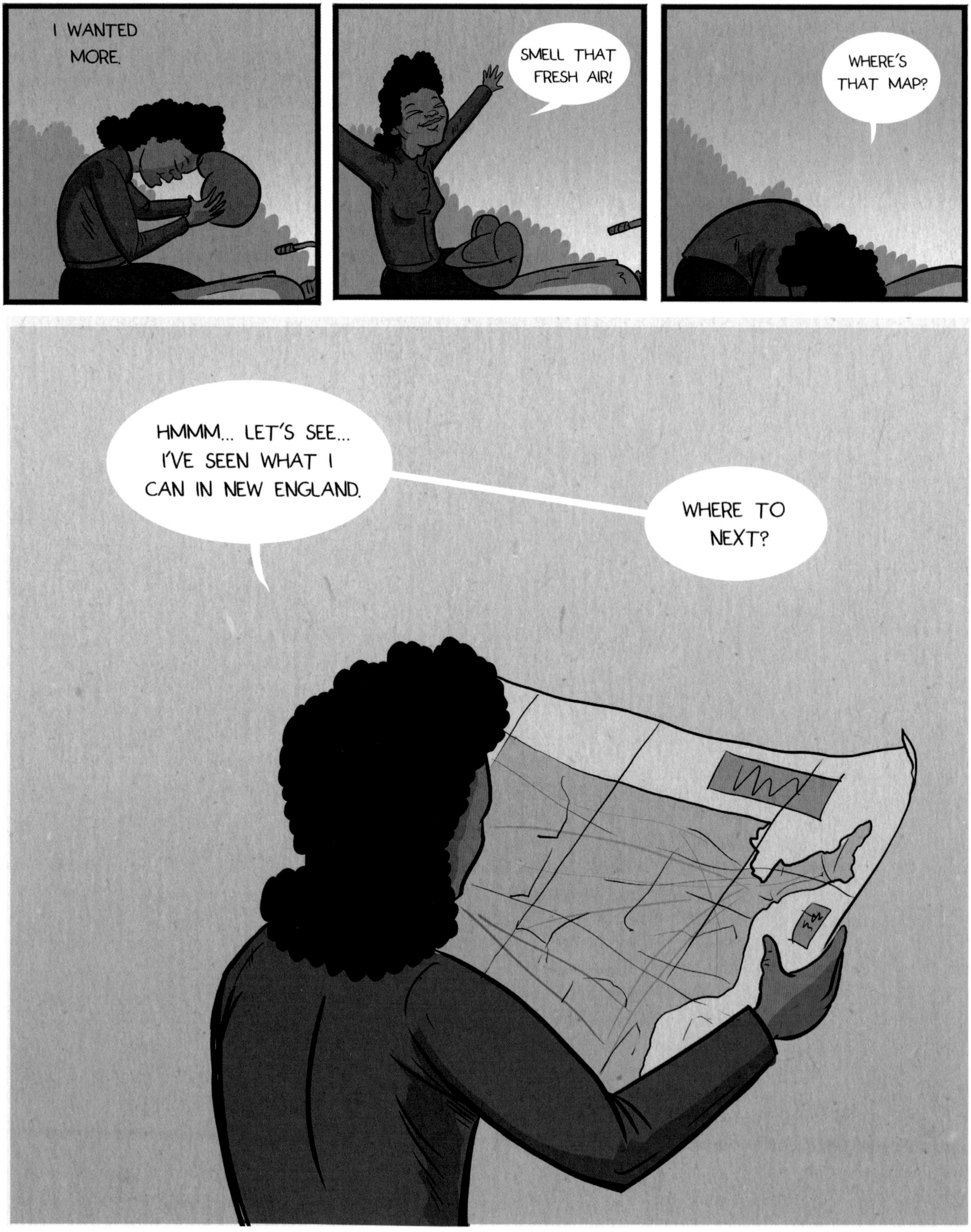
I WANTED MORE.
SMELL THAT FRESH AIR!
WHERE'S THAT MAP?
HMMM... LET'S SEE... I'VE SEEN WHAT I CAN IN NEW ENGLAND.
WHERE TO NEXT?

THIS WAS WHEN I BEGAN MY PENNY TOURS.
I TOOK A PENNY OUT OF MY POCKET...
...TOSSED IT INTO THE AIR...
...WHEREVER IT LANDED...
...WOULD BE MY NEXT STOP.

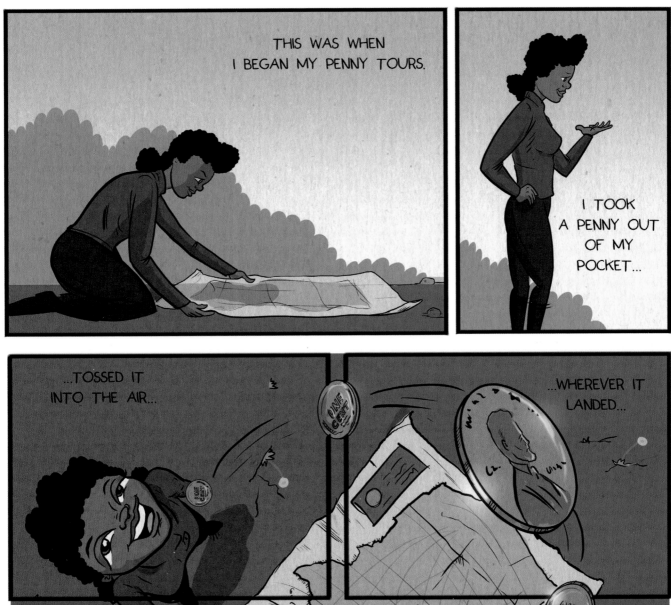

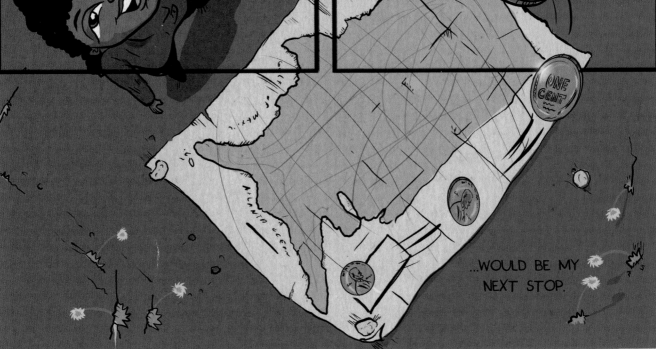

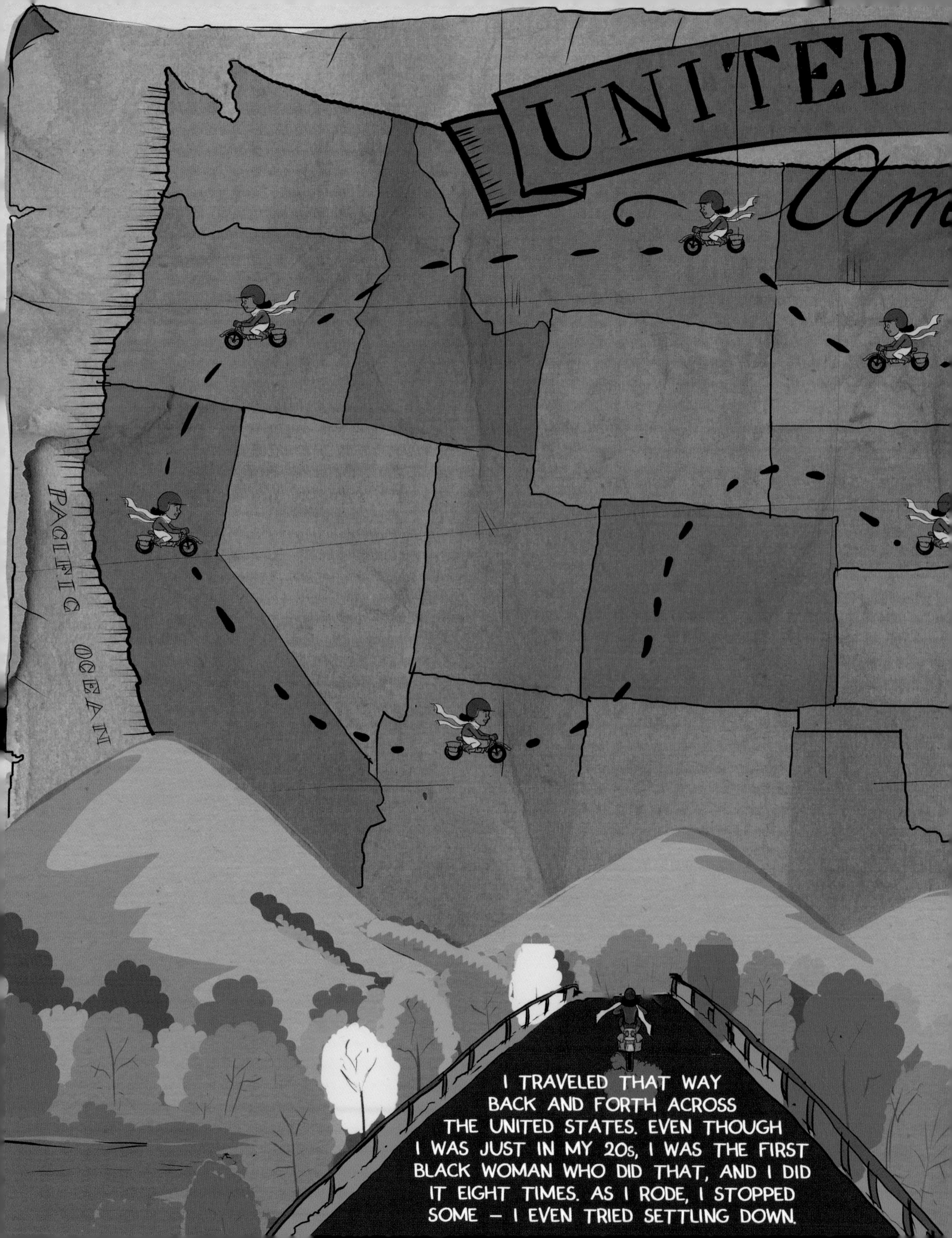
UNITED
Am
PACIFIC
OCEAN
I TRAVELED THAT WAY BACK AND FORTH ACROSS THE UNITED STATES. EVEN THOUGH I WAS JUST IN MY 20s, I WAS THE FIRST BLACK WOMAN WHO DID THAT, AND I DID IT EIGHT TIMES. AS I RODE, I STOPPED SOME — I EVEN TRIED SETTLING DOWN.

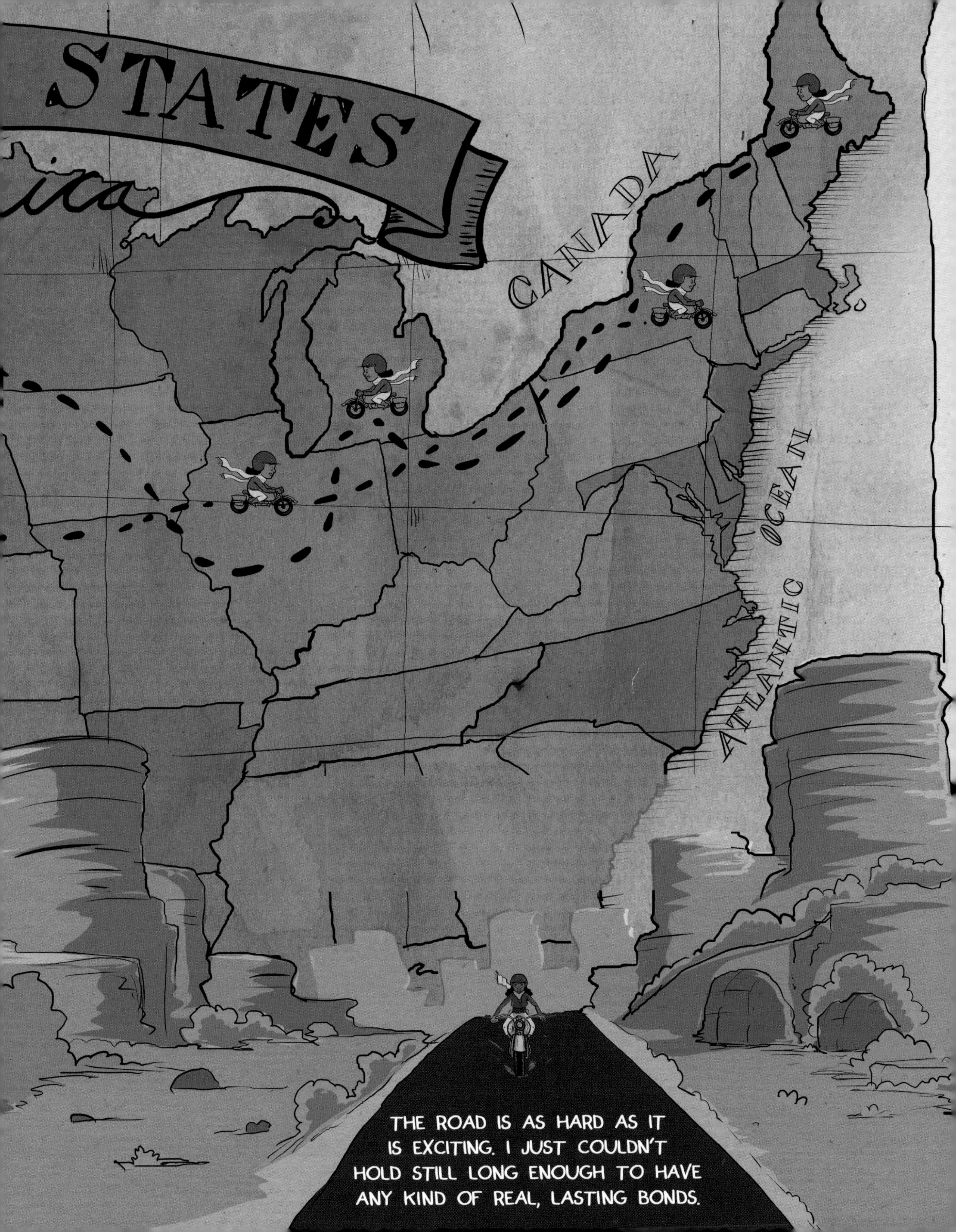
STATES
ica
CANADA
ATLANTIC OCEAN
THE ROAD IS AS HARD AS IT IS EXCITING. I JUST COULDN'T HOLD STILL LONG ENOUGH TO HAVE ANY KIND OF REAL, LASTING BONDS.

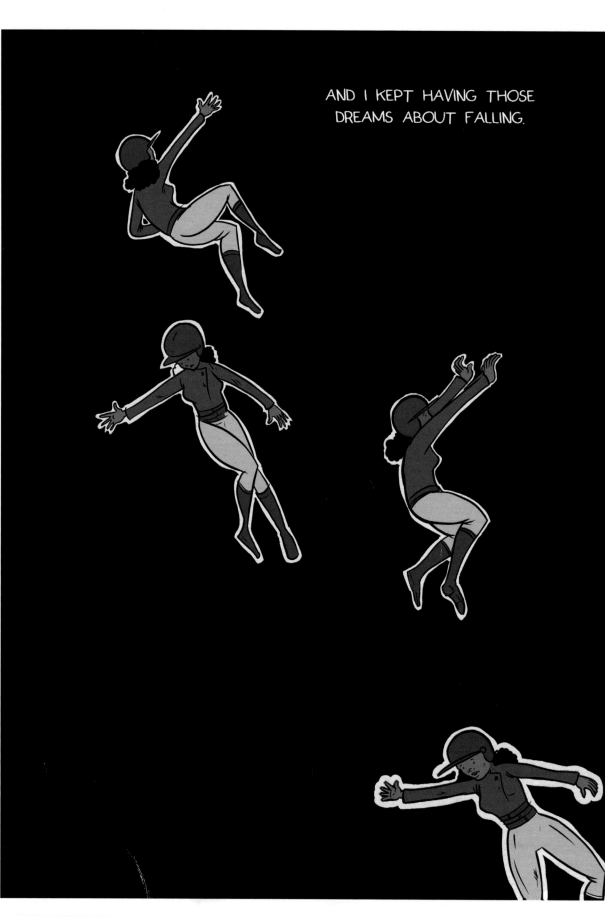

AND I KEPT HAVING THOSE
DREAMS ABOUT FALLING.

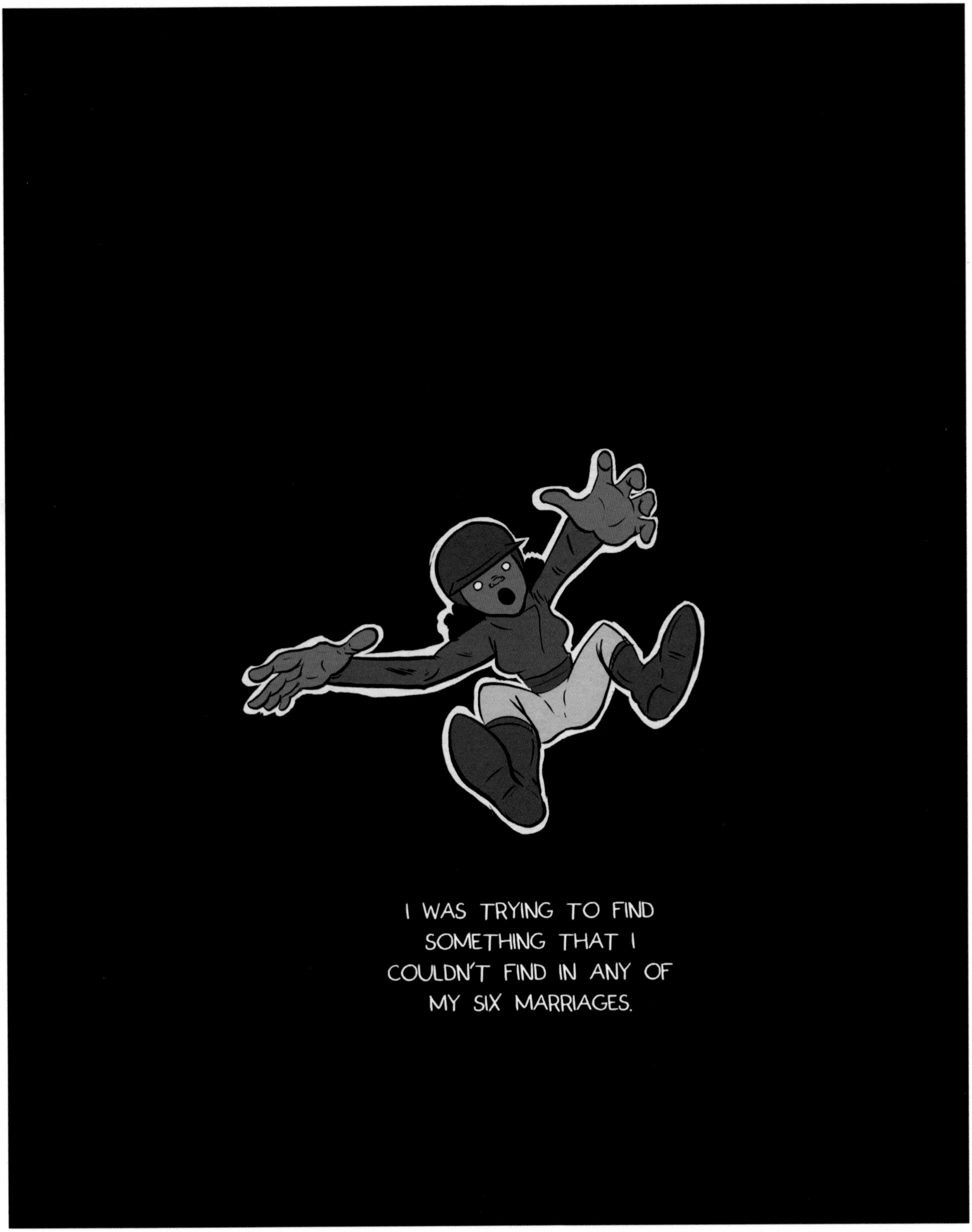
I WAS TRYING TO FIND
SOMETHING THAT I
COULDN'T FIND IN ANY OF
MY SIX MARRIAGES.

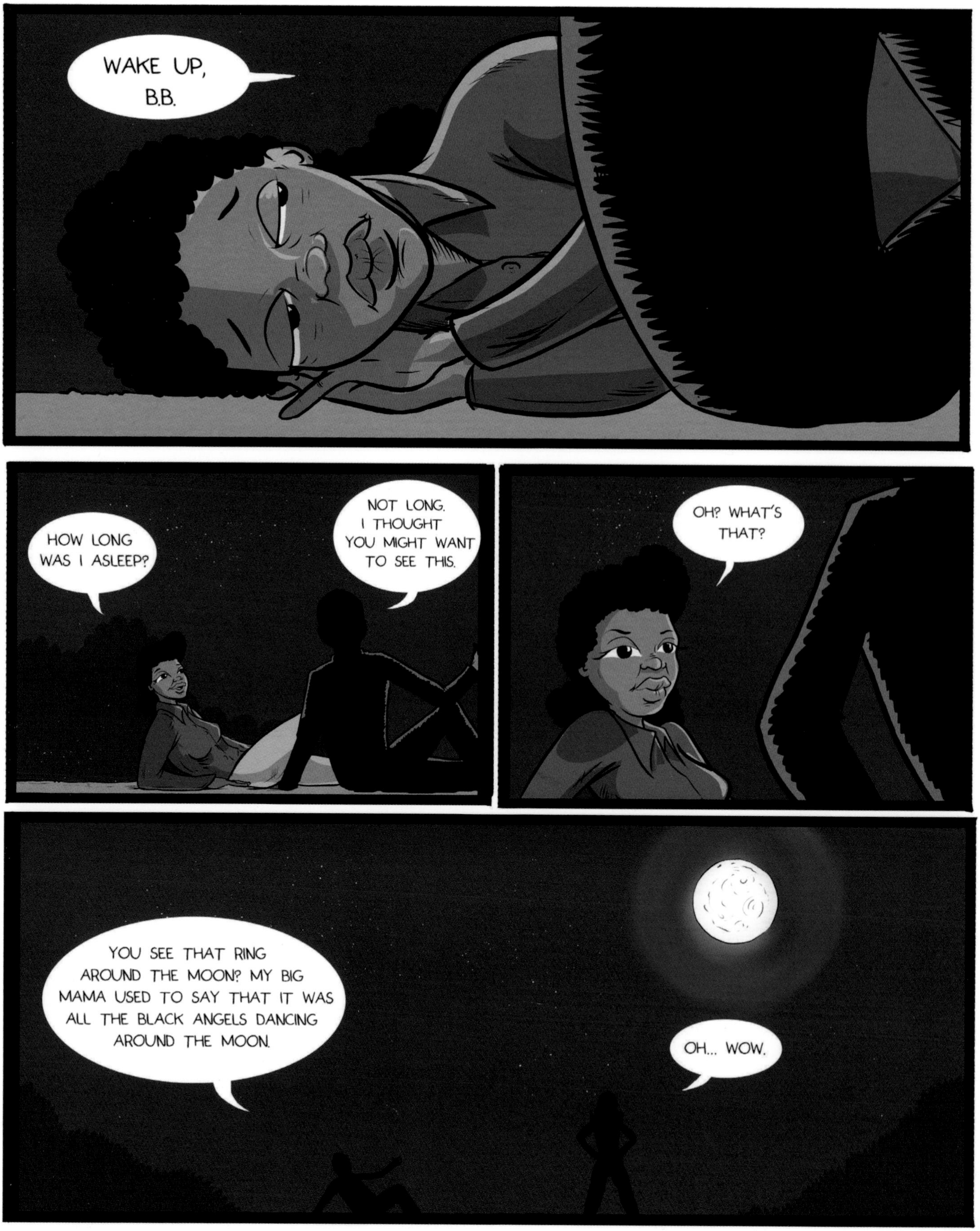
WAKE UP, B.B.
HOW LONG WAS I ASLEEP?
NOT LONG. I THOUGHT YOU MIGHT WANT TO SEE THIS.
OH? WHAT'S THAT?
YOU SEE THAT RING AROUND THE MOON? MY BIG MAMA USED TO SAY THAT IT WAS ALL THE BLACK ANGELS DANCING AROUND THE MOON.
OH... WOW.

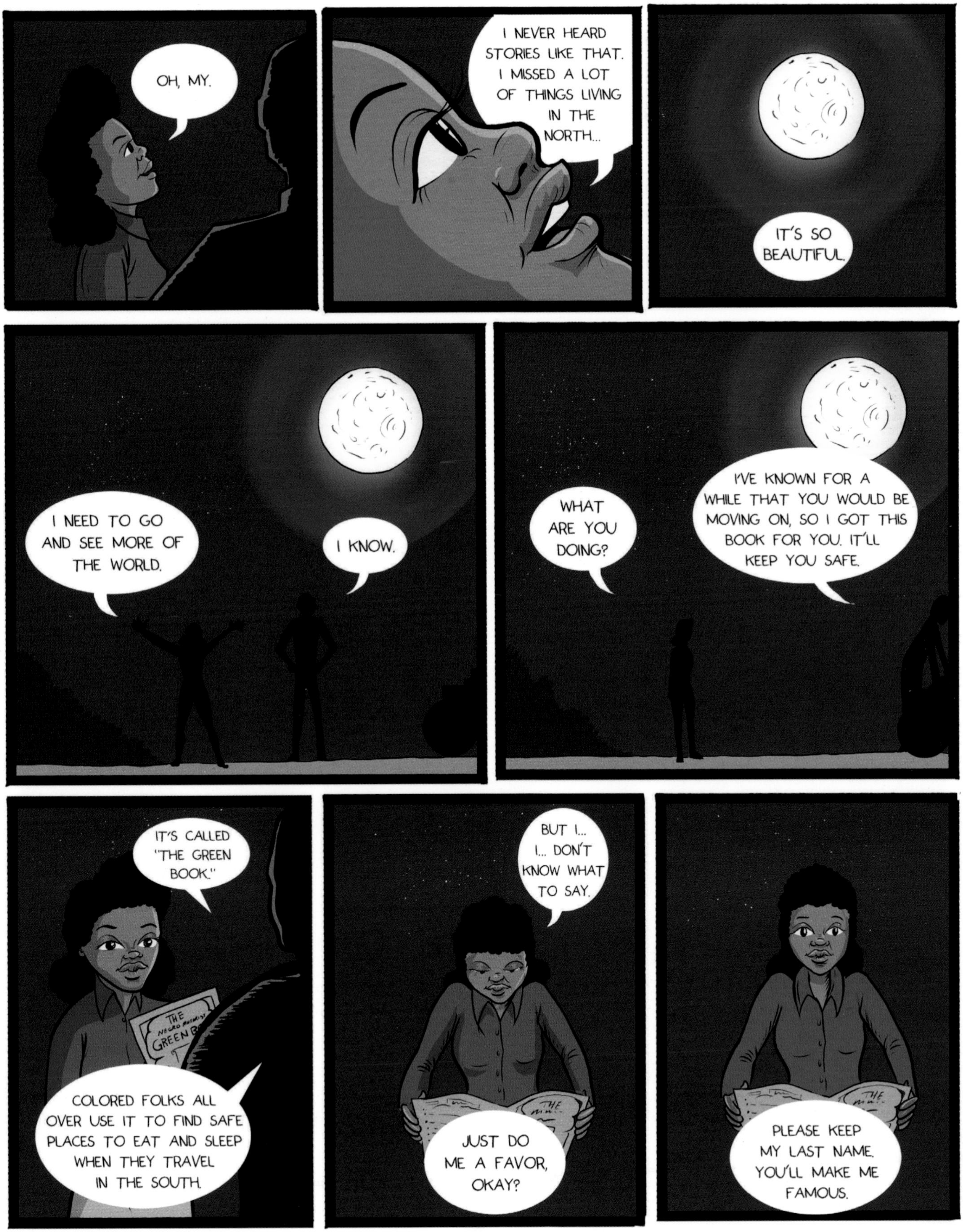
OH, MY.
I NEVER HEARD STORIES LIKE THAT. I MISSED A LOT OF THINGS LIVING IN THE NORTH...
IT'S SO BEAUTIFUL.
I NEED TO GO AND SEE MORE OF THE WORLD.
I KNOW.
WHAT ARE YOU DOING?
I'VE KNOWN FOR A WHILE THAT YOU WOULD BE MOVING ON, SO I GOT THIS BOOK FOR YOU. IT'LL KEEP YOU SAFE.
IT'S CALLED "THE GREEN BOOK."
COLORED FOLKS ALL OVER USE IT TO FIND SAFE PLACES TO EAT AND SLEEP WHEN THEY TRAVEL IN THE SOUTH.
BUT I... I... DON'T KNOW WHAT TO SAY.
JUST DO ME A FAVOR, OKAY?
PLEASE KEEP MY LAST NAME. YOU'LL MAKE ME FAMOUS.

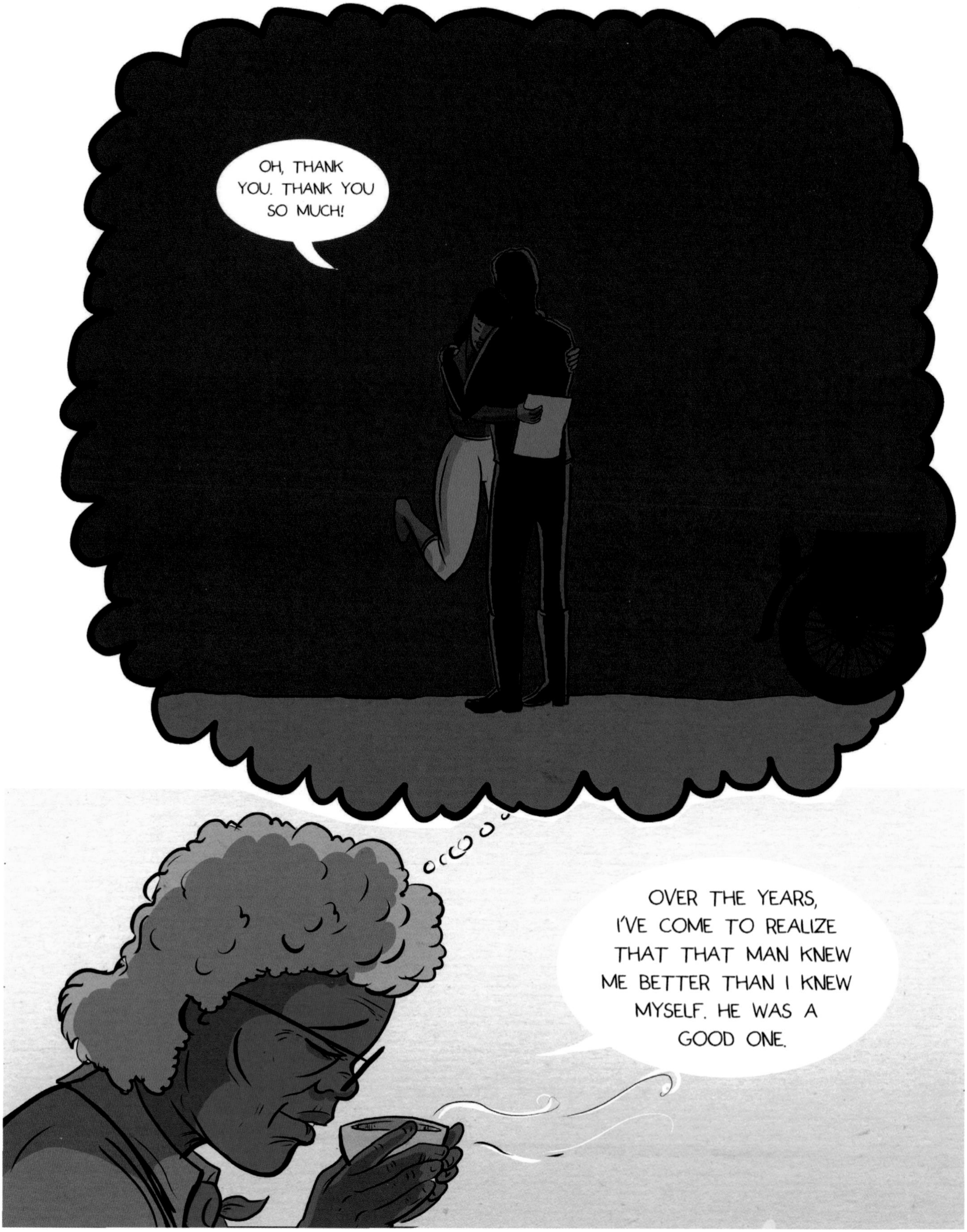
OH, THANK YOU. THANK YOU SO MUCH!
OVER THE YEARS, I'VE COME TO REALIZE THAT THAT MAN KNEW ME BETTER THAN I KNEW MYSELF. HE WAS A GOOD ONE.

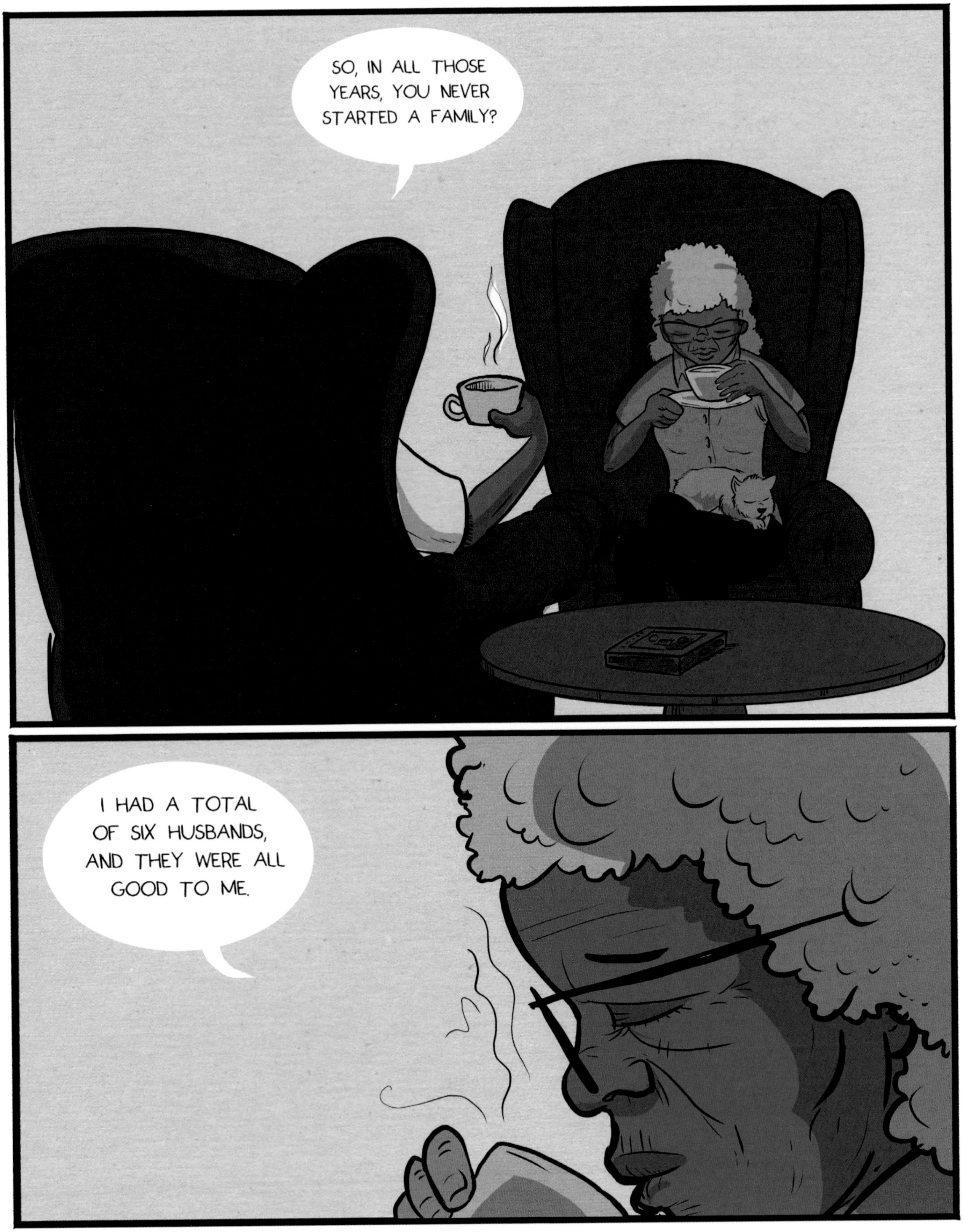
SO, IN ALL THOSE YEARS, YOU NEVER STARTED A FAMILY?
I HAD A TOTAL OF SIX HUSBANDS, AND THEY WERE ALL GOOD TO ME.

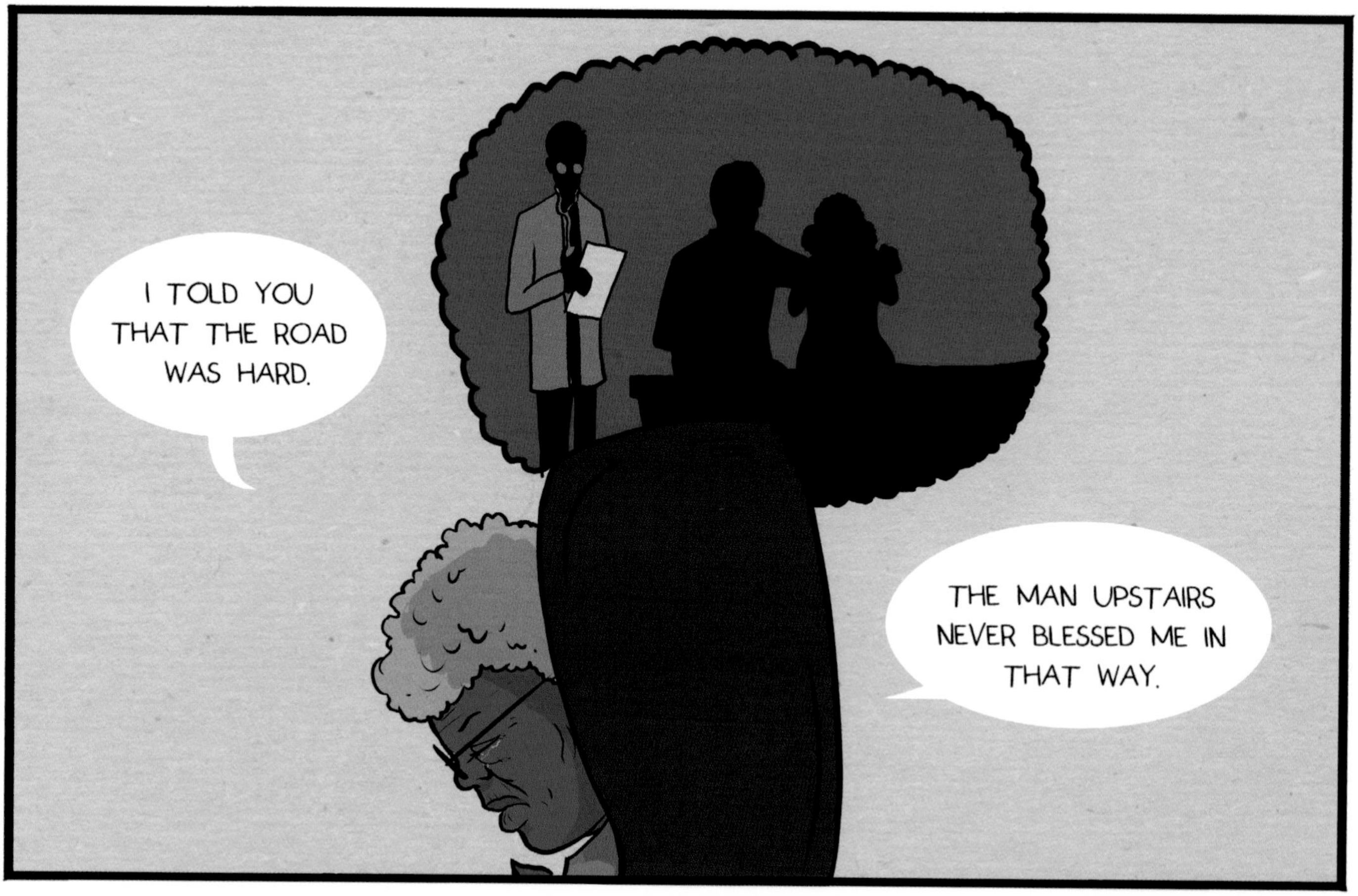
I TOLD YOU THAT THE ROAD WAS HARD.
THE MAN UPSTAIRS NEVER BLESSED ME IN THAT WAY.

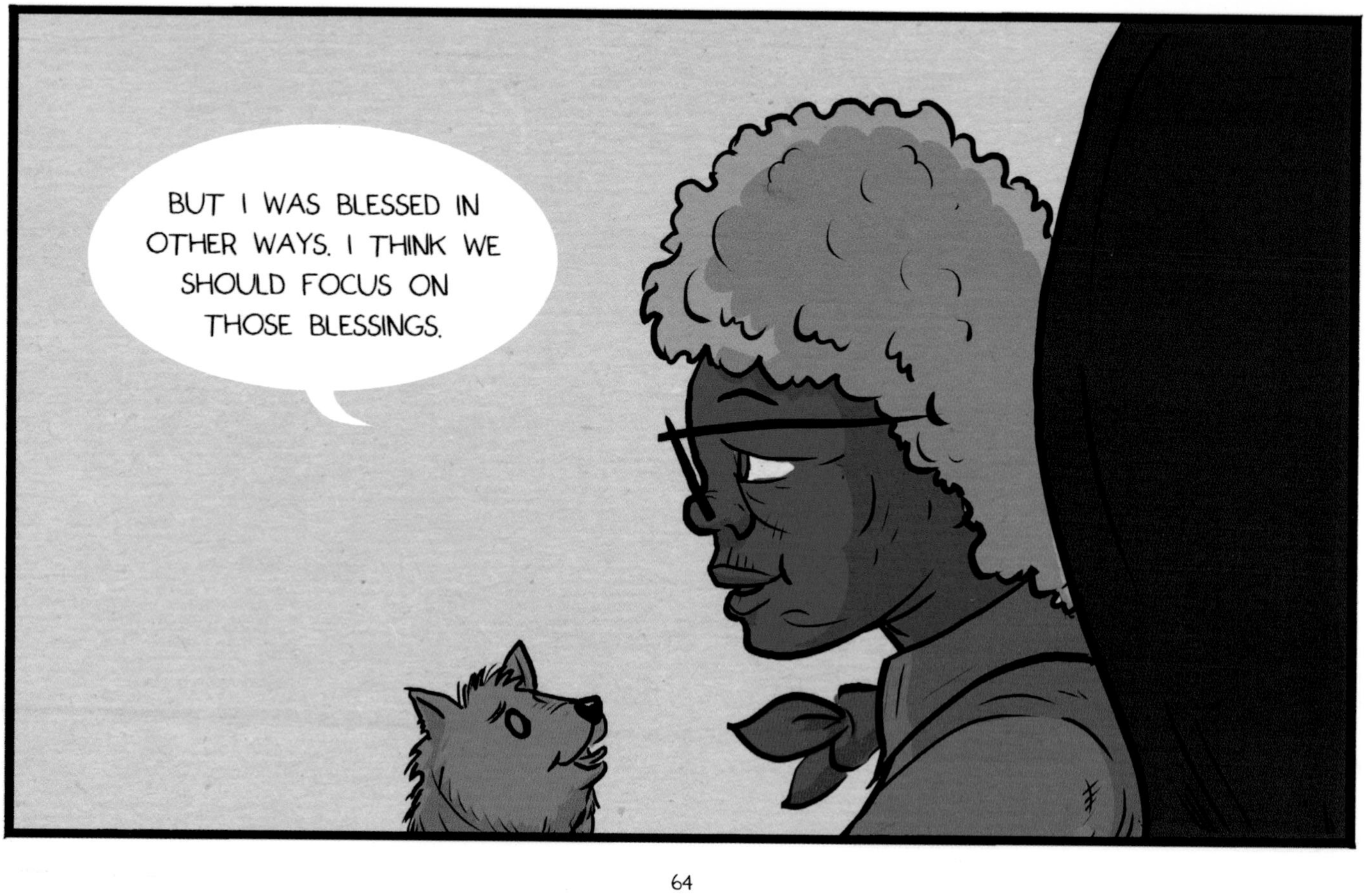
BUT I WAS BLESSED IN OTHER WAYS. I THINK WE SHOULD FOCUS ON THOSE BLESSINGS.

THE VERY NEXT
NIGHT, I HAD
ANOTHER DREAM.

CHAPTER 5

ADVENTURE

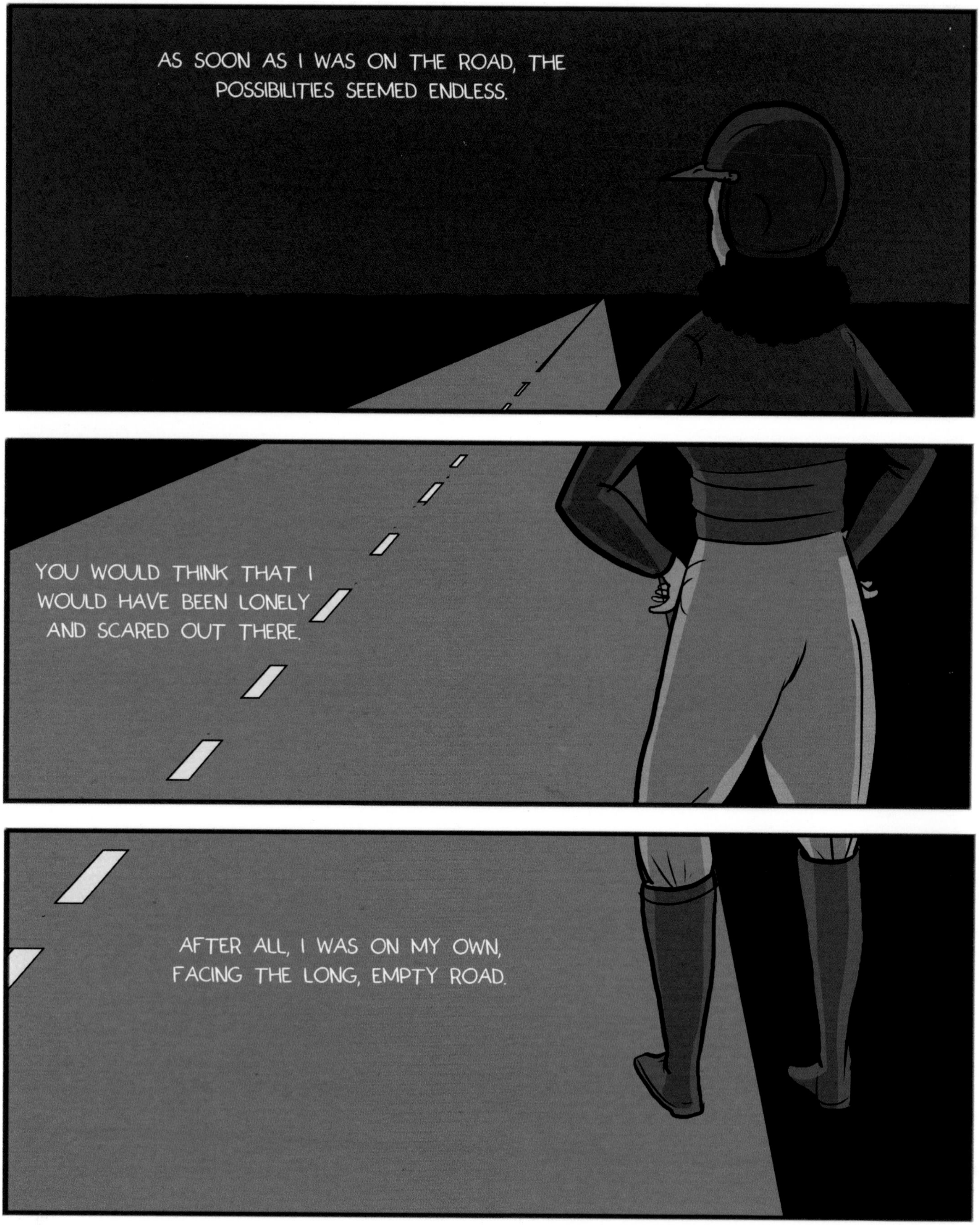
AS SOON AS I WAS ON THE ROAD, THE POSSIBILITIES SEEMED ENDLESS.
YOU WOULD THINK THAT I WOULD HAVE BEEN LONELY AND SCARED OUT THERE.
AFTER ALL, I WAS ON MY OWN, FACING THE LONG, EMPTY ROAD.

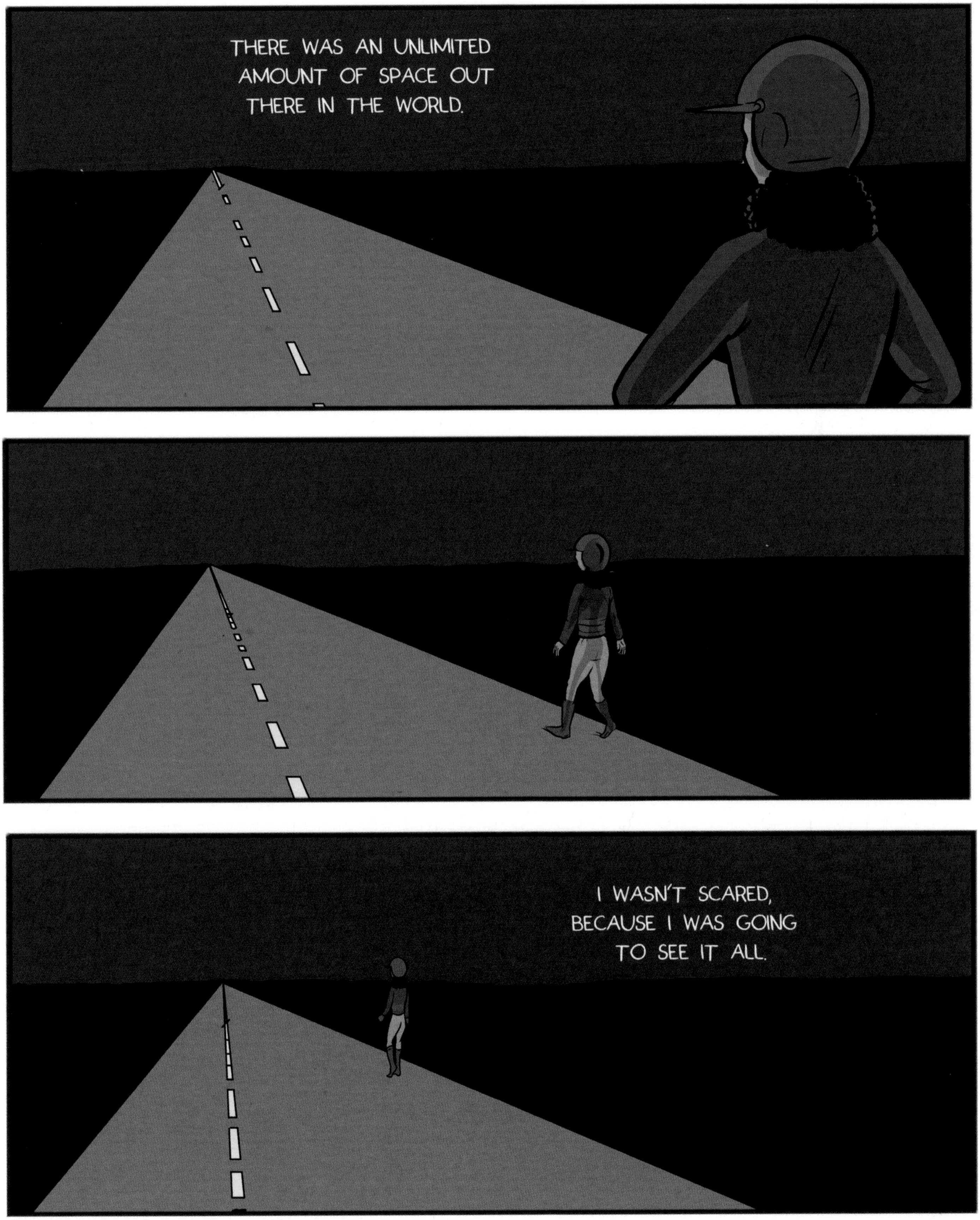
THERE WAS AN UNLIMITED AMOUNT OF SPACE OUT THERE IN THE WORLD.
I WASN'T SCARED, BECAUSE I WAS GOING TO SEE IT ALL.

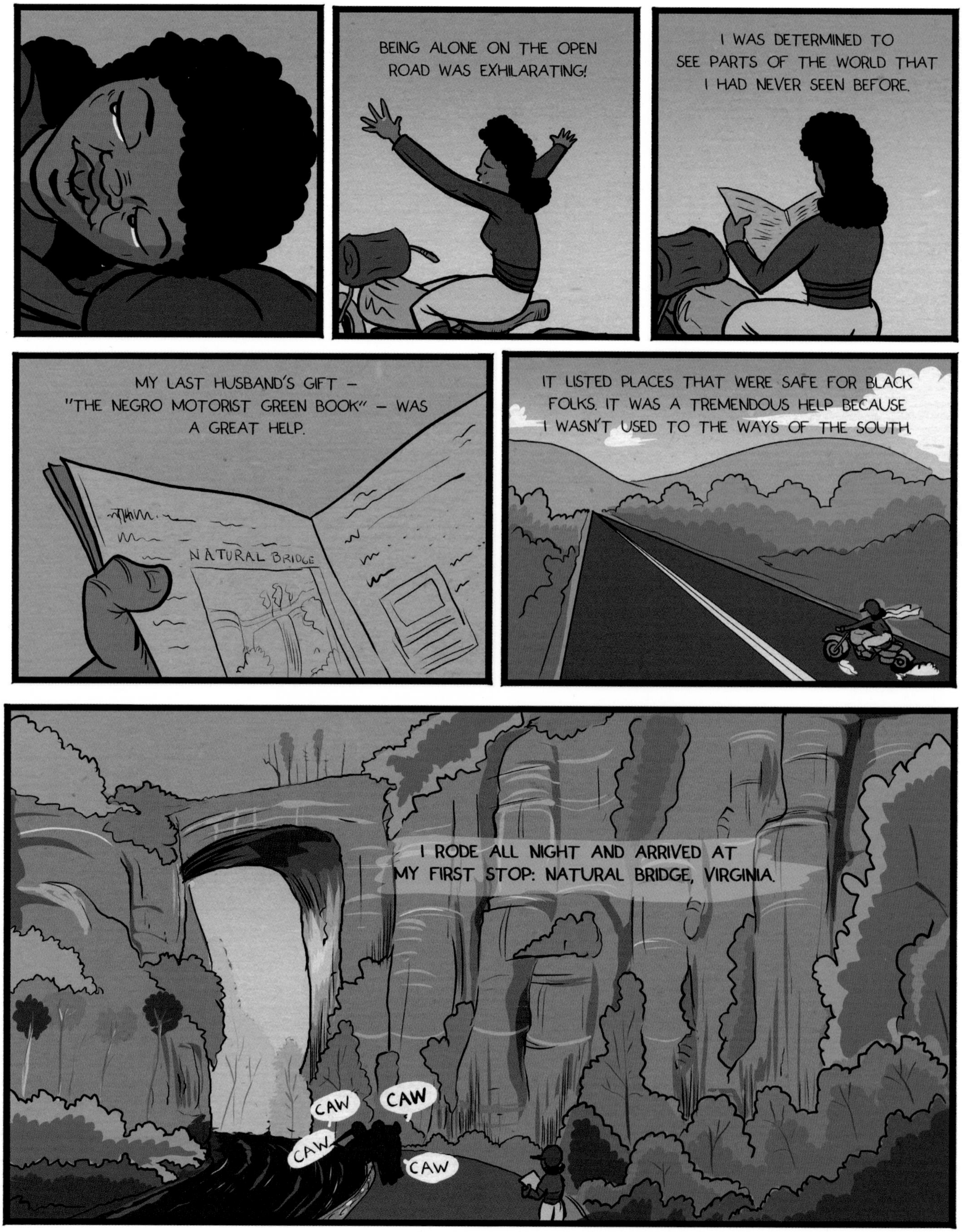

BEING ALONE ON THE OPEN ROAD WAS EXHILARATING!
I WAS DETERMINED TO SEE PARTS OF THE WORLD THAT I HAD NEVER SEEN BEFORE.
MY LAST HUSBAND'S GIFT — "THE NEGRO MOTORIST GREEN BOOK" — WAS A GREAT HELP.
NATURAL BRIDGE
IT LISTED PLACES THAT WERE SAFE FOR BLACK FOLKS. IT WAS A TREMENDOUS HELP BECAUSE I WASN'T USED TO THE WAYS OF THE SOUTH.
I RODE ALL NIGHT AND ARRIVED AT MY FIRST STOP: NATURAL BRIDGE, VIRGINIA.
CAW
CAW
CAW
CAW

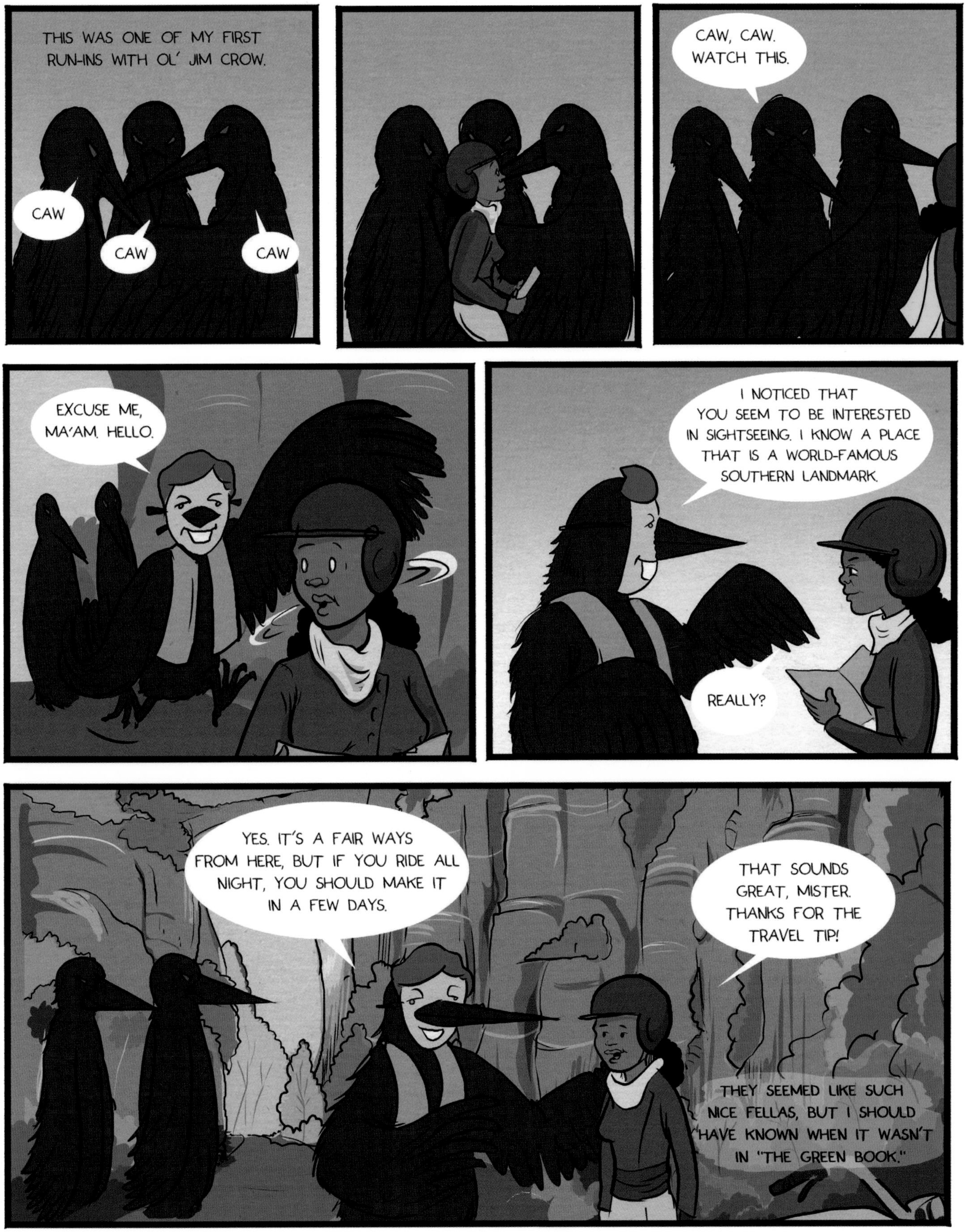
THIS WAS ONE OF MY FIRST RUN-INS WITH OL' JIM CROW.
CAW
CAW
CAW
CAW, CAW. WATCH THIS.
EXCUSE ME, MA'AM. HELLO.
I NOTICED THAT YOU SEEM TO BE INTERESTED IN SIGHTSEEING. I KNOW A PLACE THAT IS A WORLD-FAMOUS SOUTHERN LANDMARK.
REALLY?
YES. IT'S A FAIR WAYS FROM HERE, BUT IF YOU RIDE ALL NIGHT, YOU SHOULD MAKE IT IN A FEW DAYS.
THAT SOUNDS GREAT, MISTER. THANKS FOR THE TRAVEL TIP!
THEY SEEMED LIKE SUCH NICE FELLAS, BUT I SHOULD HAVE KNOWN WHEN IT WASN'T IN "THE GREEN BOOK."

THE NEXT FEW DAYS WERE A WHIRLWIND OF TROUBLE. I SEEMED TO BE DOGGED BY JIM CROW THE WHOLE WAY.

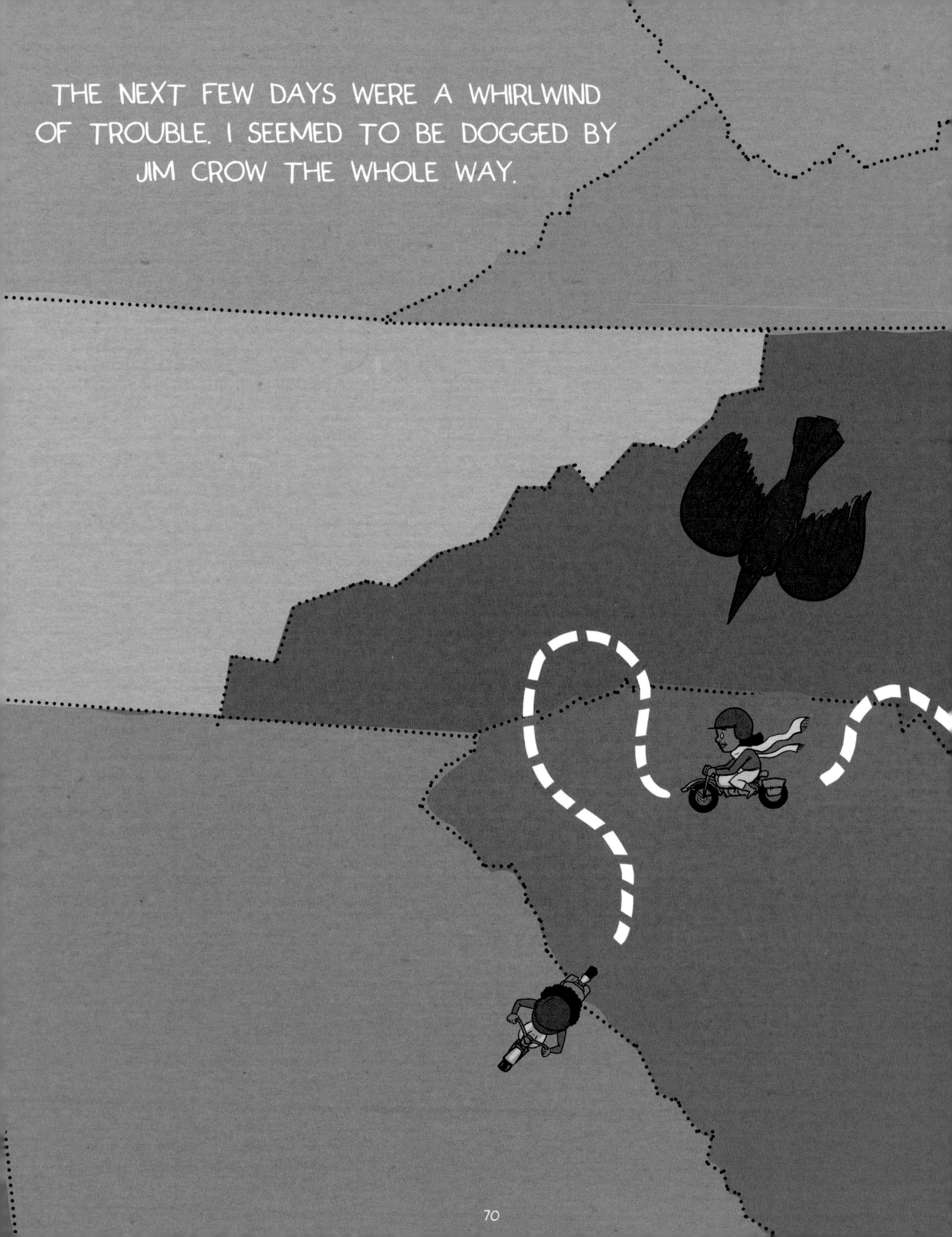

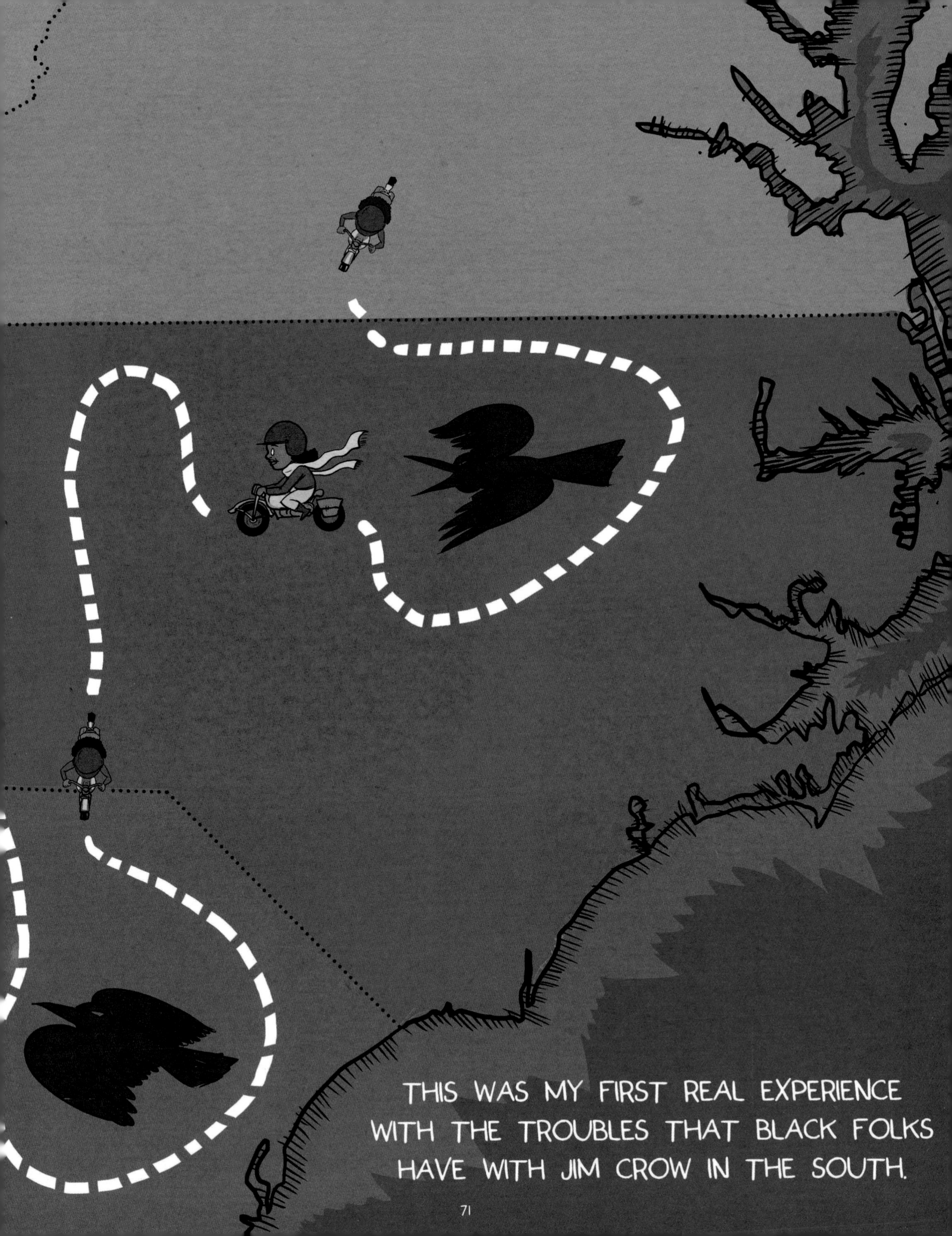
THIS WAS MY FIRST REAL EXPERIENCE
WITH THE TROUBLES THAT BLACK FOLKS
HAVE WITH JIM CROW IN THE SOUTH.

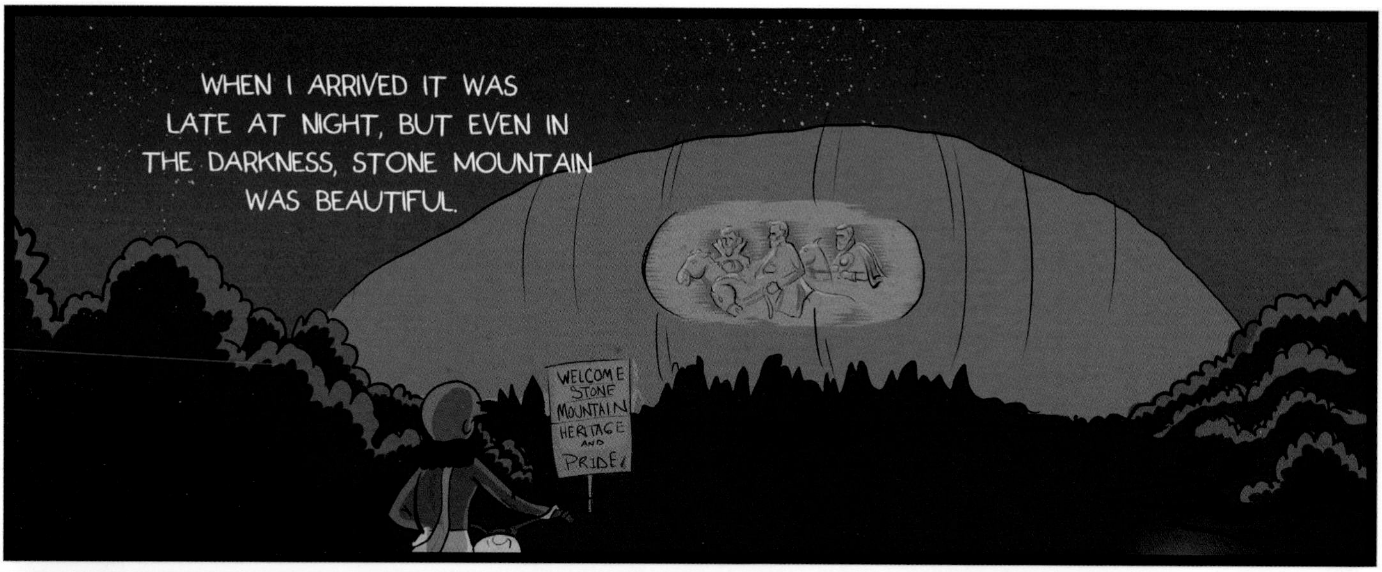
WHEN I ARRIVED IT WAS LATE AT NIGHT, BUT EVEN IN THE DARKNESS, STONE MOUNTAIN WAS BEAUTIFUL.
WELCOME STONE MOUNTAIN HERITAGE AND PRIDE!

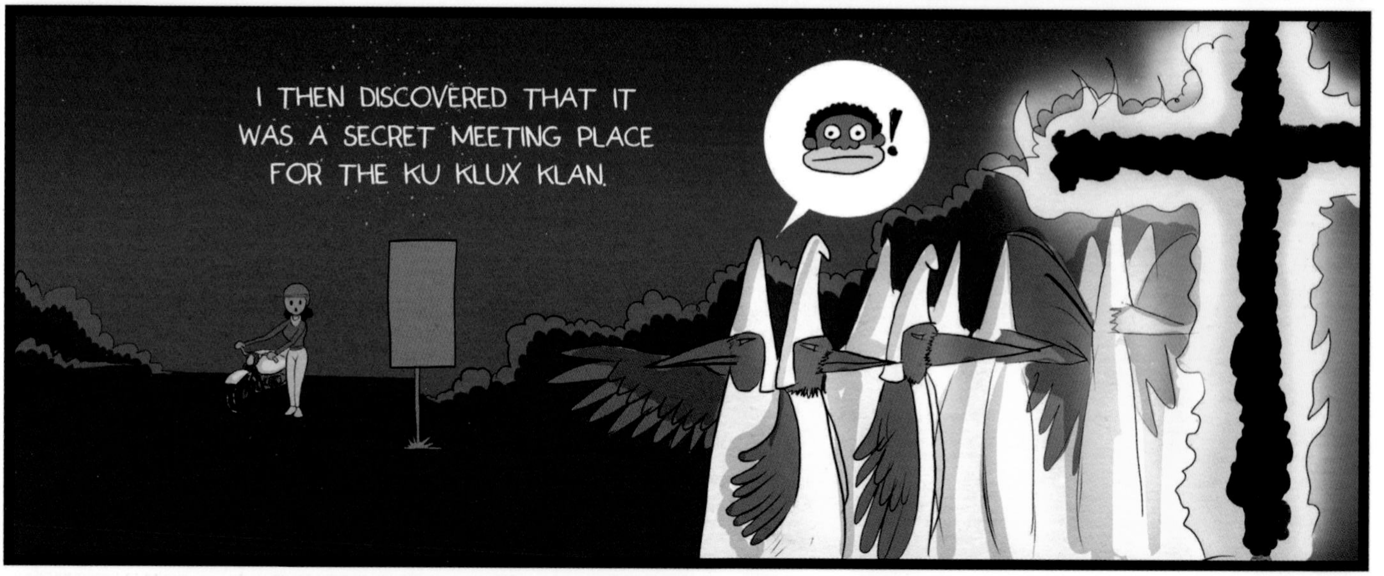
I THEN DISCOVERED THAT IT WAS A SECRET MEETING PLACE FOR THE KU KLUX KLAN.
!

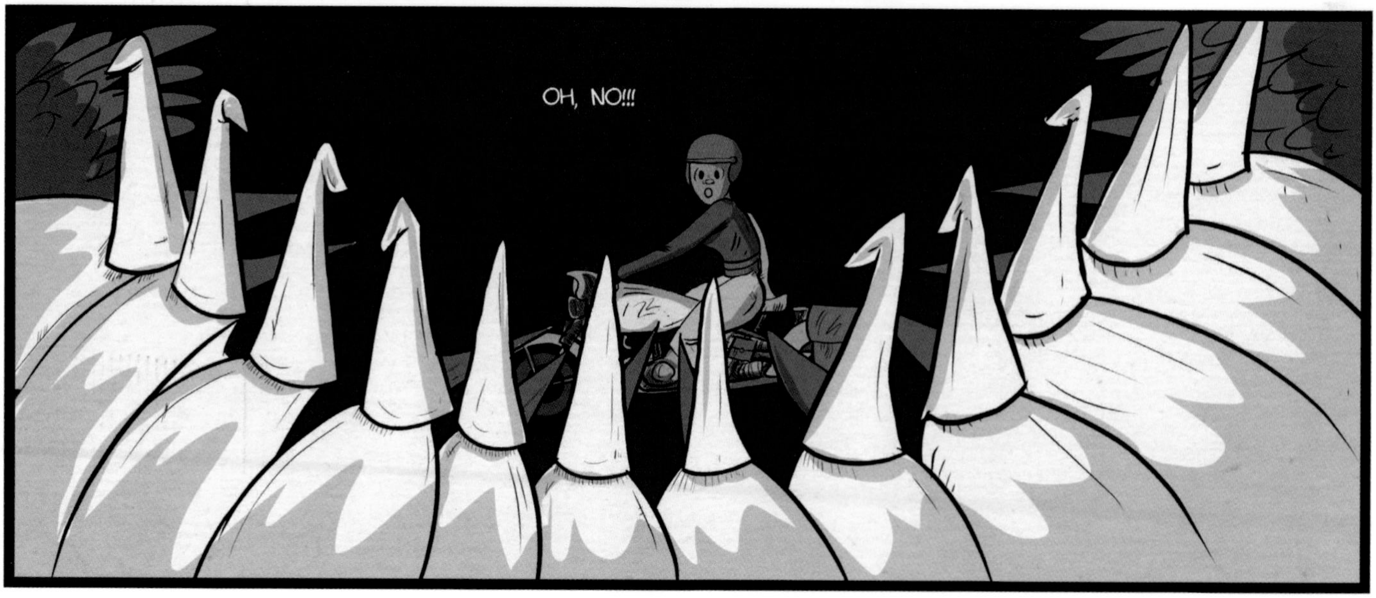
OH, NO!!!

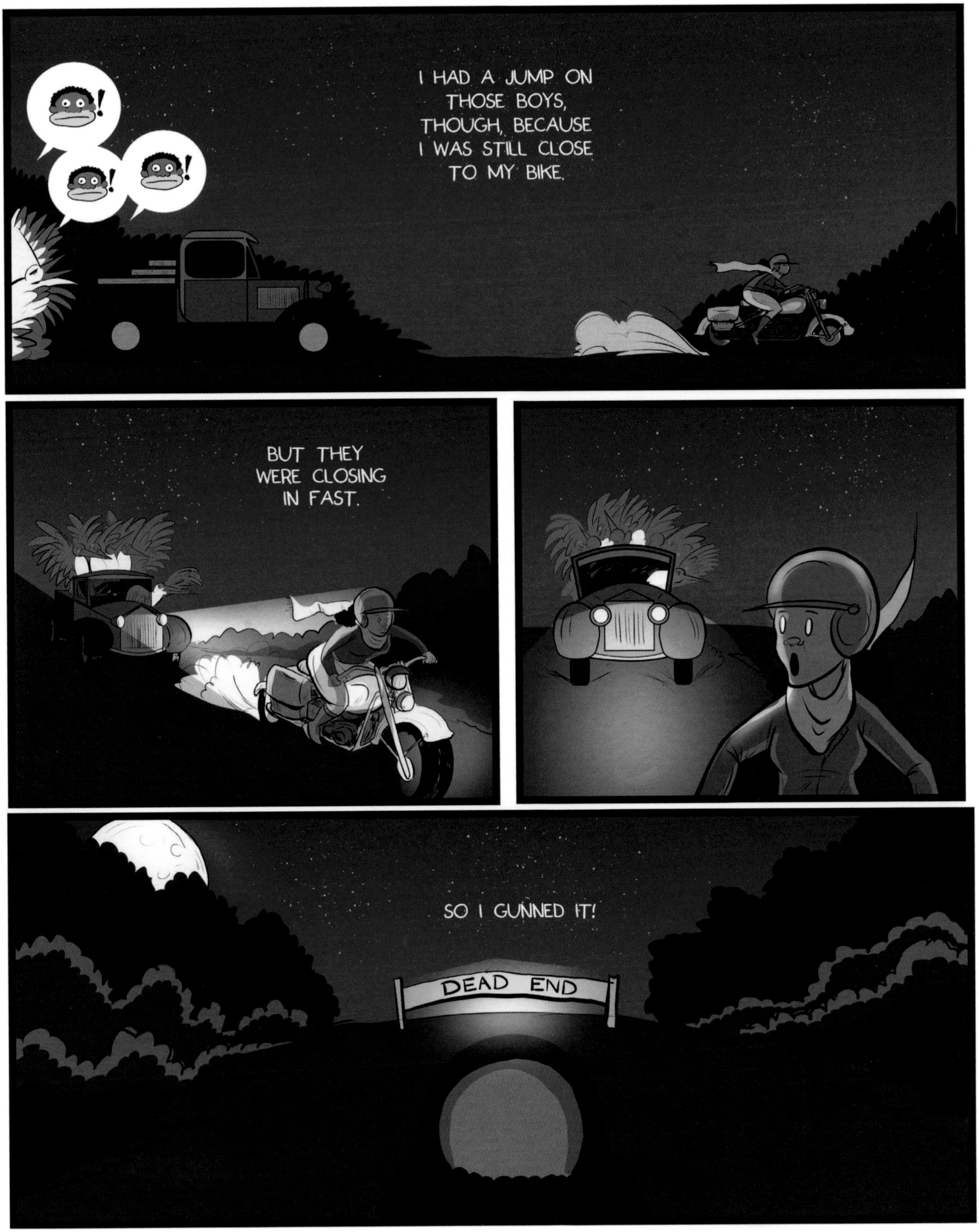
I HAD A JUMP ON THOSE BOYS, THOUGH, BECAUSE I WAS STILL CLOSE TO MY BIKE.
BUT THEY WERE CLOSING IN FAST.
SO I GUNNED IT!
DEAD END

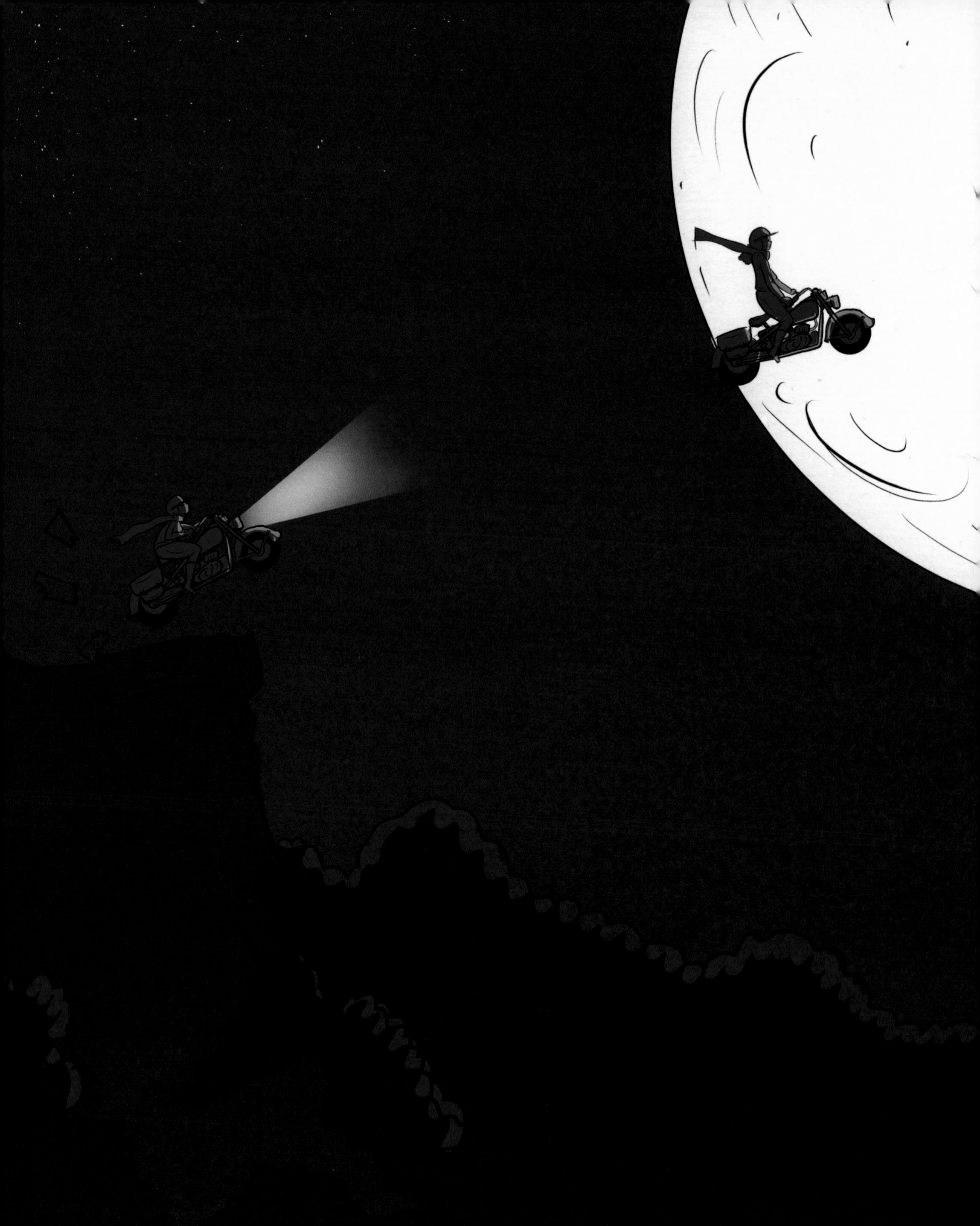

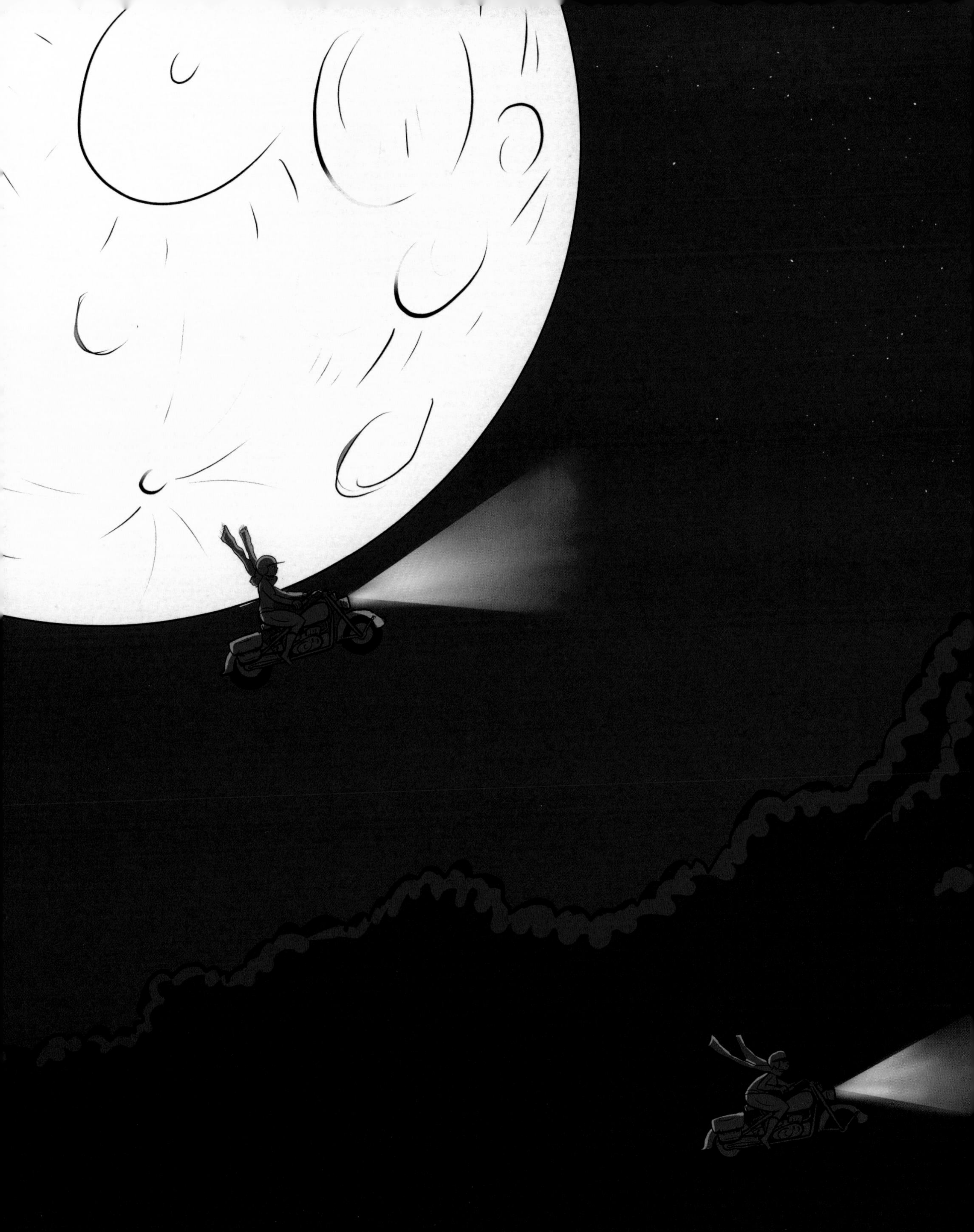

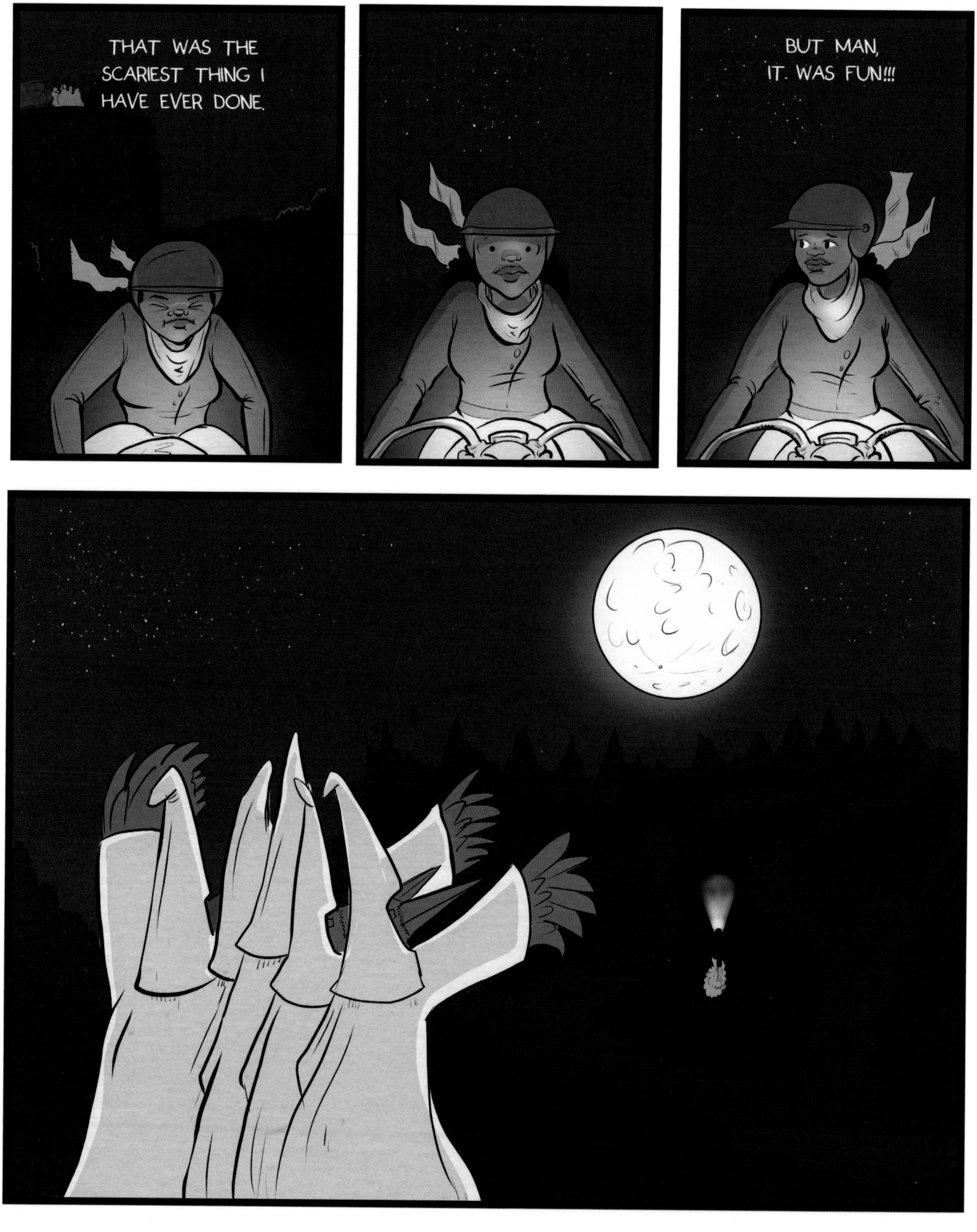
THAT WAS THE SCARIEST THING I HAVE EVER DONE.
BUT MAN, IT. WAS FUN!!!

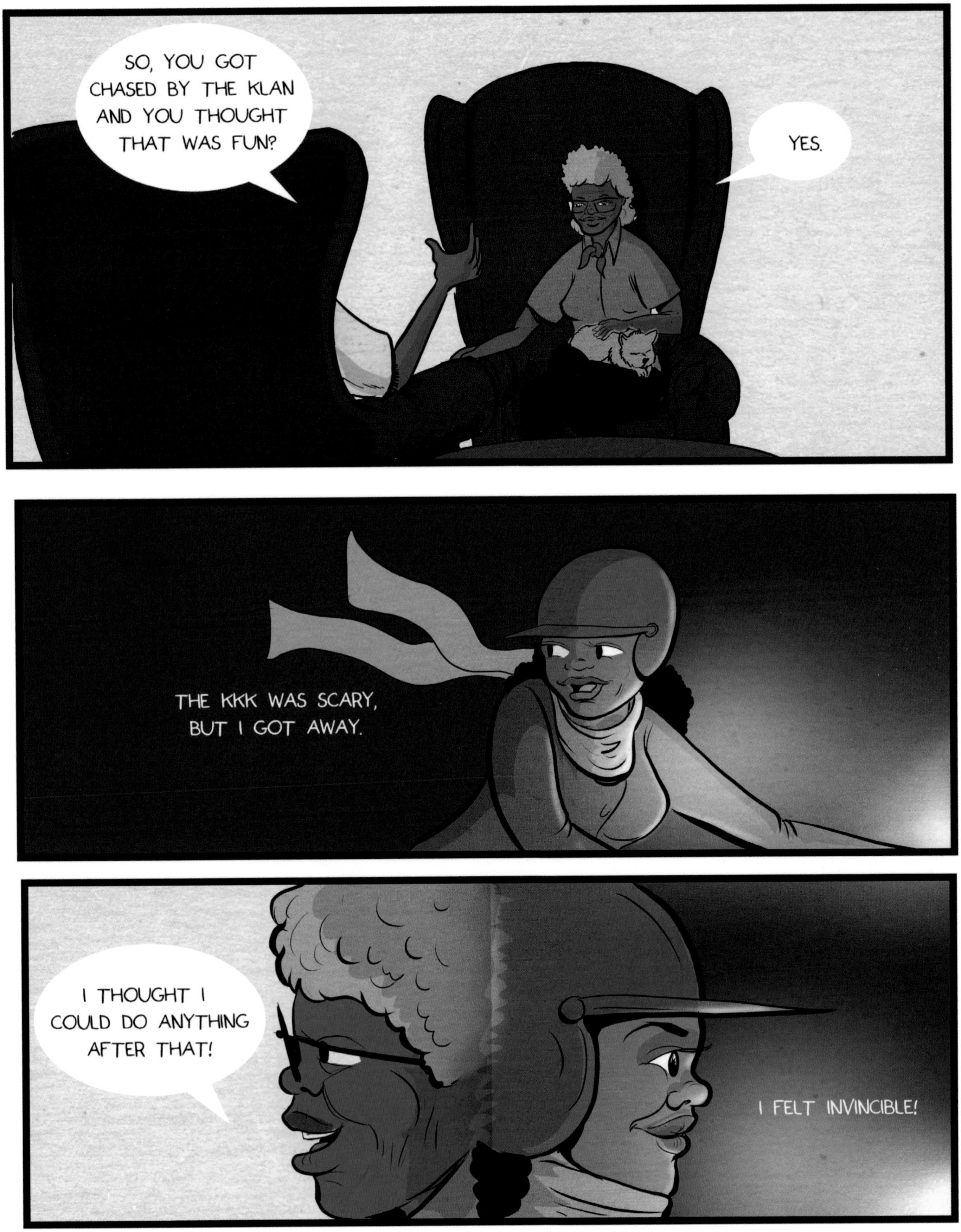
SO, YOU GOT CHASED BY THE KLAN AND YOU THOUGHT THAT WAS FUN?
YES.
THE KKK WAS SCARY, BUT I GOT AWAY.
I THOUGHT I COULD DO ANYTHING AFTER THAT!
I FELT INVINCIBLE!

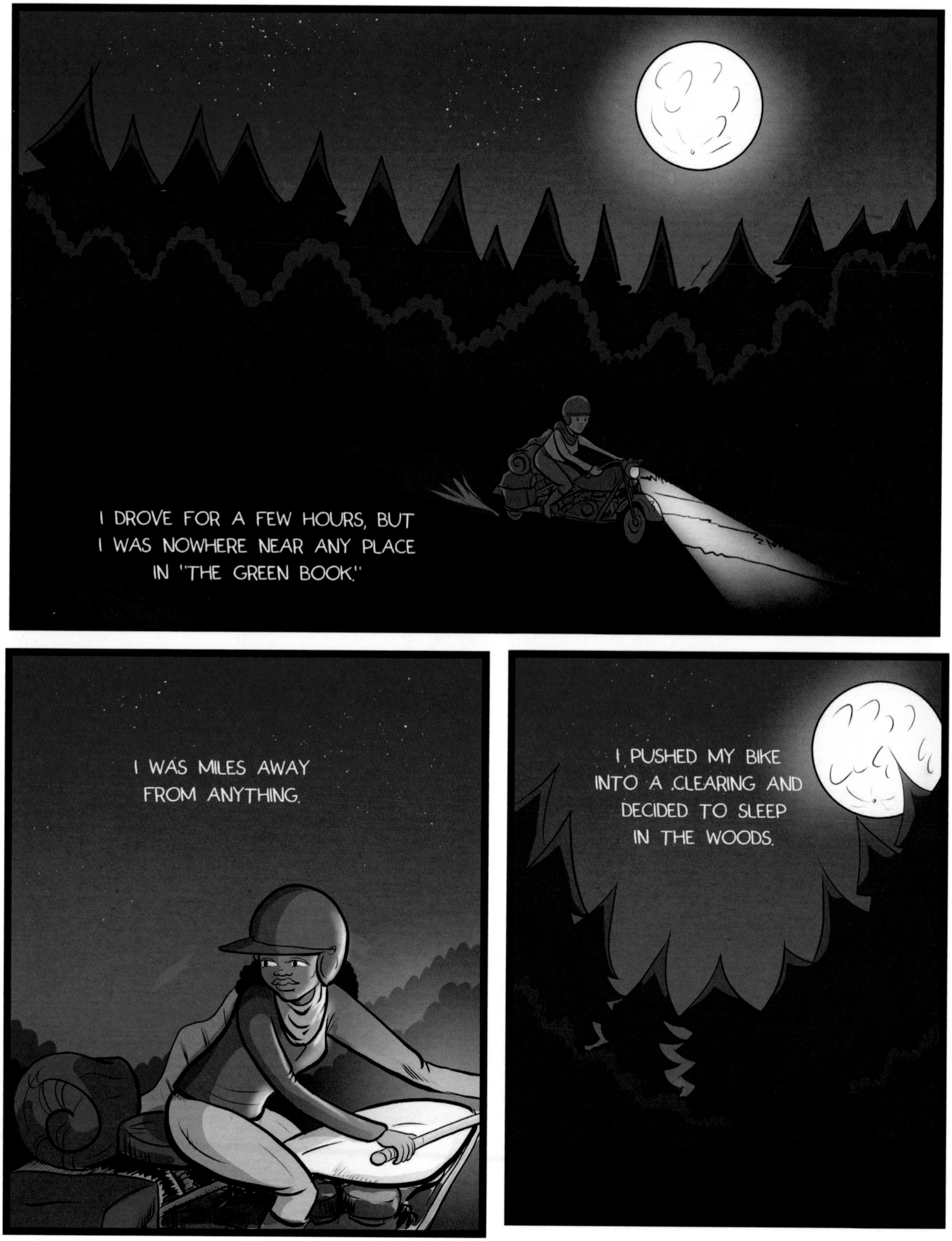
I DROVE FOR A FEW HOURS, BUT
I WAS NOWHERE NEAR ANY PLACE
IN "THE GREEN BOOK."
I WAS MILES AWAY
FROM ANYTHING.
I PUSHED MY BIKE
INTO A CLEARING AND
DECIDED TO SLEEP
IN THE WOODS.

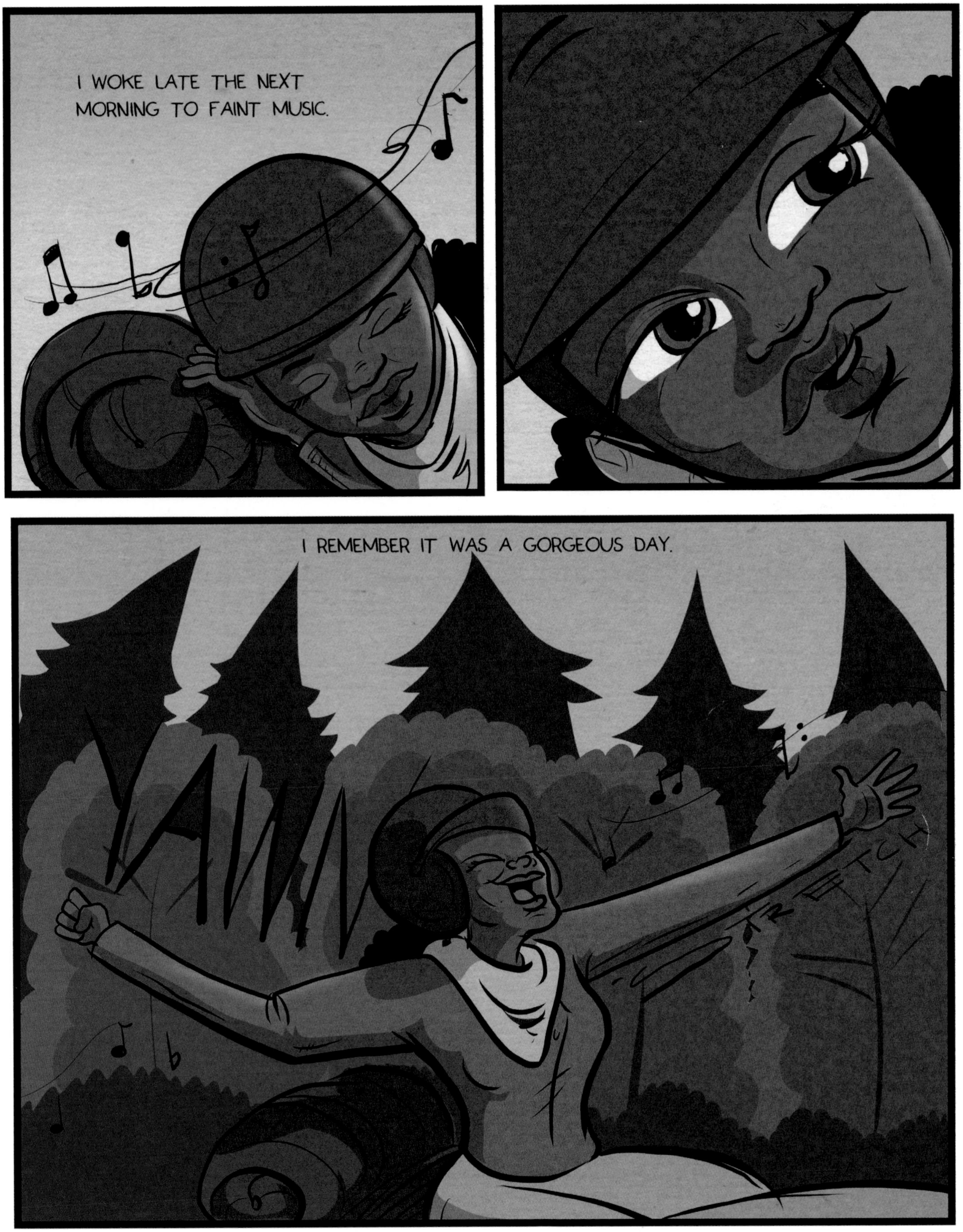
I WOKE LATE THE NEXT MORNING TO FAINT MUSIC.
I REMEMBER IT WAS A GORGEOUS DAY.
YAWN

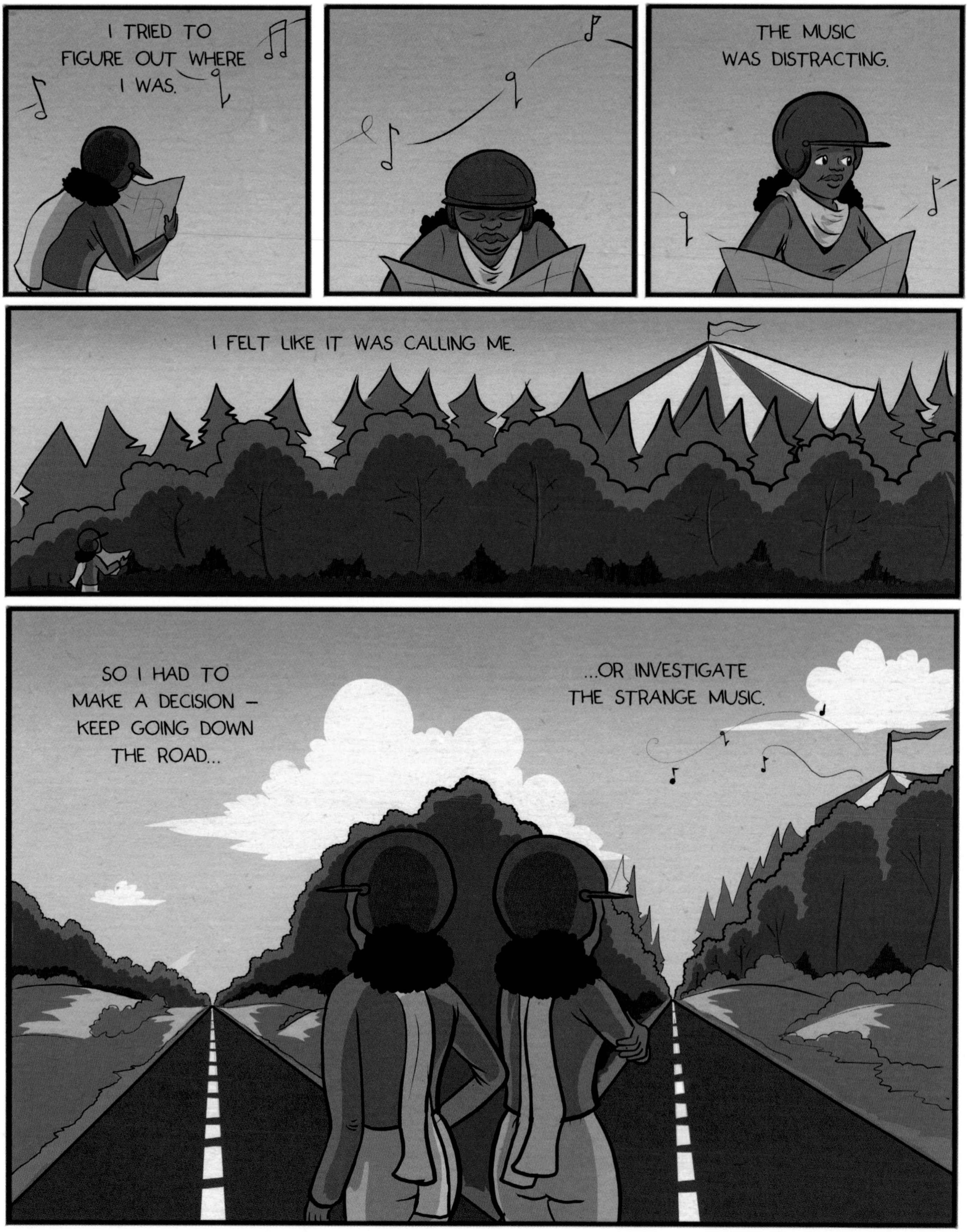
I TRIED TO FIGURE OUT WHERE I WAS.
THE MUSIC WAS DISTRACTING.
I FELT LIKE IT WAS CALLING ME.
SO I HAD TO MAKE A DECISION – KEEP GOING DOWN THE ROAD...
...OR INVESTIGATE THE STRANGE MUSIC.

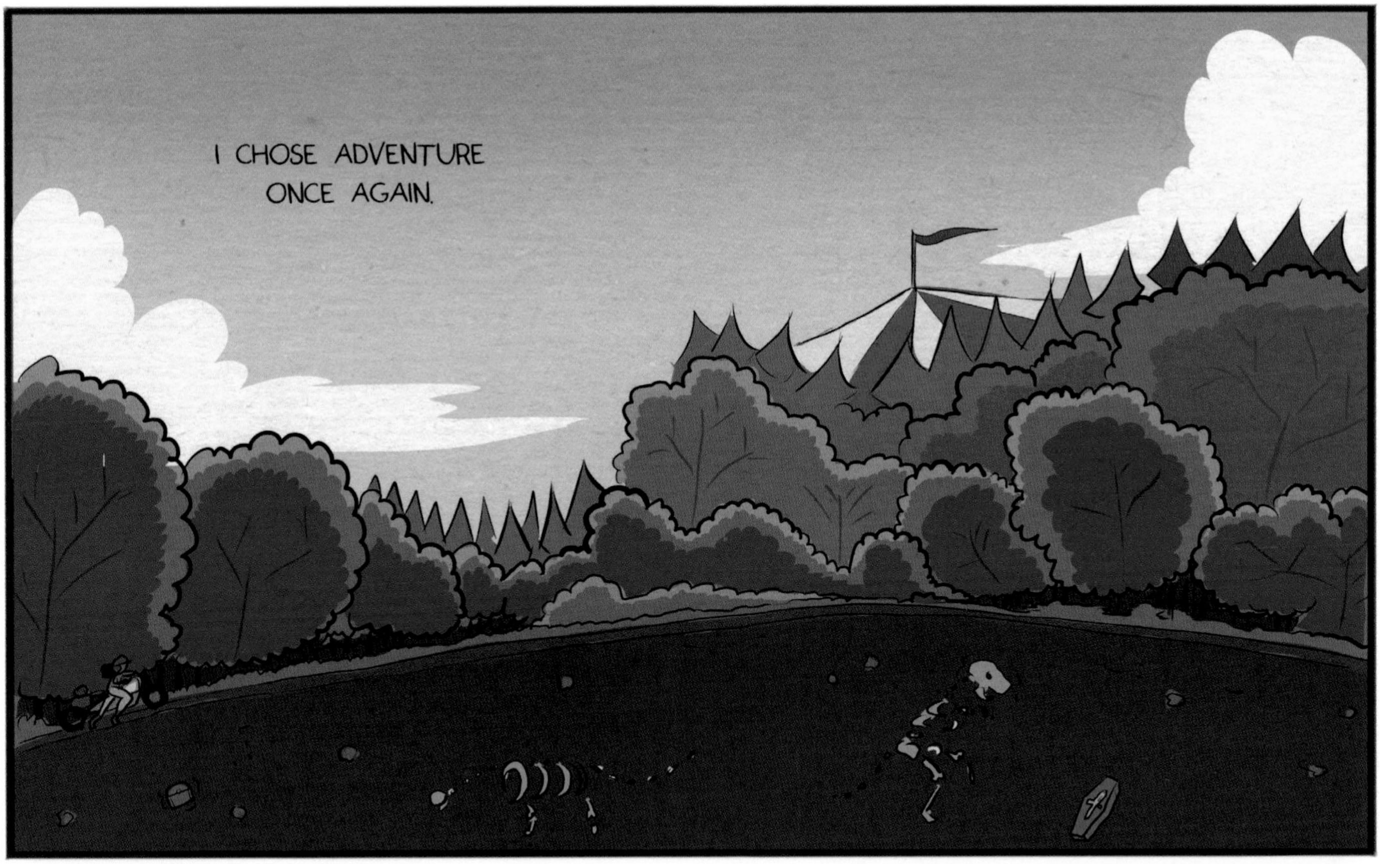
I CHOSE ADVENTURE ONCE AGAIN.

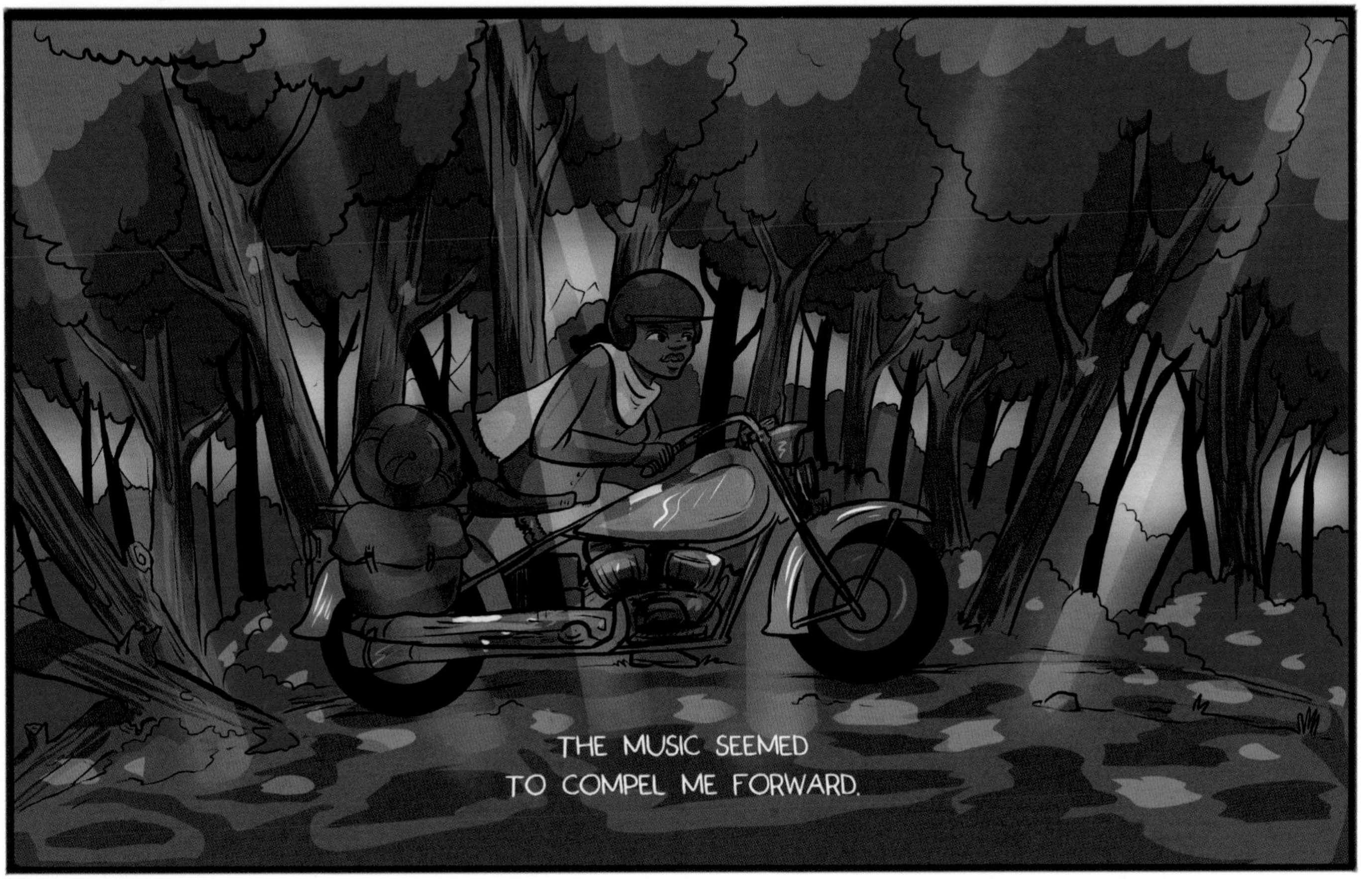
THE MUSIC SEEMED TO COMPEL ME FORWARD.

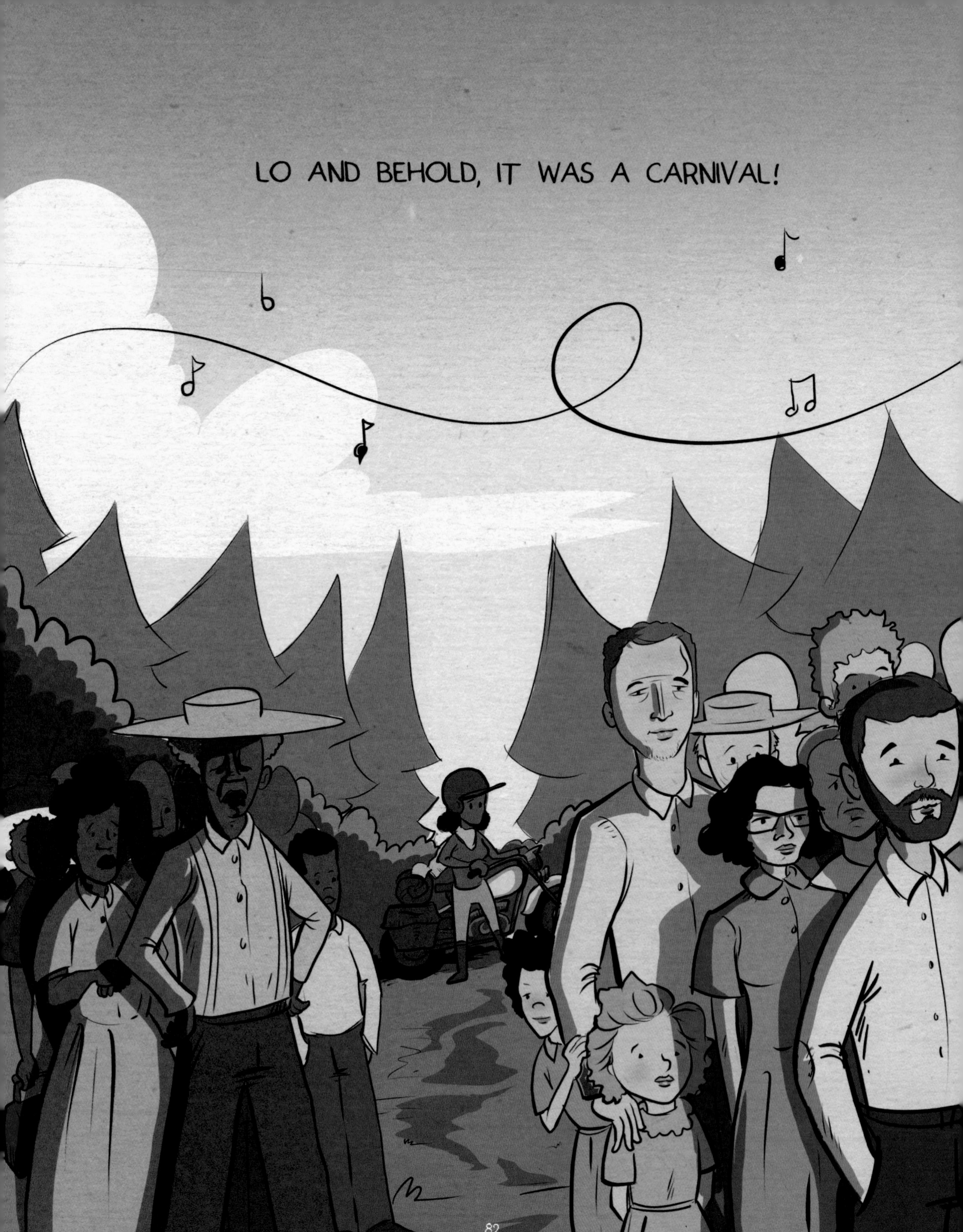
LO AND BEHOLD, IT WAS A CARNIVAL!

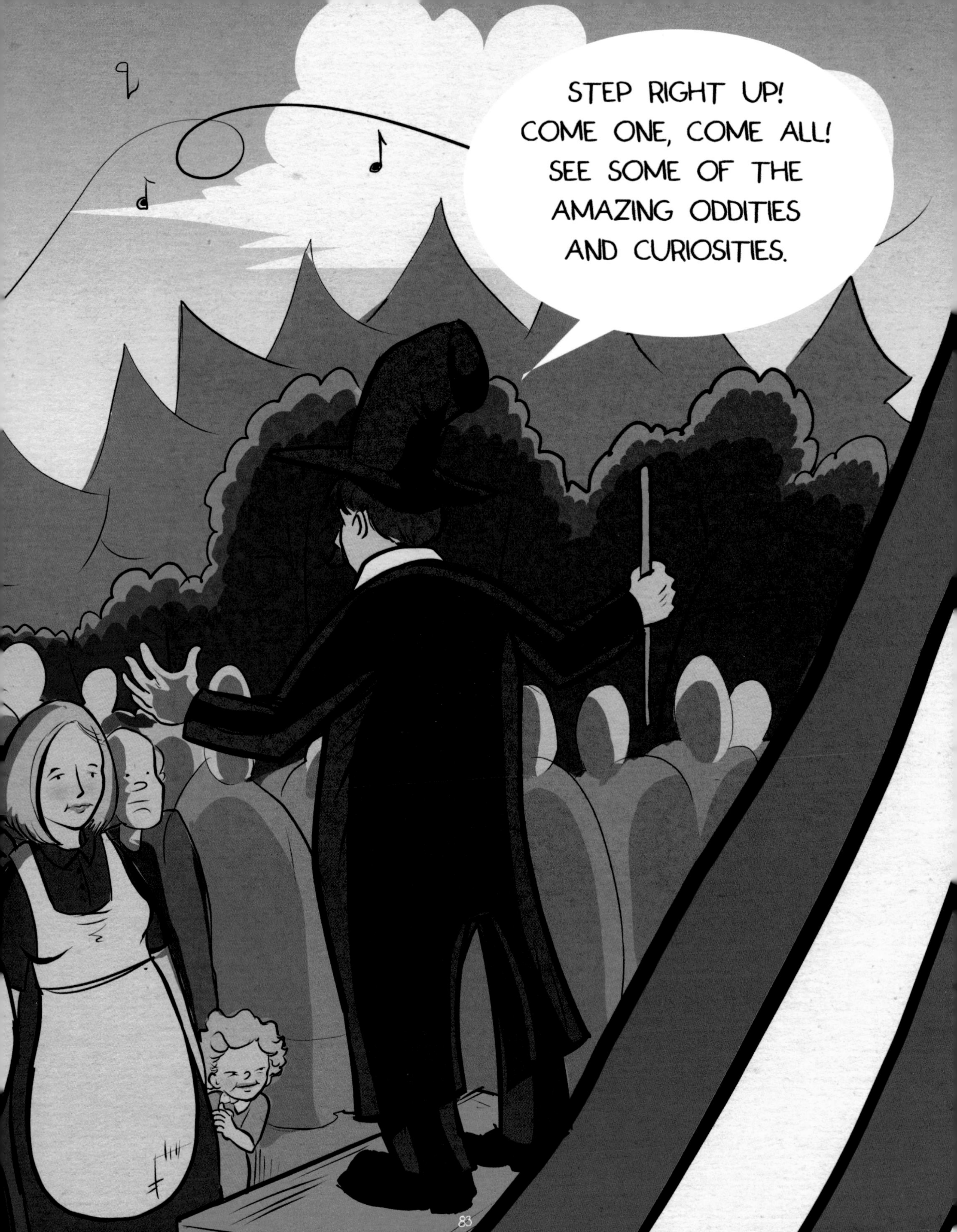
STEP RIGHT UP! COME ONE, COME ALL! SEE SOME OF THE AMAZING ODDITIES AND CURIOSITIES.

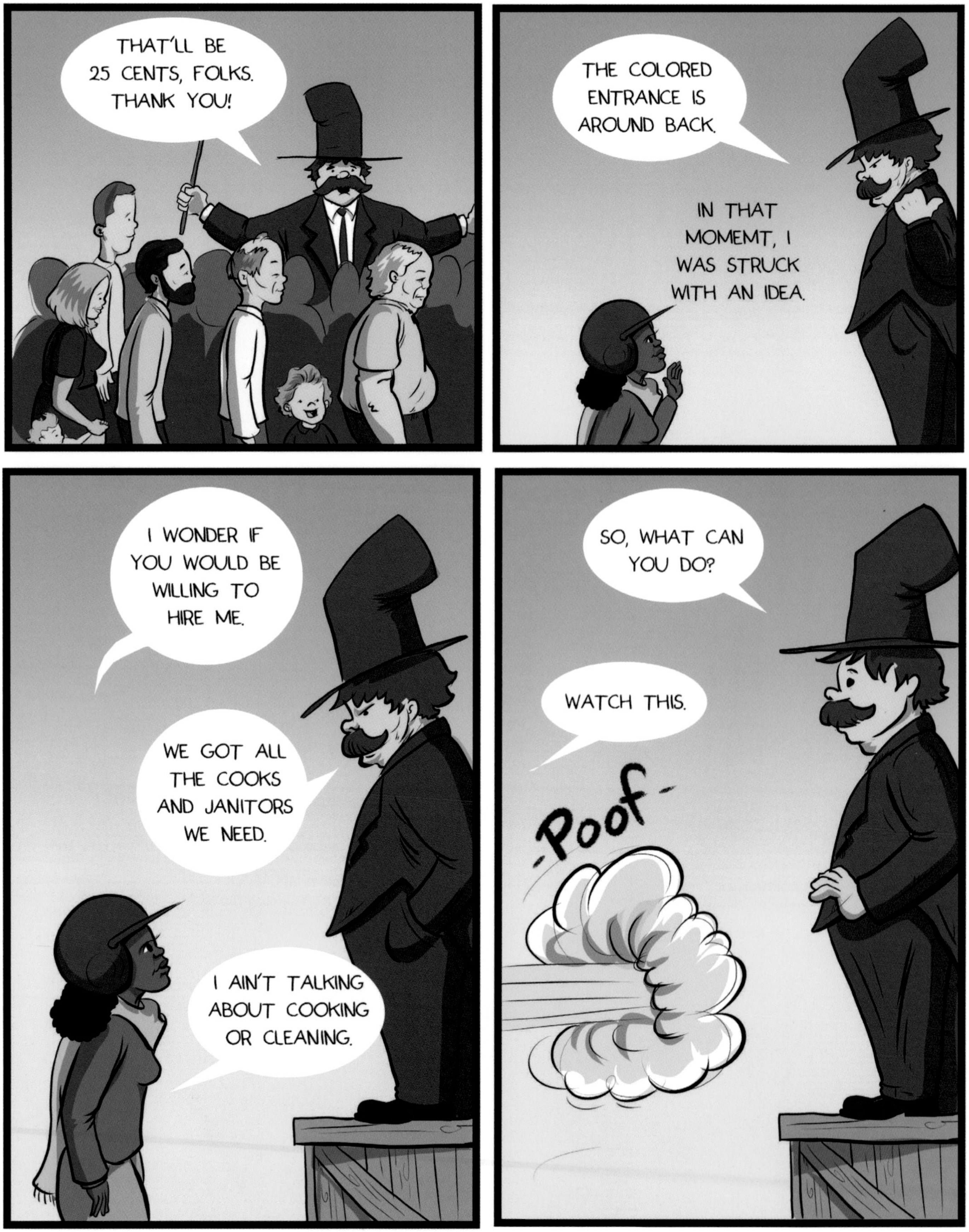
THAT'LL BE 25 CENTS, FOLKS. THANK YOU!
THE COLORED ENTRANCE IS AROUND BACK.
IN THAT MOMEMT, I WAS STRUCK WITH AN IDEA.
I WONDER IF YOU WOULD BE WILLING TO HIRE ME.
WE GOT ALL THE COOKS AND JANITORS WE NEED.
I AIN'T TALKING ABOUT COOKING OR CLEANING.
SO, WHAT CAN YOU DO?
WATCH THIS.
Poof

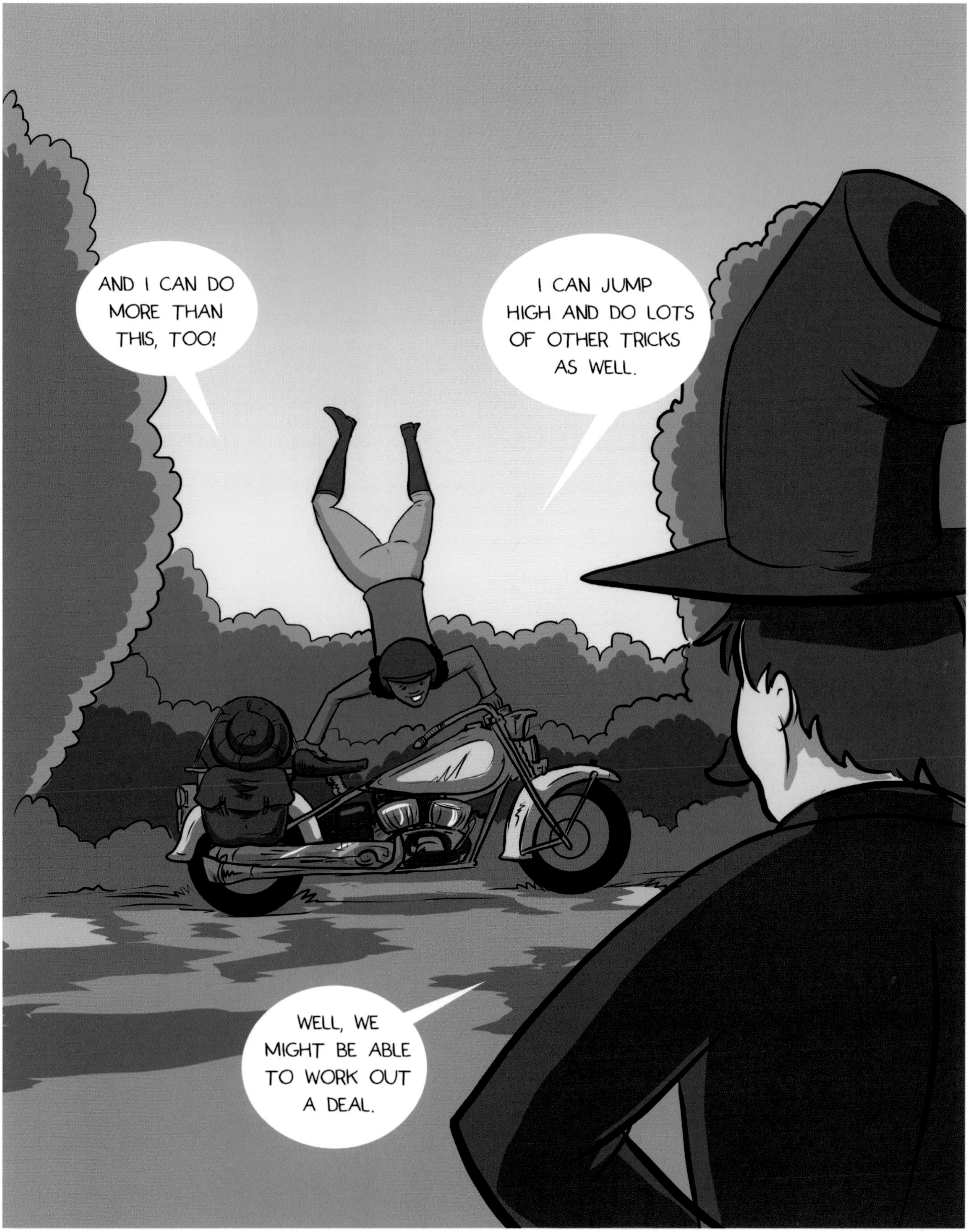
AND I CAN DO MORE THAN THIS, TOO!
I CAN JUMP HIGH AND DO LOTS OF OTHER TRICKS AS WELL.
WELL, WE MIGHT BE ABLE TO WORK OUT A DEAL.

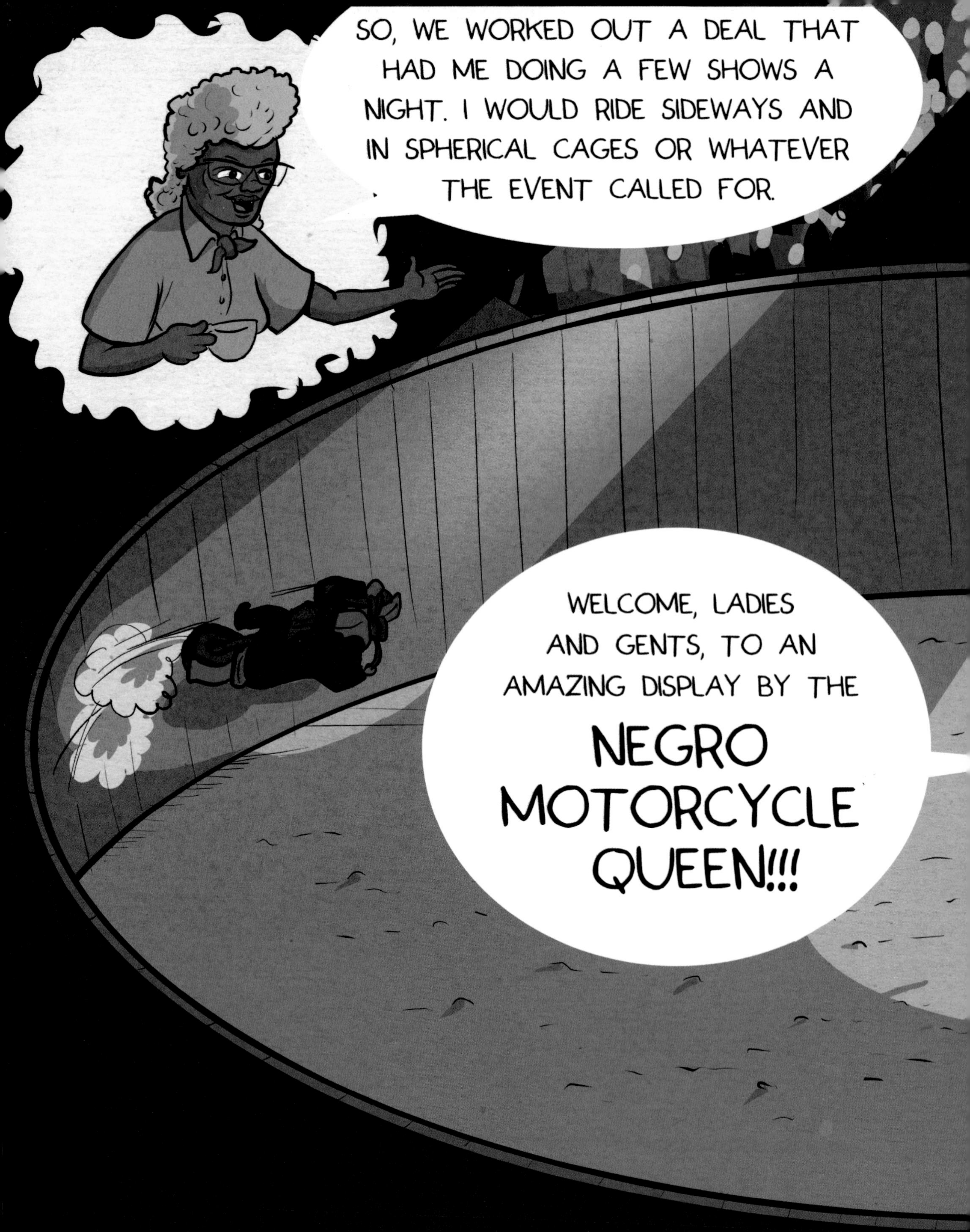
SO, WE WORKED OUT A DEAL THAT HAD ME DOING A FEW SHOWS A NIGHT. I WOULD RIDE SIDEWAYS AND IN SPHERICAL CAGES OR WHATEVER THE EVENT CALLED FOR.
WELCOME, LADIES AND GENTS, TO AN AMAZING DISPLAY BY THE NEGRO MOTORCYCLE QUEEN!!!

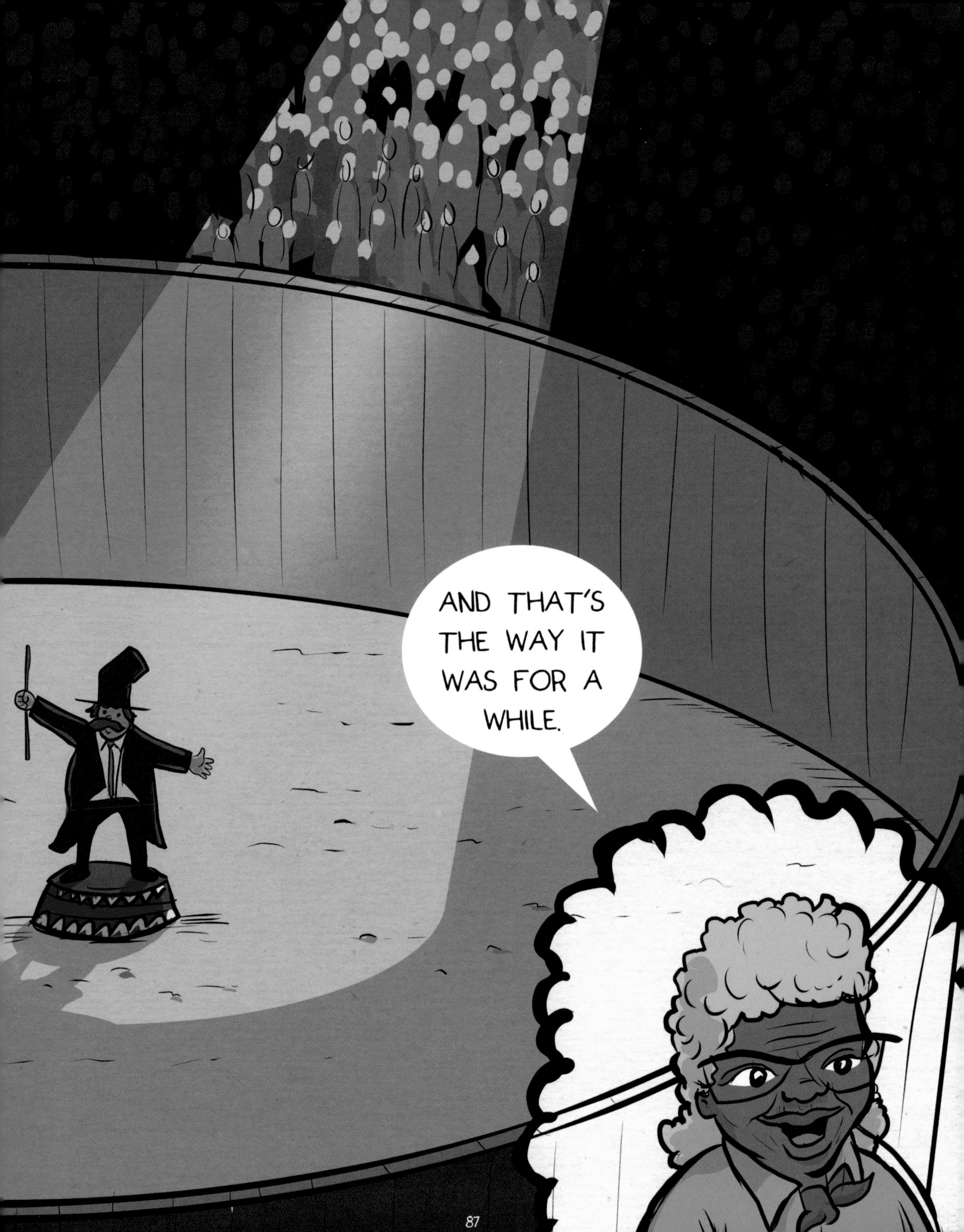
AND THAT'S THE WAY IT WAS FOR A WHILE.

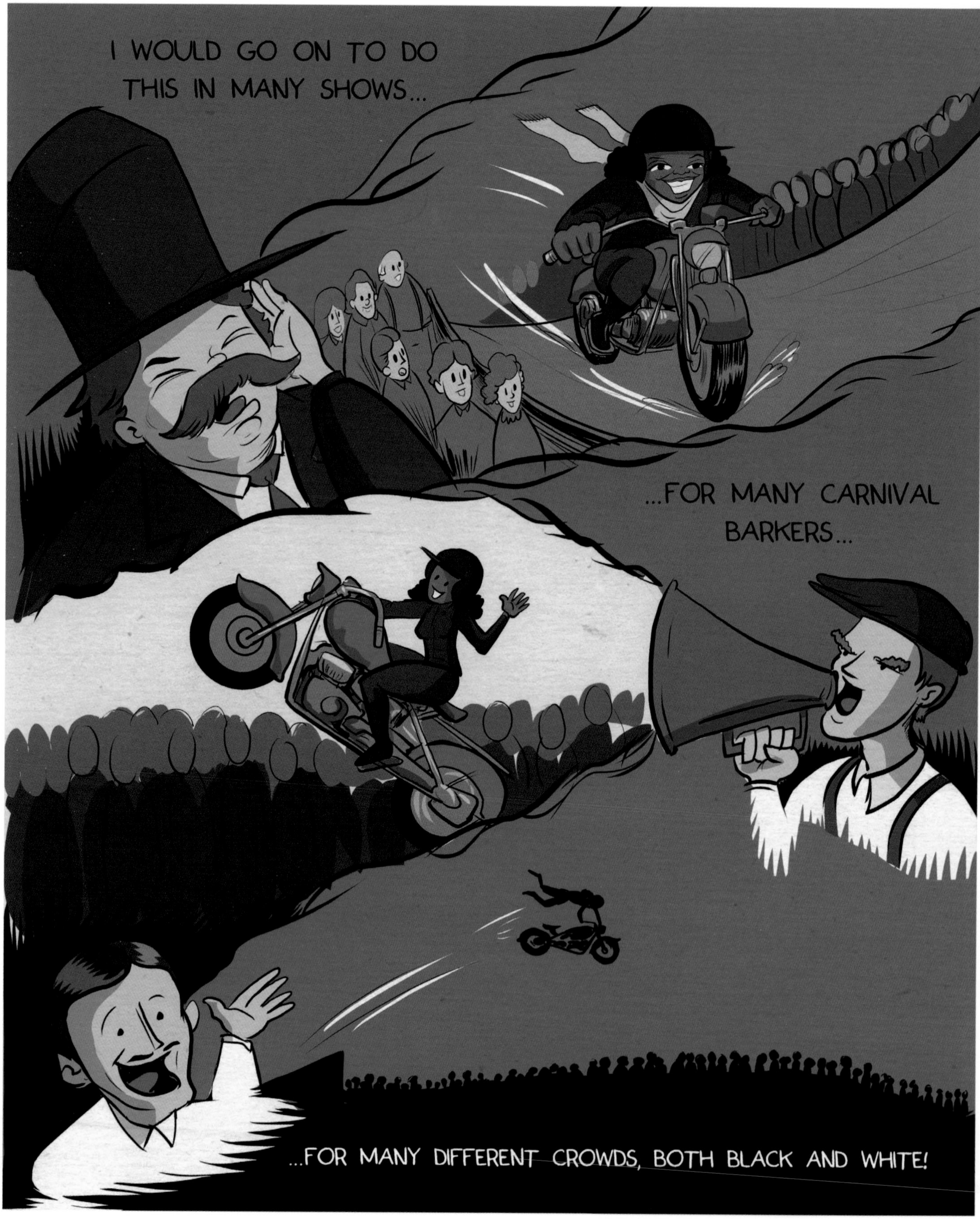
I WOULD GO ON TO DO THIS IN MANY SHOWS...
...FOR MANY CARNIVAL BARKERS...
...FOR MANY DIFFERENT CROWDS, BOTH BLACK AND WHITE!

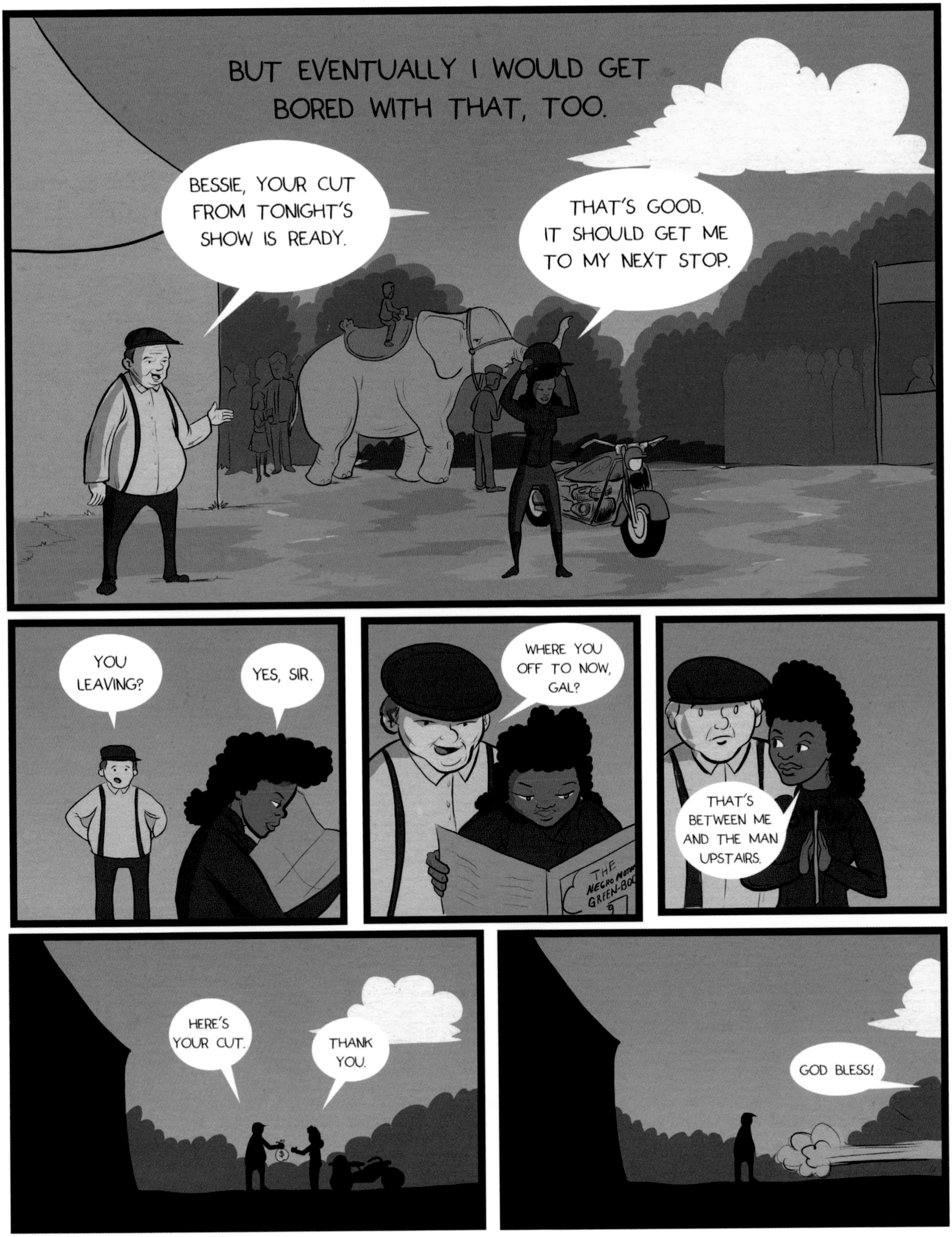
BUT EVENTUALLY I WOULD GET BORED WITH THAT, TOO.
BESSIE, YOUR CUT FROM TONIGHT'S SHOW IS READY.
THAT'S GOOD. IT SHOULD GET ME TO MY NEXT STOP.
YOU LEAVING?
YES, SIR.
WHERE YOU OFF TO NOW, GAL?
THAT'S BETWEEN ME AND THE MAN UPSTAIRS.
HERE'S YOUR CUT.
THANK YOU.
GOD BLESS!

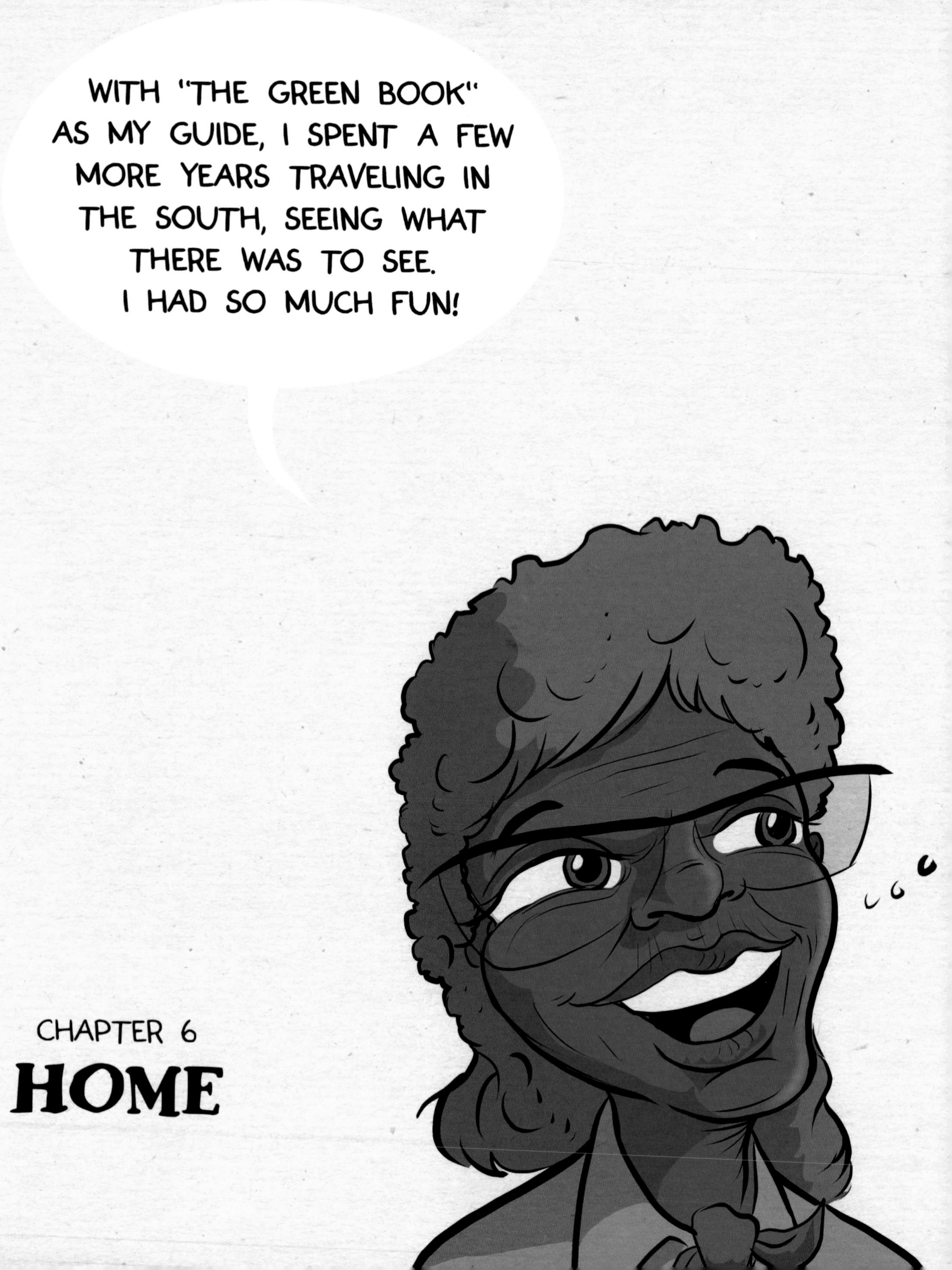
WITH "THE GREEN BOOK" AS MY GUIDE, I SPENT A FEW MORE YEARS TRAVELING IN THE SOUTH, SEEING WHAT THERE WAS TO SEE. I HAD SO MUCH FUN!

CHAPTER 6

HOME

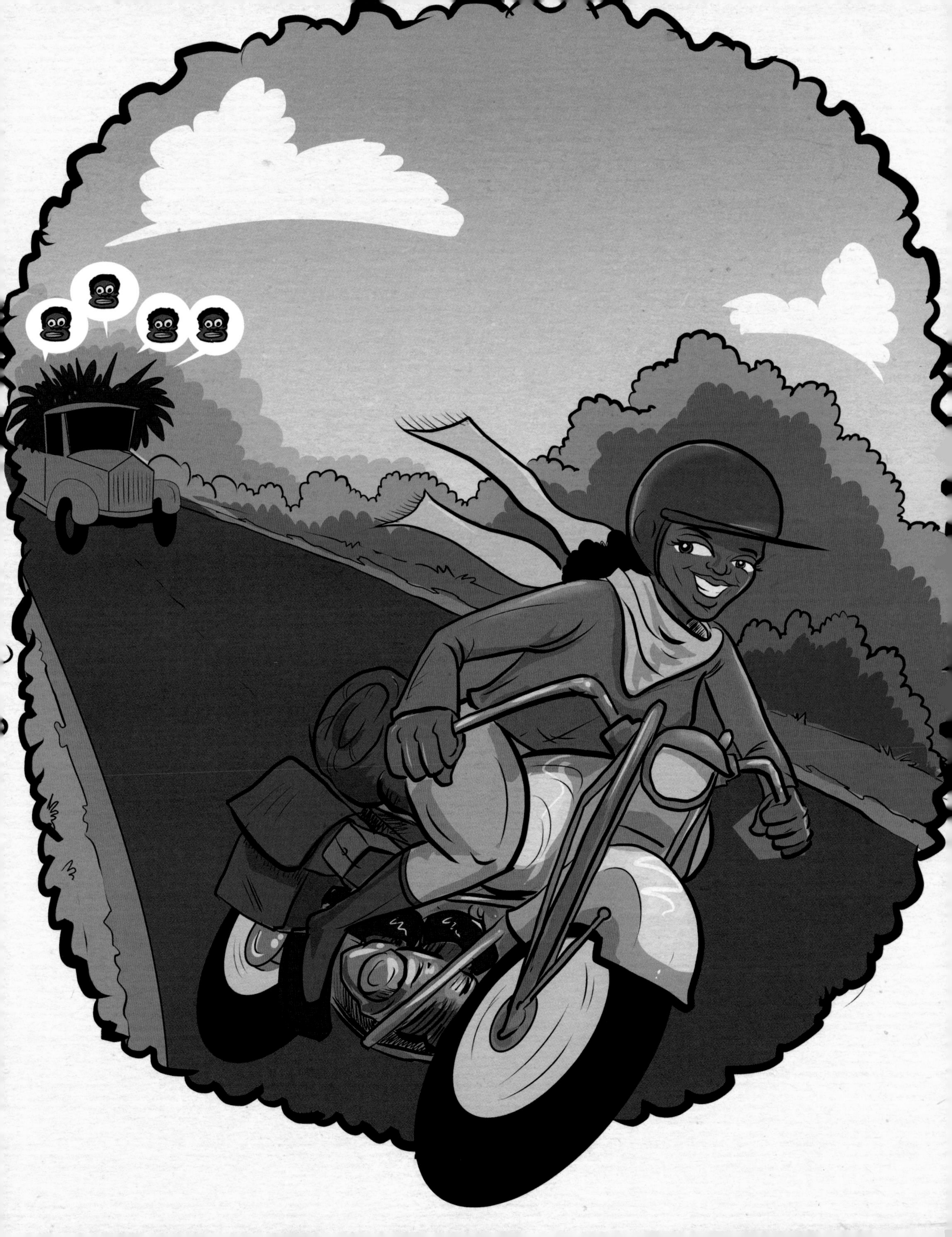

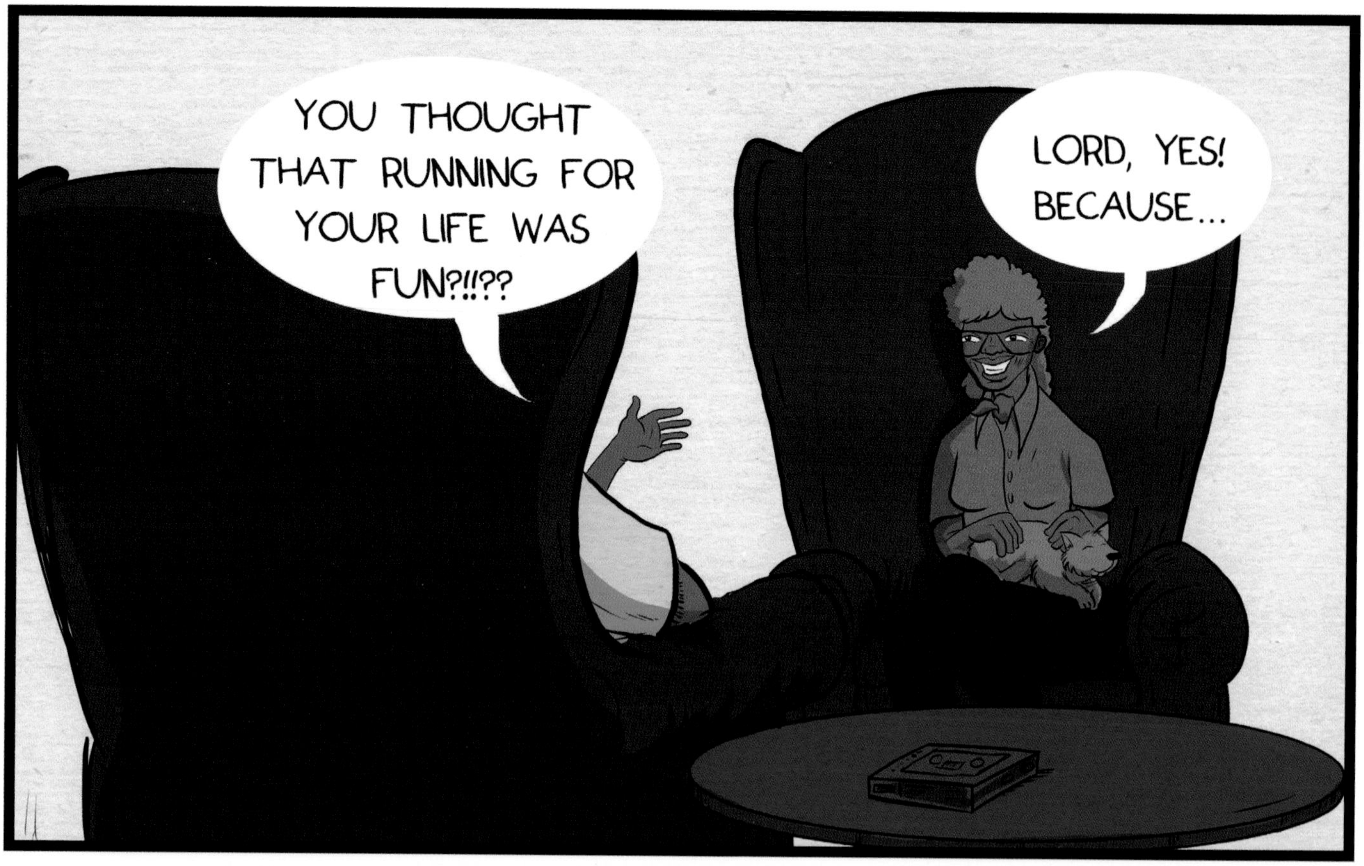
YOU THOUGHT THAT RUNNING FOR YOUR LIFE WAS FUN?!!??
LORD, YES! BECAUSE...

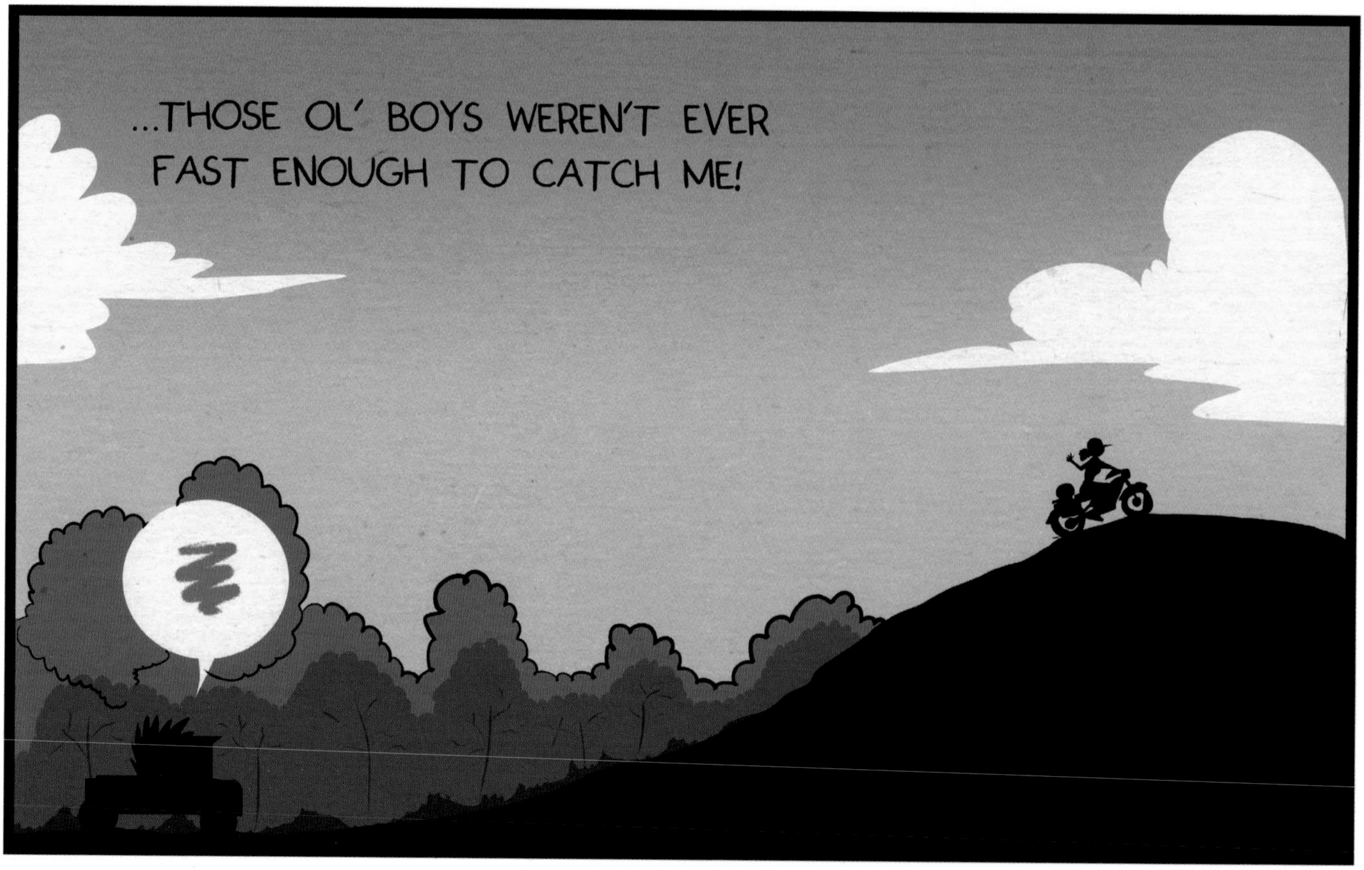
...THOSE OL' BOYS WEREN'T EVER FAST ENOUGH TO CATCH ME!

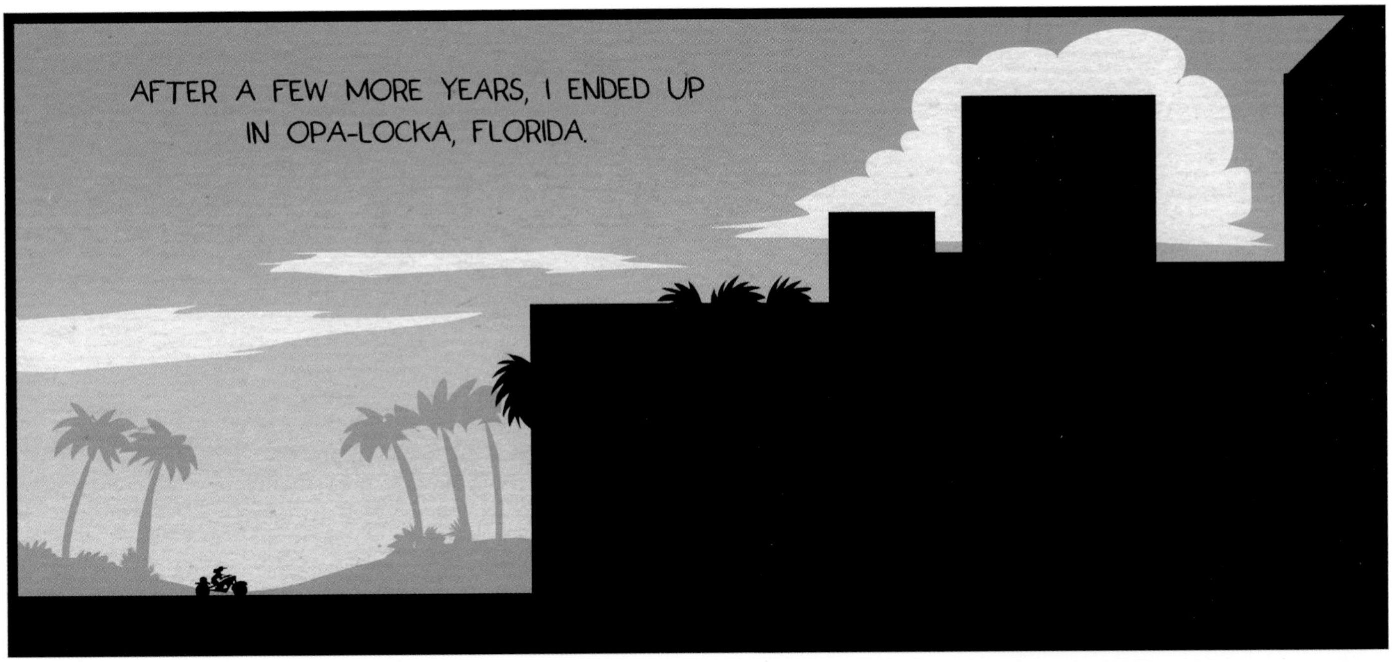
AFTER A FEW MORE YEARS, I ENDED UP IN OPA-LOCKA, FLORIDA.

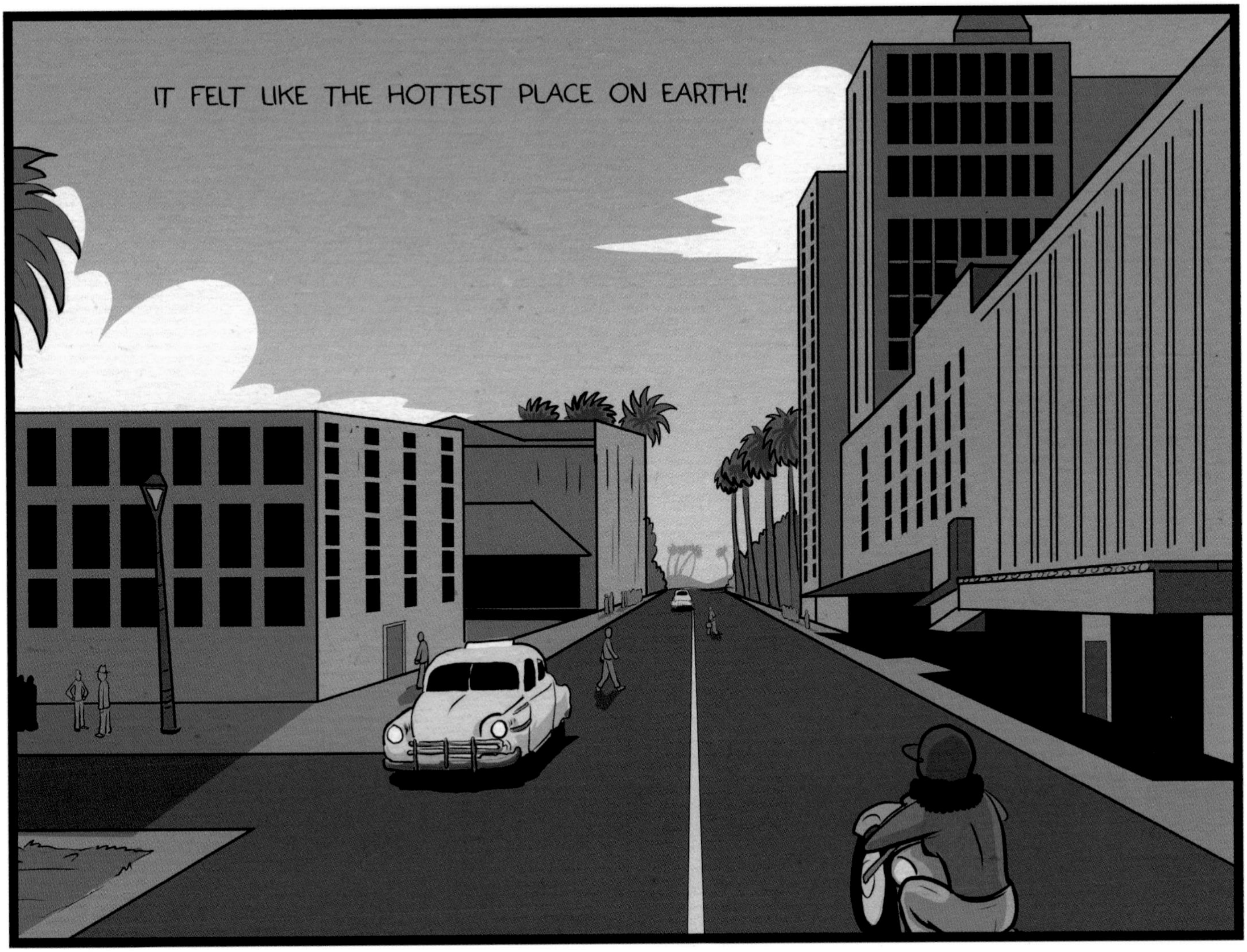
IT FELT LIKE THE HOTTEST PLACE ON EARTH!

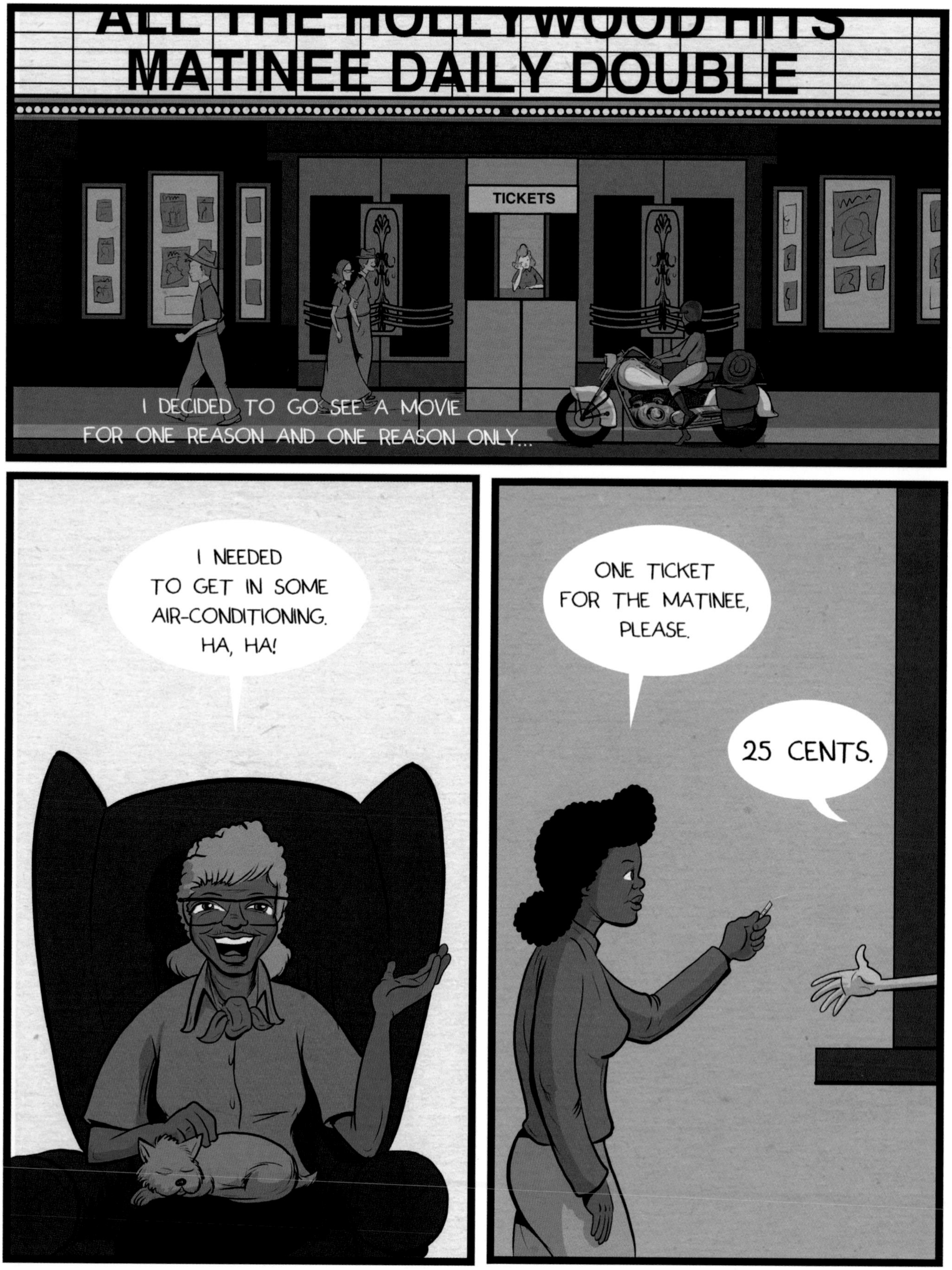
ALL THE HOLLYWOOD HITS
MATINEE DAILY DOUBLE
TICKETS
I DECIDED TO GO SEE A MOVIE FOR ONE REASON AND ONE REASON ONLY...
I NEEDED TO GET IN SOME AIR-CONDITIONING. HA, HA!
ONE TICKET FOR THE MATINEE, PLEASE.
25 CENTS.

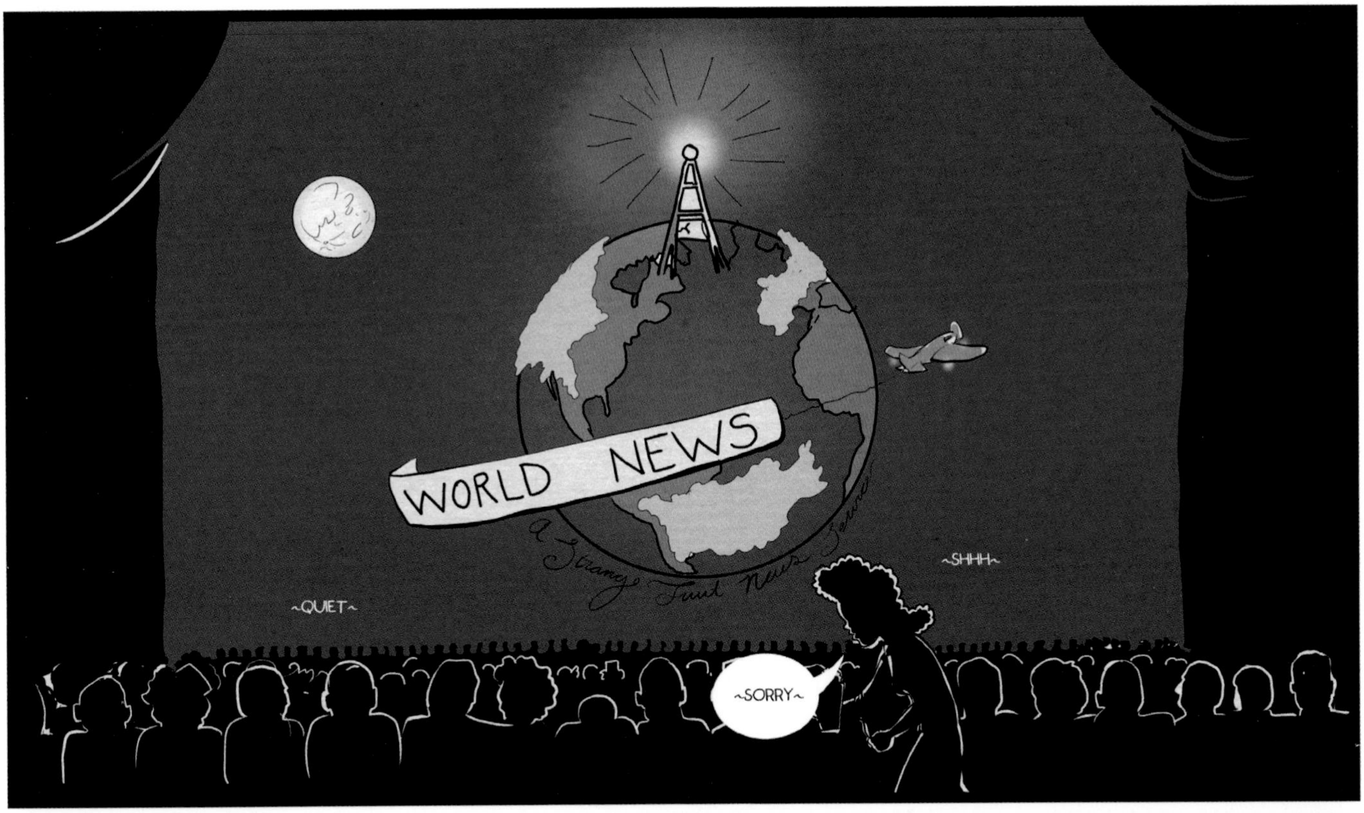
WORLD NEWS
~QUIET~
~SHHH~
~SORRY~

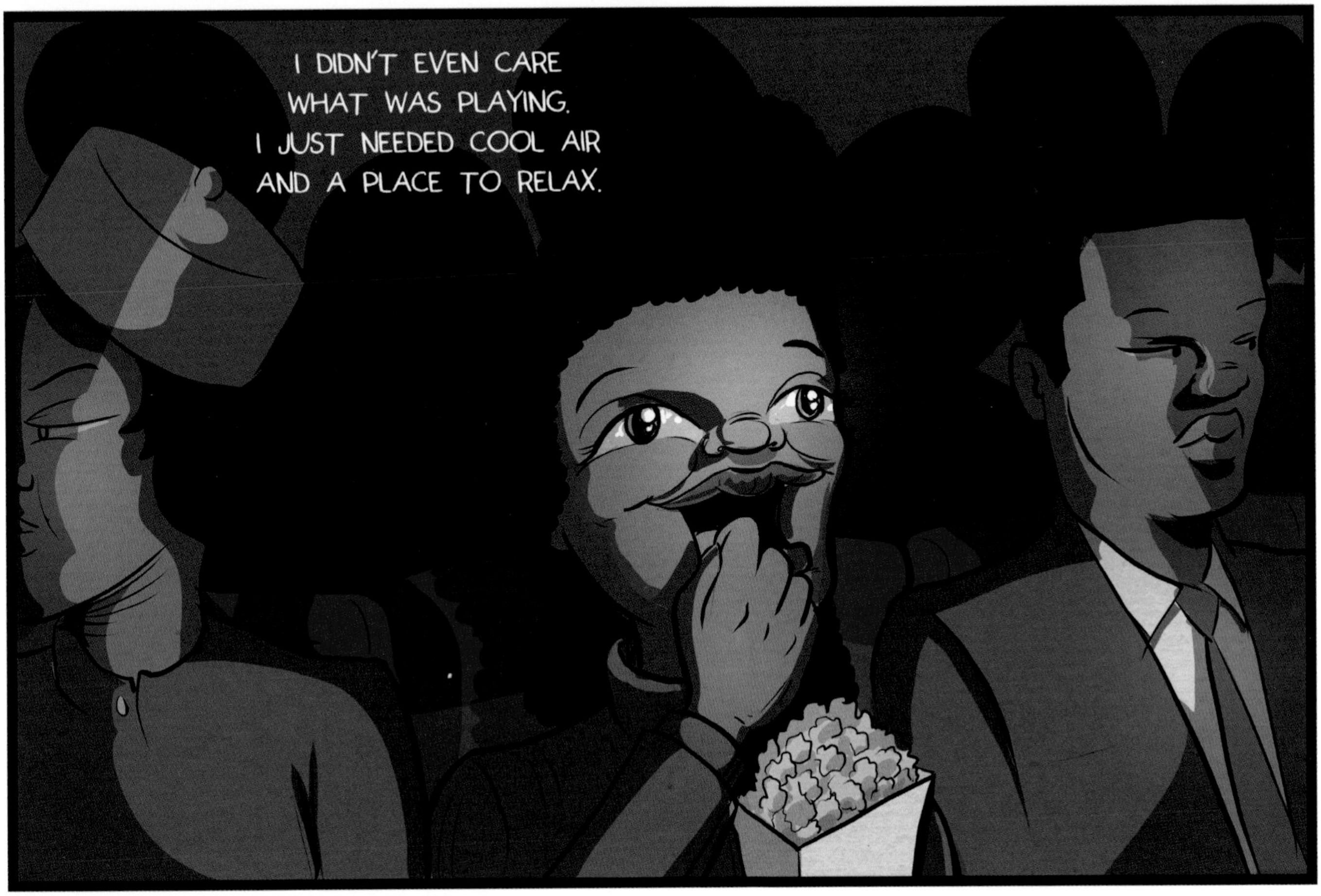
I DIDN'T EVEN CARE
WHAT WAS PLAYING.
I JUST NEEDED COOL AIR
AND A PLACE TO RELAX.

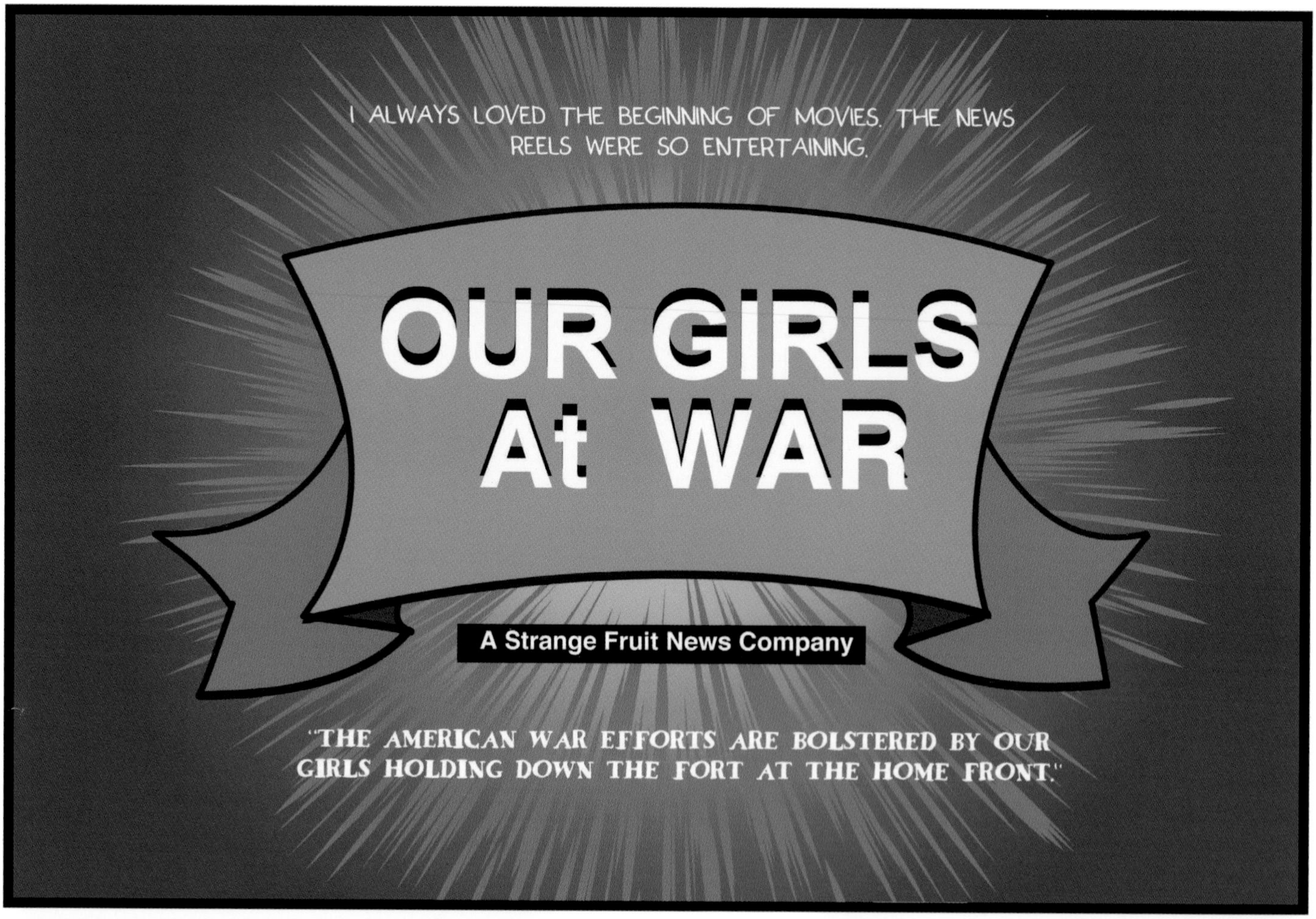
I ALWAYS LOVED THE BEGINNING OF MOVIES. THE NEWS REELS WERE SO ENTERTAINING.
OUR GIRLS At WAR
A Strange Fruit News Company
"THE AMERICAN WAR EFFORTS ARE BOLSTERED BY OUR GIRLS HOLDING DOWN THE FORT AT THE HOME FRONT."

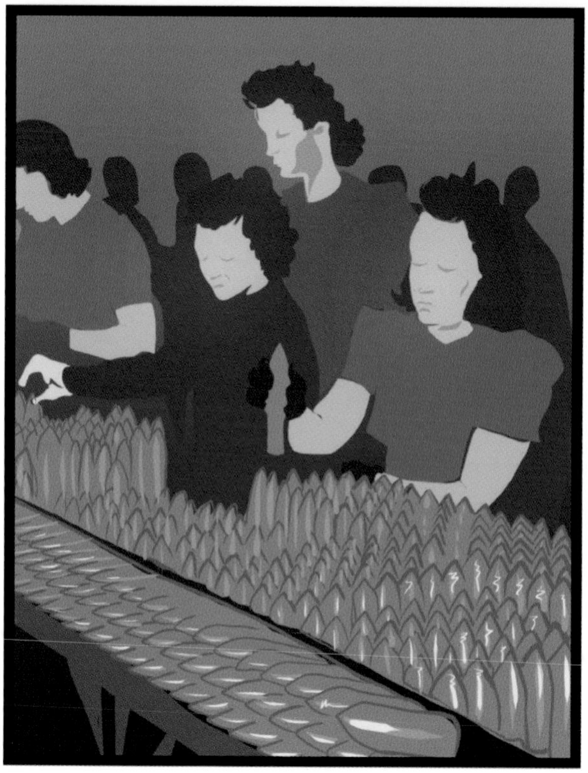

"HERE YOU CAN SEE OUR GIRLS DOING THEIR PART IN THE WAR EFFORT.

WITH ALL THE BOYS OVERSEAS GIVING THE WHAT-FOR TO HITLER AND HIS KRAUT ARMY, WE NEED SOMEONE TO DO THE WORK THAT IS USUALLY DONE BY MEN."

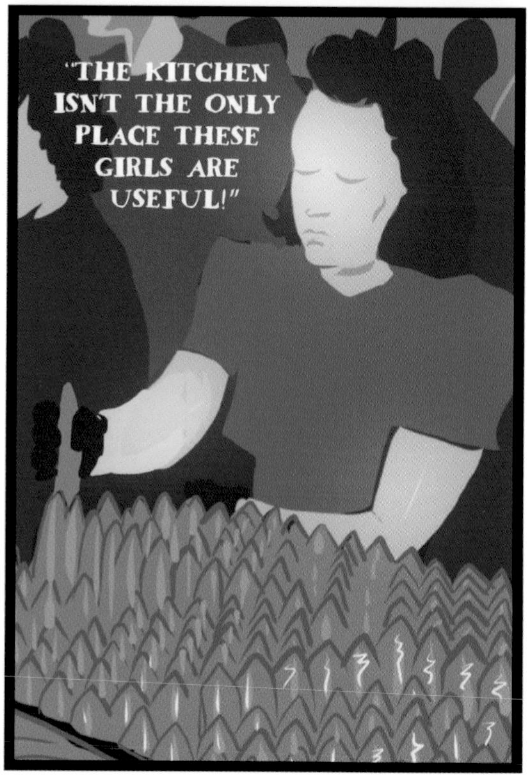
"THE KITCHEN ISN'T THE ONLY PLACE THESE GIRLS ARE USEFUL!"

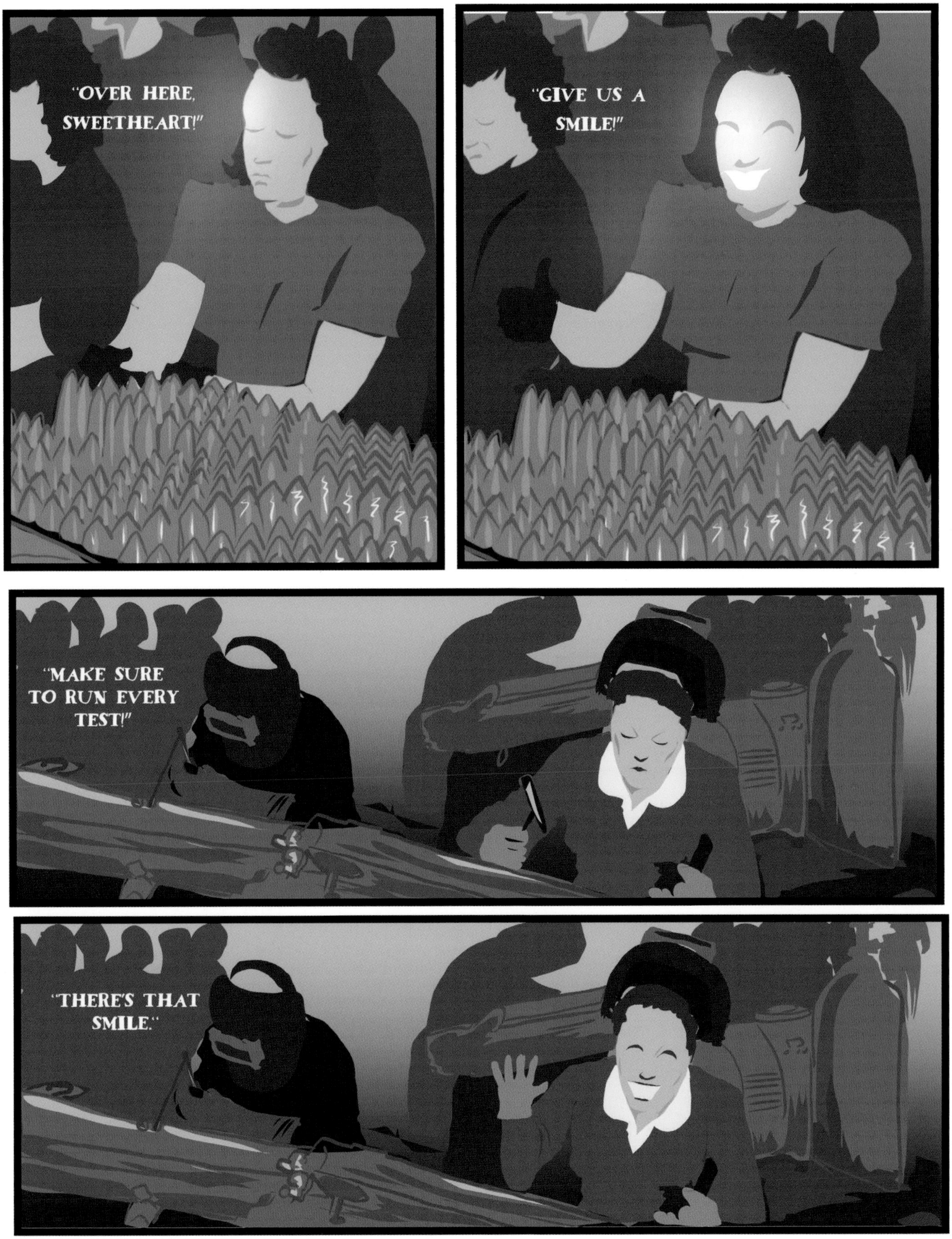
"OVER HERE, SWEETHEART!"
"GIVE US A SMILE!"
"MAKE SURE TO RUN EVERY TEST!"
"THERE'S THAT SMILE."

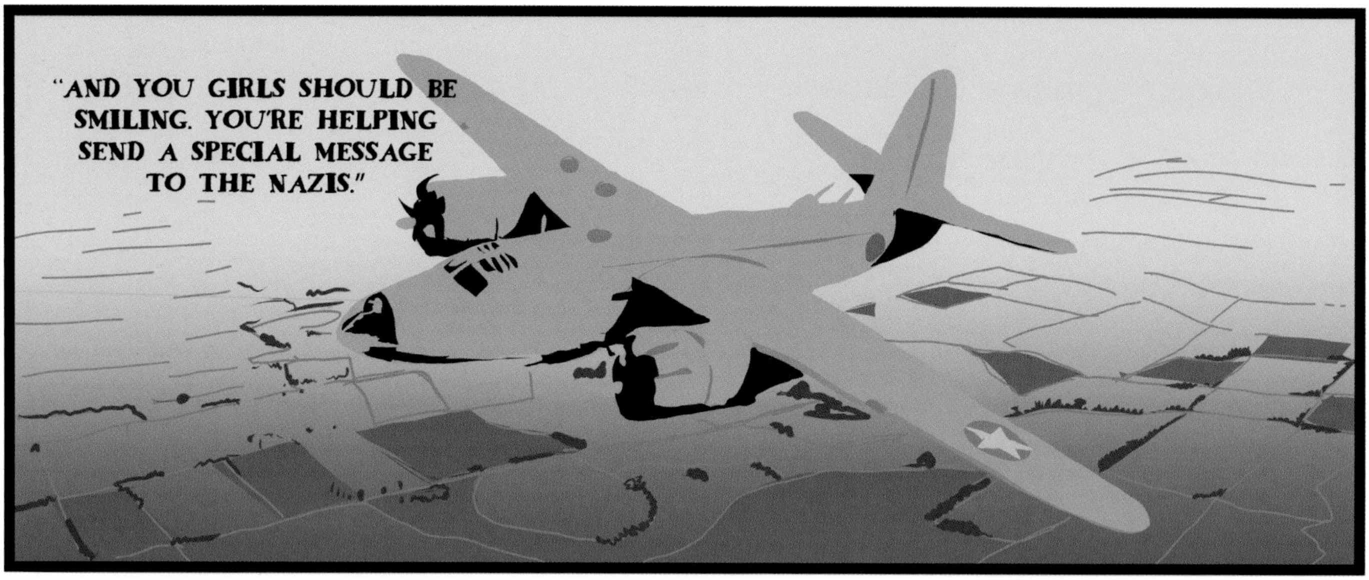
"AND YOU GIRLS SHOULD BE SMILING. YOU'RE HELPING SEND A SPECIAL MESSAGE TO THE NAZIS."

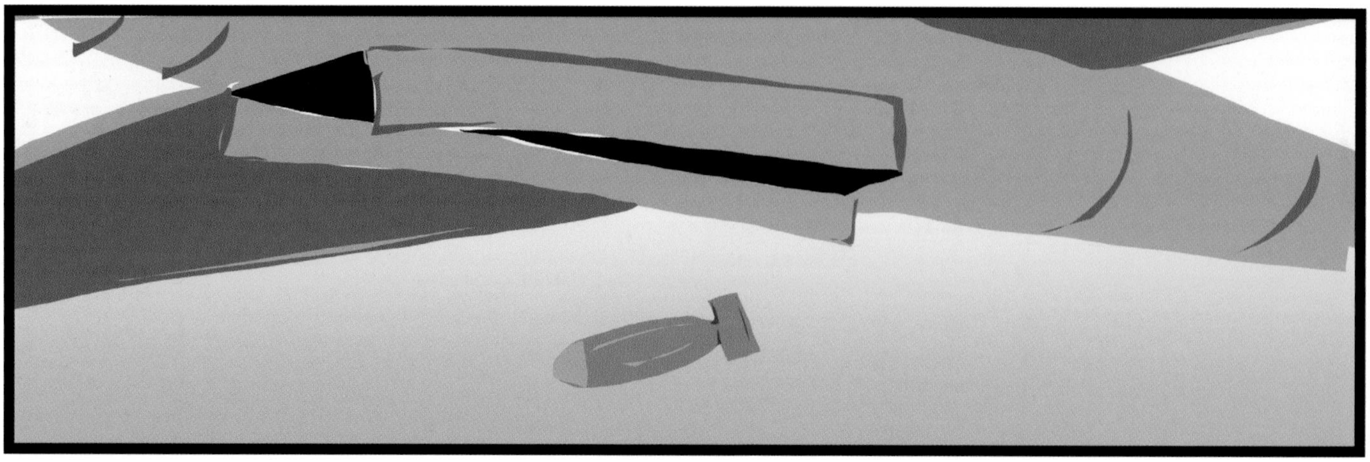

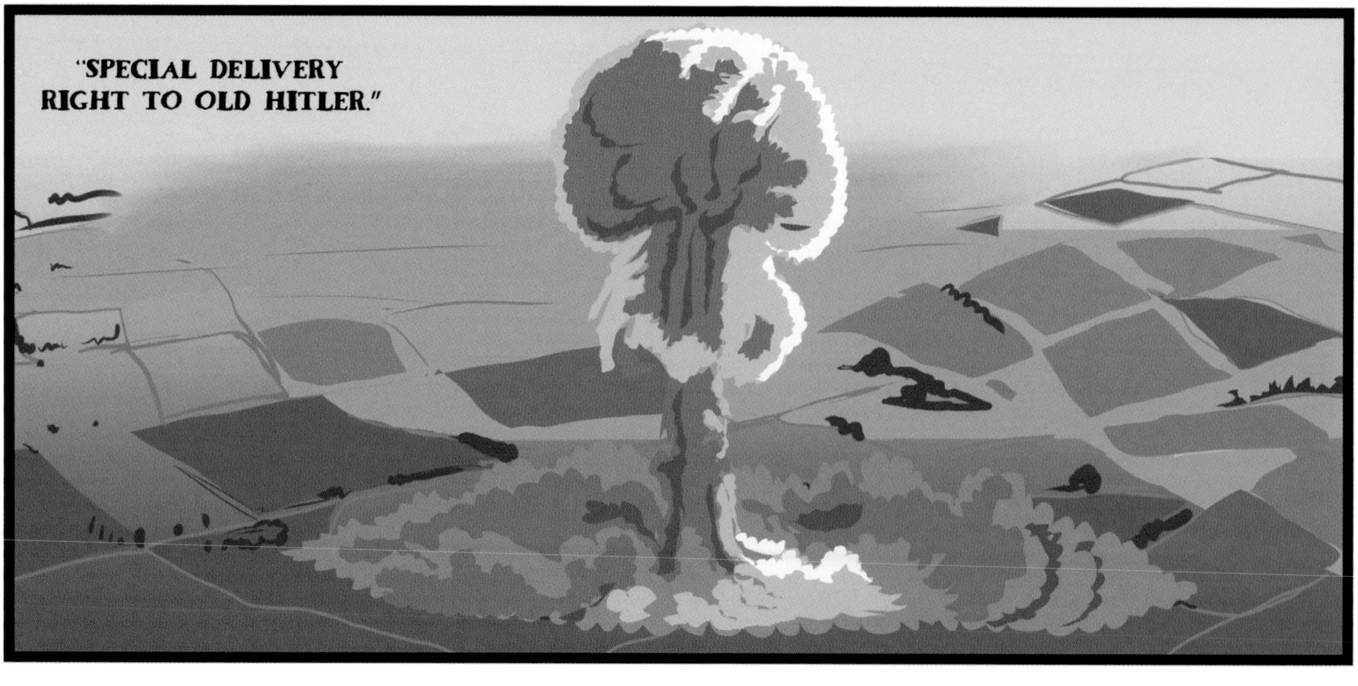
"SPECIAL DELIVERY RIGHT TO OLD HITLER."

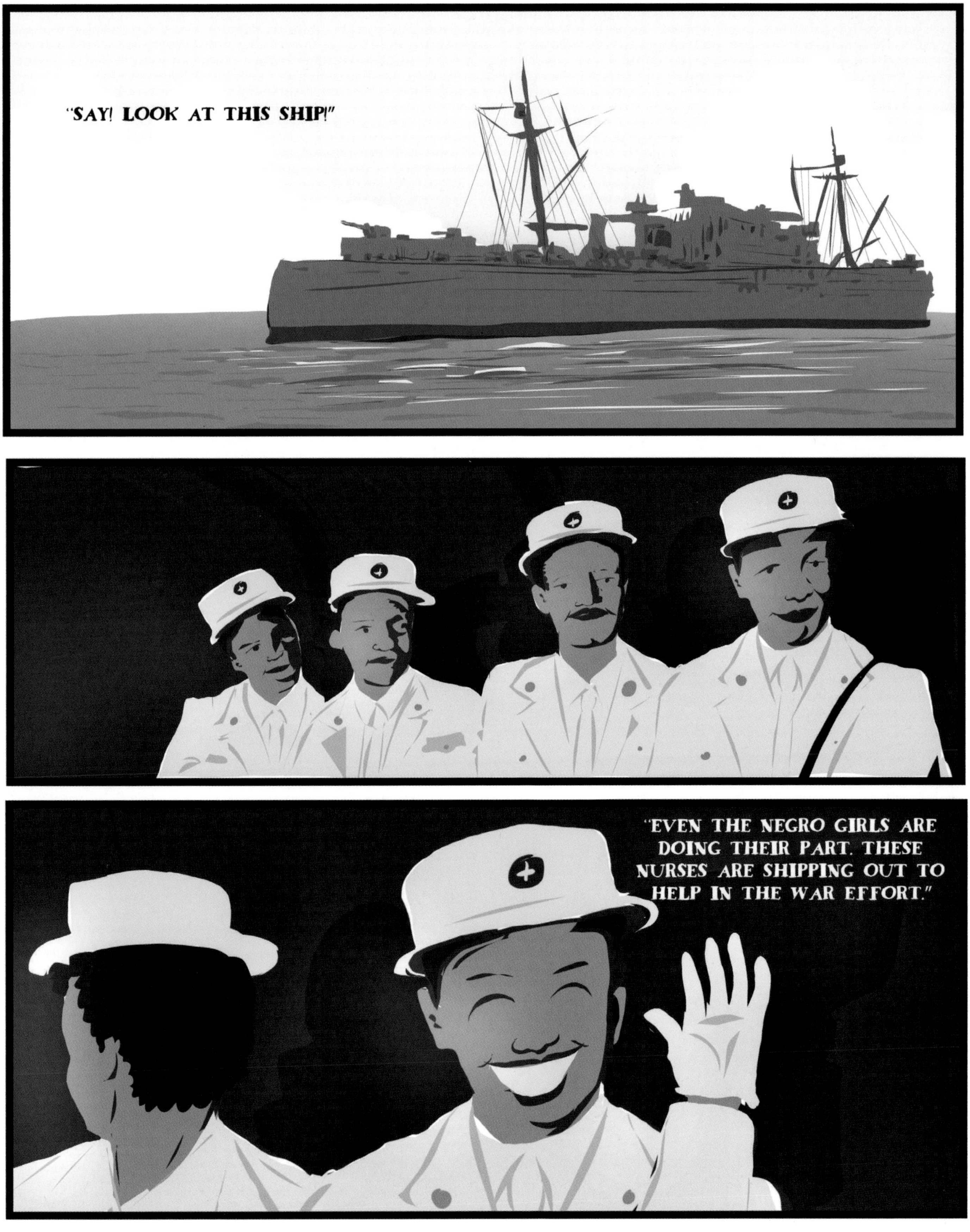
"SAY! LOOK AT THIS SHIP!"
"EVEN THE NEGRO GIRLS ARE DOING THEIR PART. THESE NURSES ARE SHIPPING OUT TO HELP IN THE WAR EFFORT."

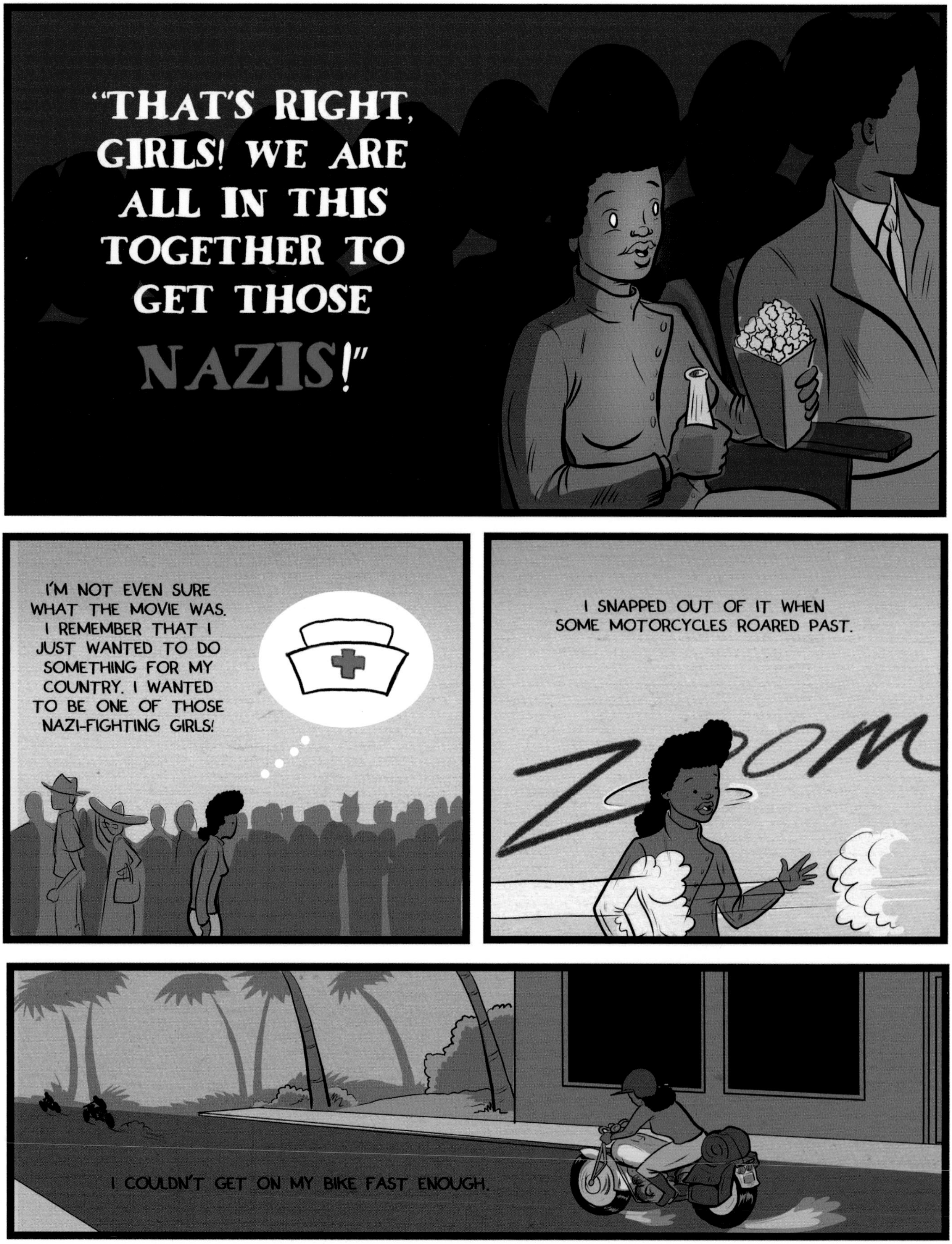
"THAT'S RIGHT, GIRLS! WE ARE ALL IN THIS TOGETHER TO GET THOSE NAZIS!"
I'M NOT EVEN SURE WHAT THE MOVIE WAS. I REMEMBER THAT I JUST WANTED TO DO SOMETHING FOR MY COUNTRY. I WANTED TO BE ONE OF THOSE NAZI-FIGHTING GIRLS!
I SNAPPED OUT OF IT WHEN SOME MOTORCYCLES ROARED PAST.
ZOOM
I COULDN'T GET ON MY BIKE FAST ENOUGH.

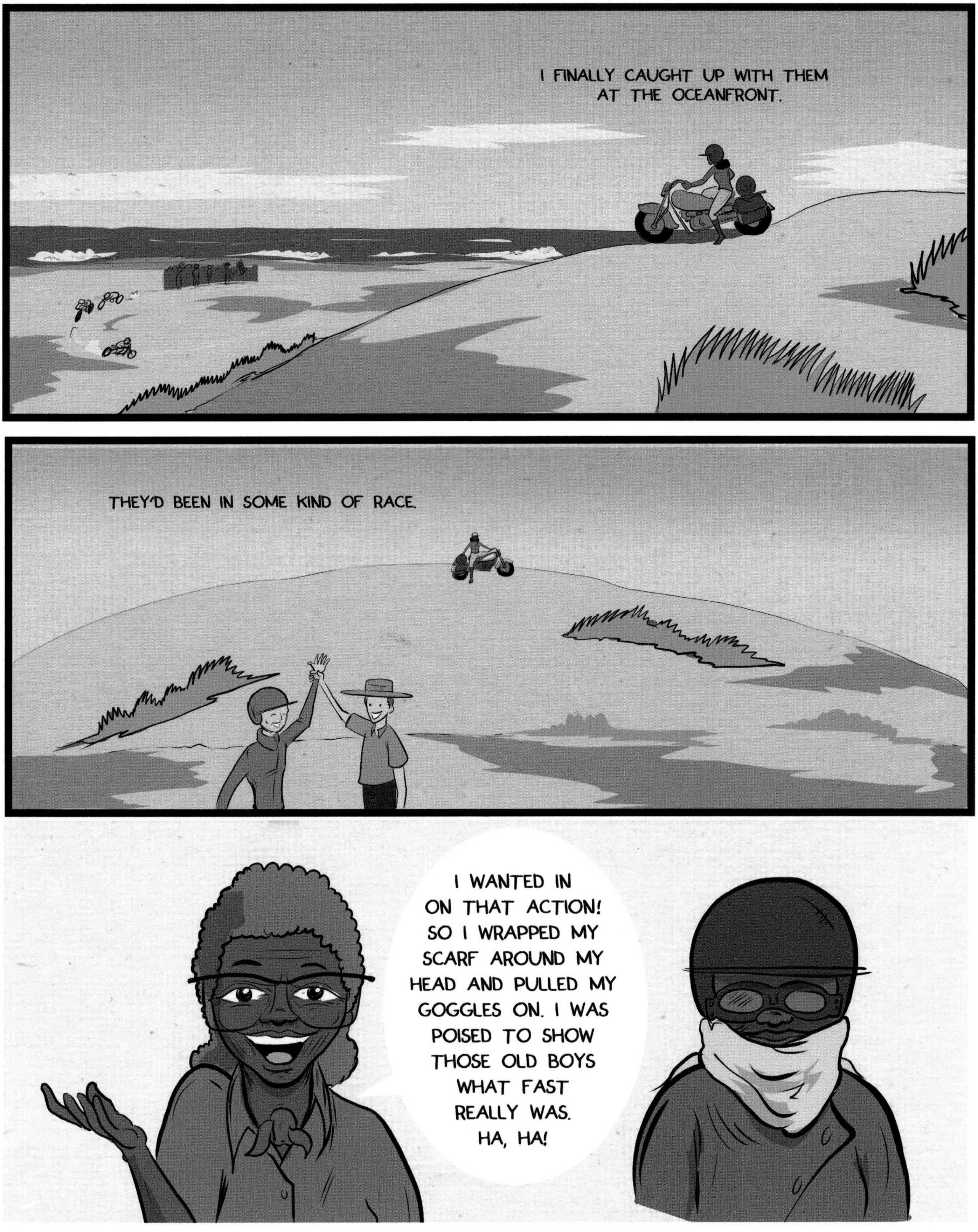
I FINALLY CAUGHT UP WITH THEM AT THE OCEANFRONT.
THEY'D BEEN IN SOME KIND OF RACE.
I WANTED IN ON THAT ACTION! SO I WRAPPED MY SCARF AROUND MY HEAD AND PULLED MY GOGGLES ON. I WAS POISED TO SHOW THOSE OLD BOYS WHAT FAST REALLY WAS. HA, HA!

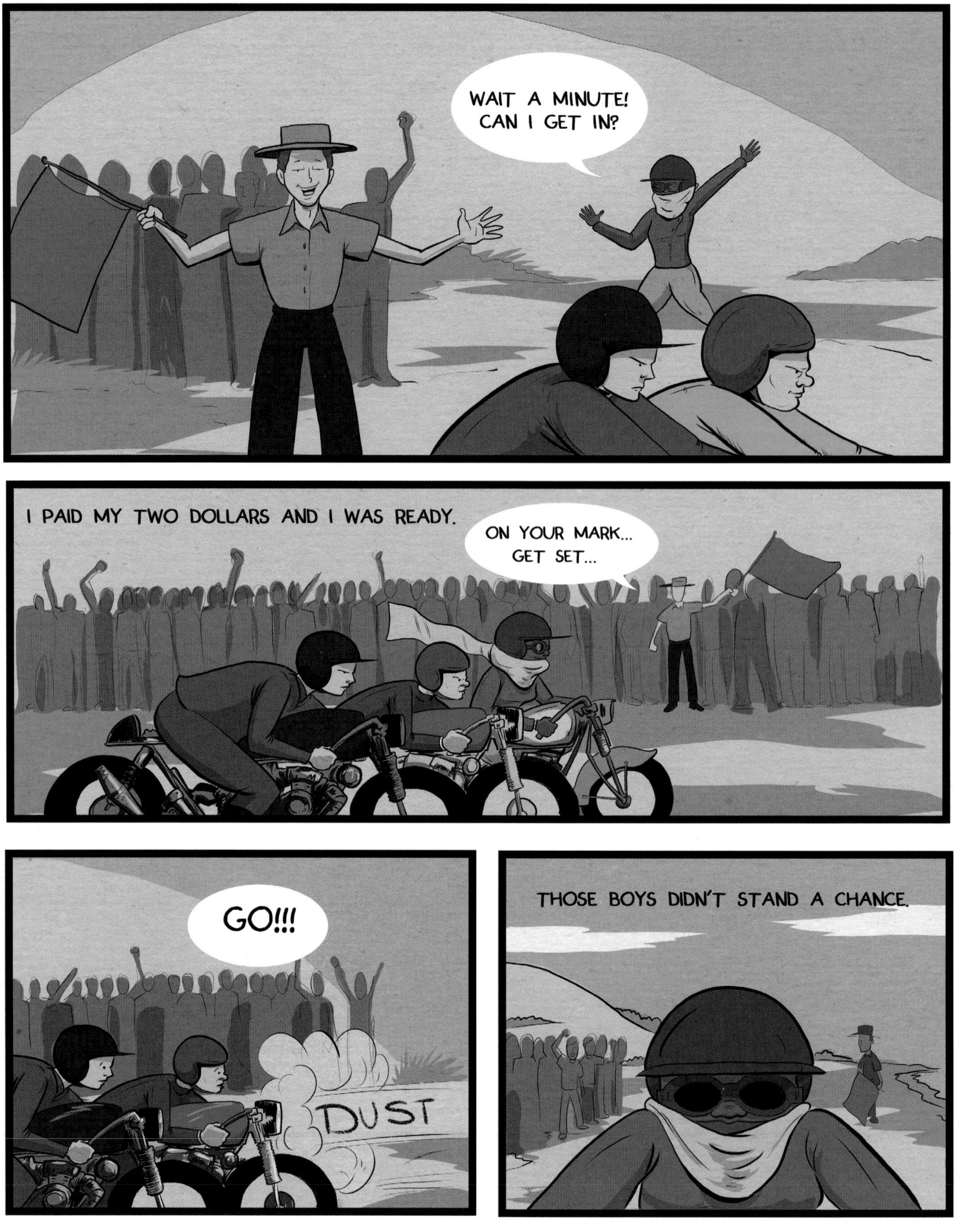
WAIT A MINUTE! CAN I GET IN?
I PAID MY TWO DOLLARS AND I WAS READY.
ON YOUR MARK... GET SET...
GO!!!
DUST
THOSE BOYS DIDN'T STAND A CHANCE.

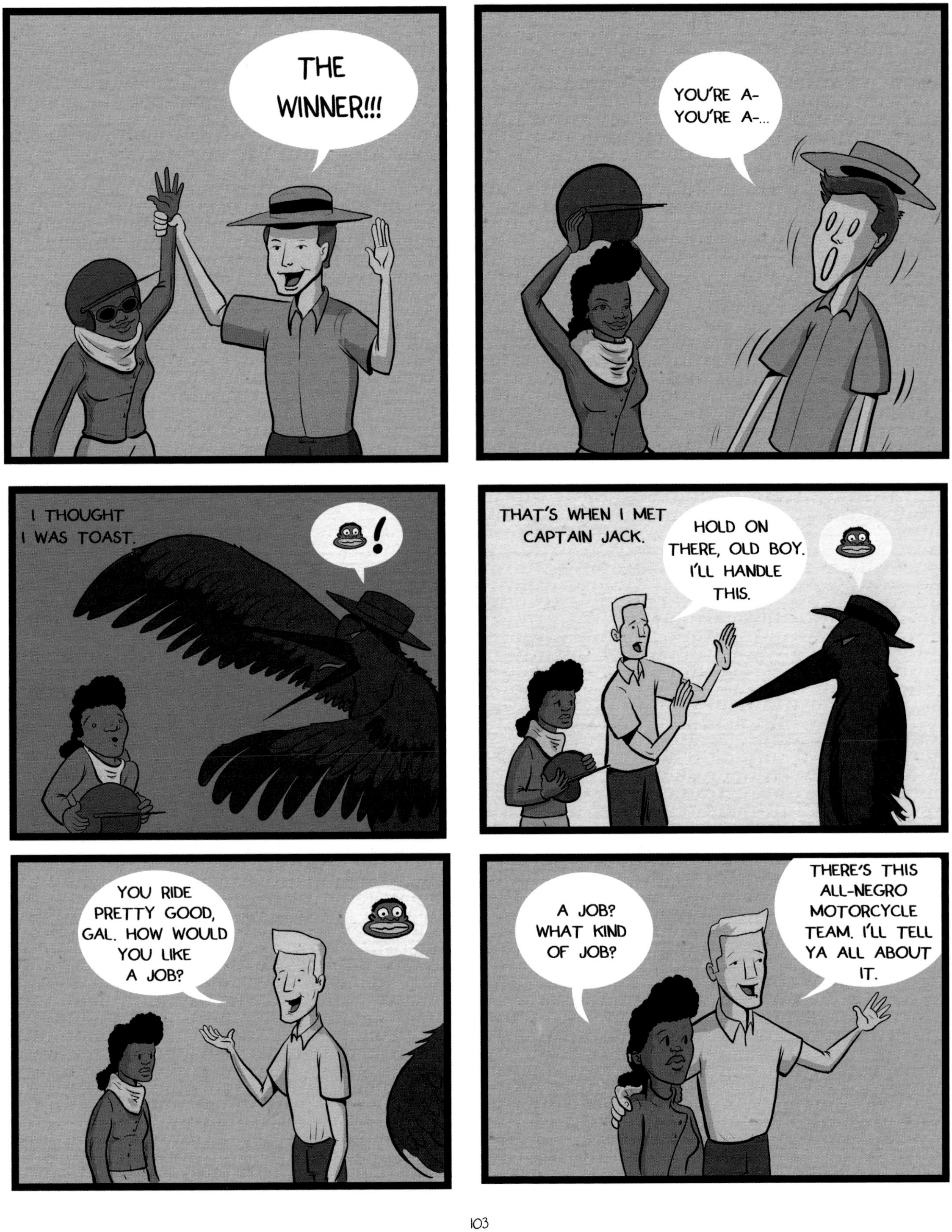
THE WINNER!!!
YOU'RE A- YOU'RE A-...
I THOUGHT I WAS TOAST.
!
THAT'S WHEN I MET CAPTAIN JACK.
HOLD ON THERE, OLD BOY. I'LL HANDLE THIS.
YOU RIDE PRETTY GOOD, GAL. HOW WOULD YOU LIKE A JOB?
A JOB? WHAT KIND OF JOB?
THERE'S THIS ALL-NEGRO MOTORCYCLE TEAM. I'LL TELL YA ALL ABOUT IT.

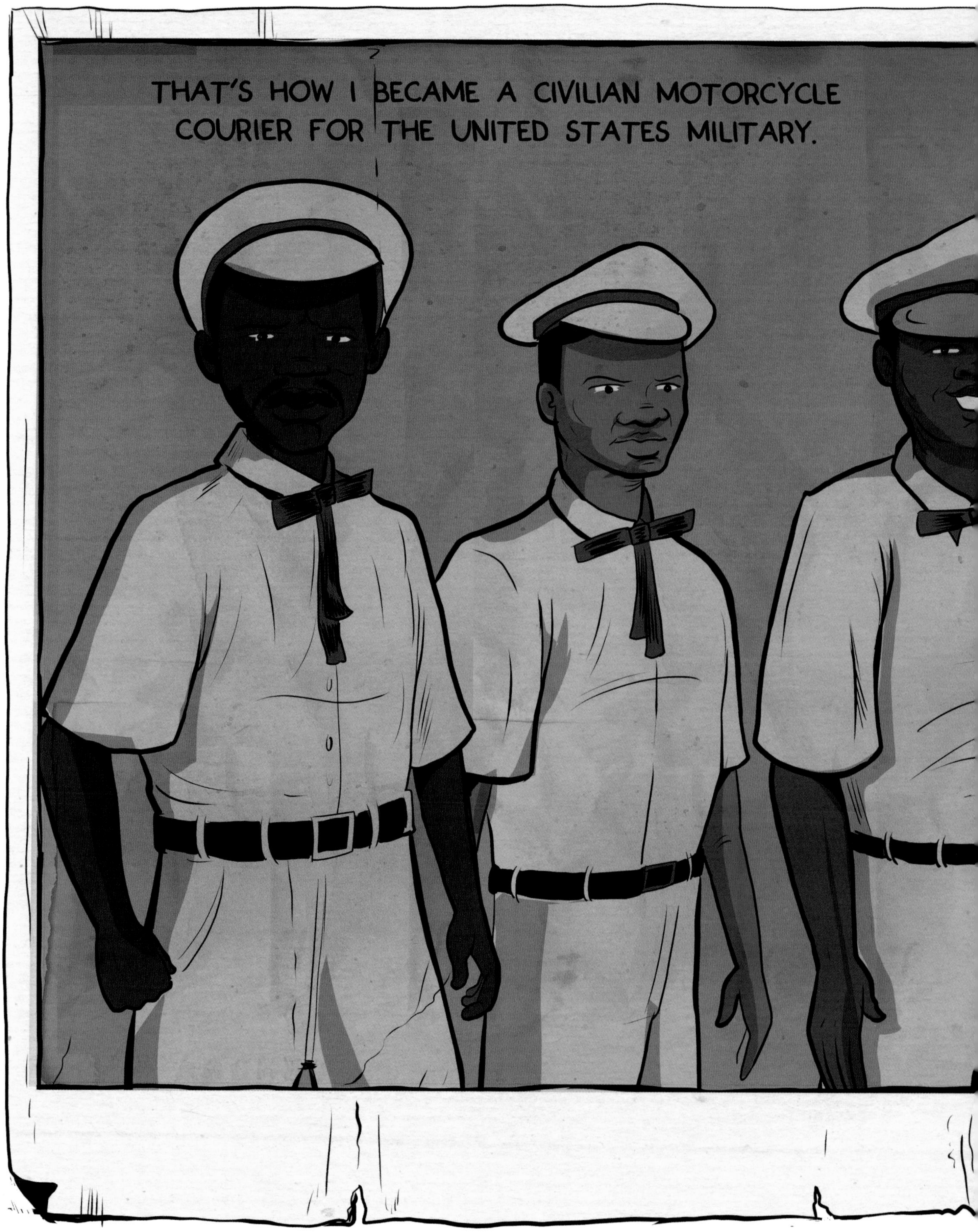
THAT'S HOW I BECAME A CIVILIAN MOTORCYCLE COURIER FOR THE UNITED STATES MILITARY.

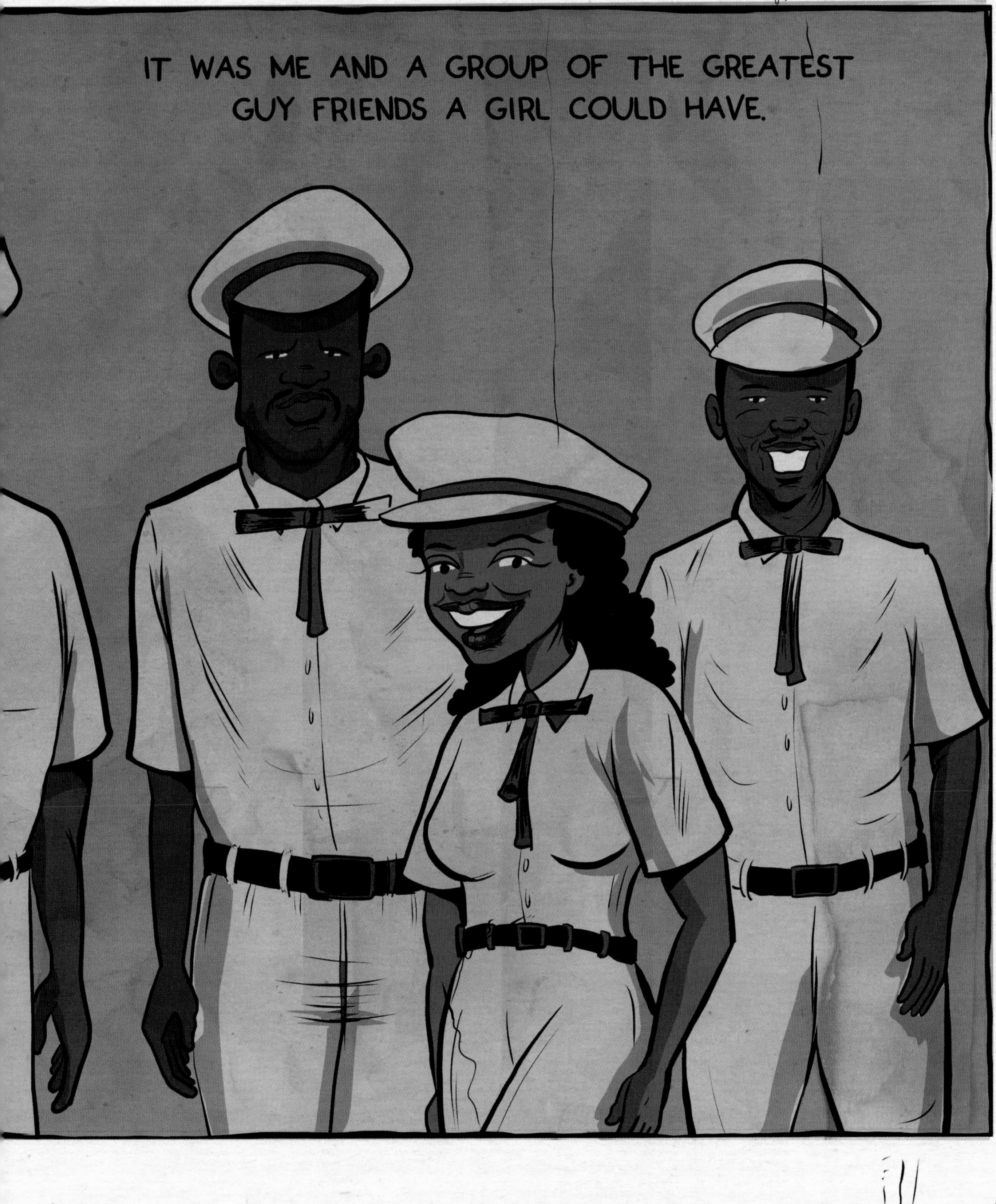
IT WAS ME AND A GROUP OF THE GREATEST GUY FRIENDS A GIRL COULD HAVE.

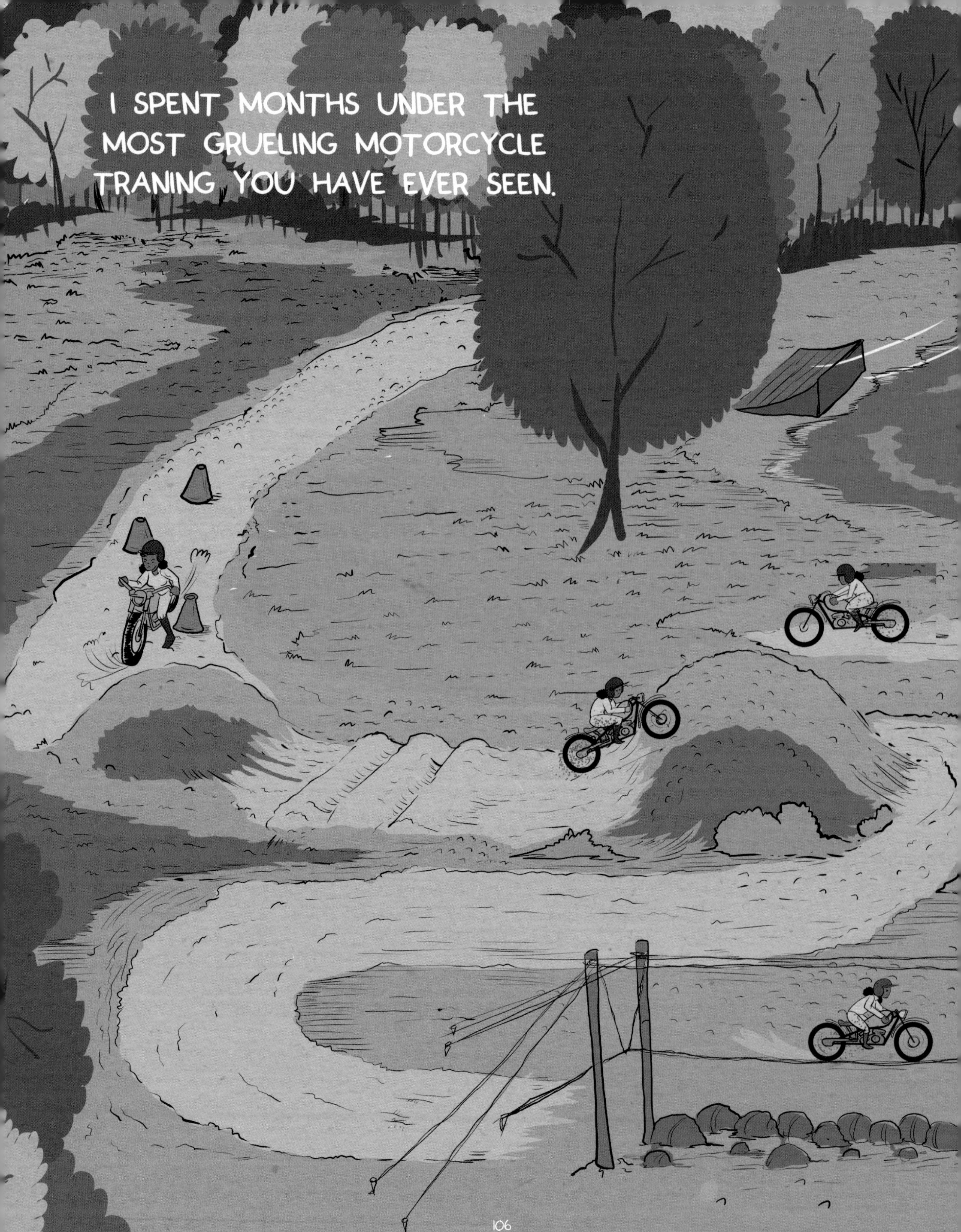
I SPENT MONTHS UNDER THE MOST GRUELING MOTORCYCLE TRANING YOU HAVE EVER SEEN.

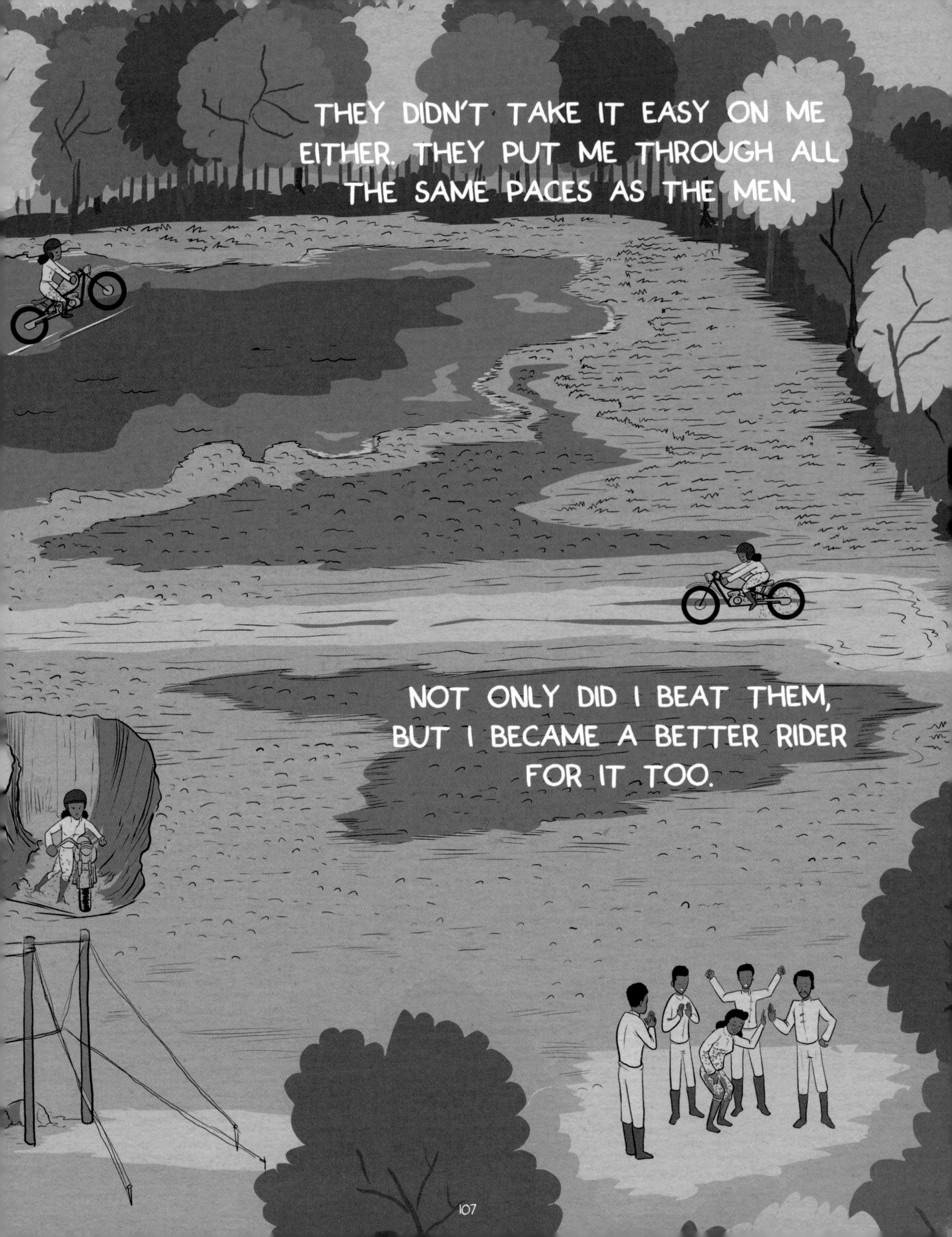
THEY DIDN'T TAKE IT EASY ON ME EITHER. THEY PUT ME THROUGH ALL THE SAME PACES AS THE MEN.
NOT ONLY DID I BEAT THEM, BUT I BECAME A BETTER RIDER FOR IT TOO.

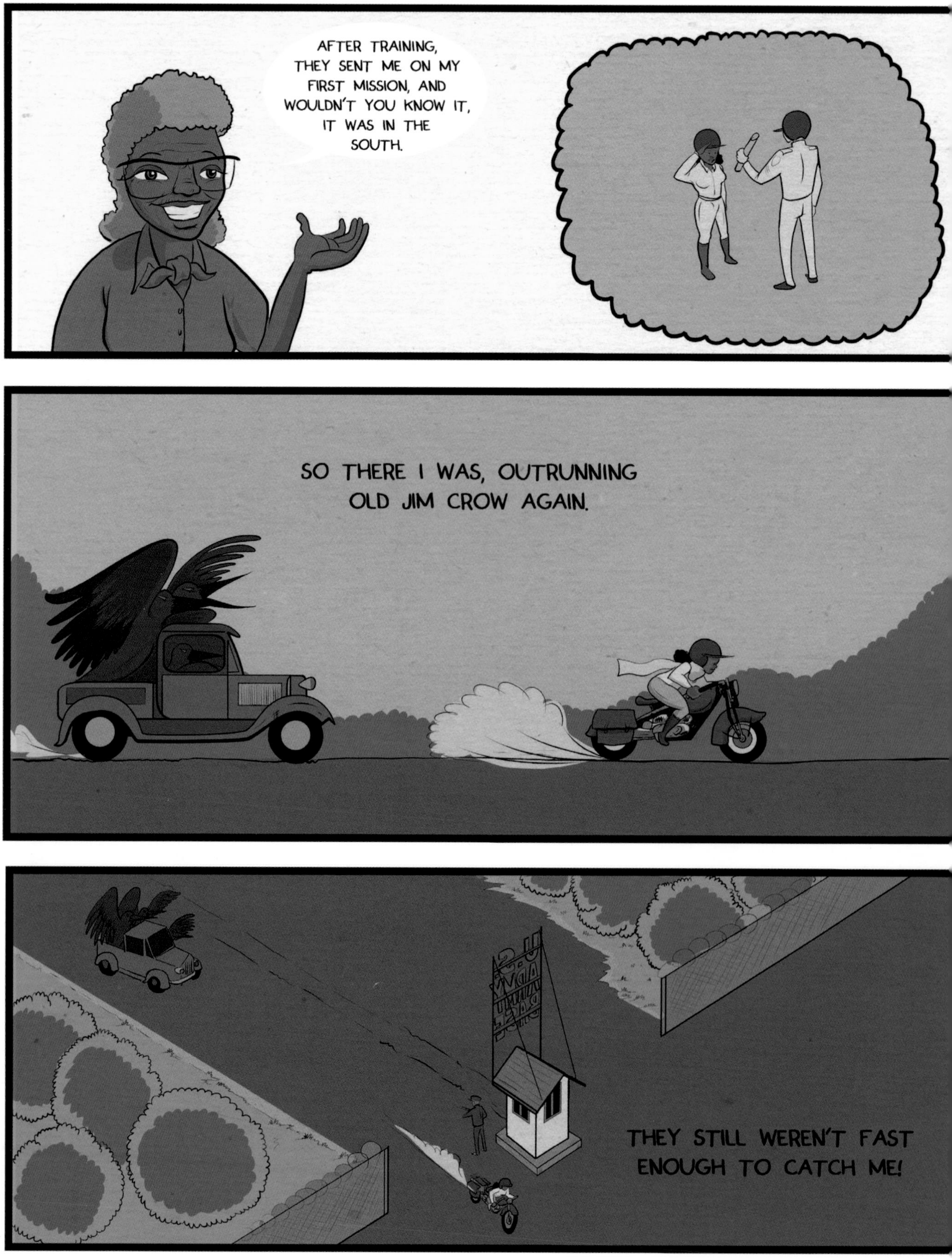
AFTER TRAINING, THEY SENT ME ON MY FIRST MISSION, AND WOULDN'T YOU KNOW IT, IT WAS IN THE SOUTH.
SO THERE I WAS, OUTRUNNING OLD JIM CROW AGAIN.
THEY STILL WEREN'T FAST ENOUGH TO CATCH ME!

AND THAT WAS PRETTY MUCH MY LIFE FOR A SPELL...

RUNNING FROM BASE TO BASE,

ALWAYS AHEAD OF OLD JIM CROW.

IT BECAME EASY AFTER A WHILE.

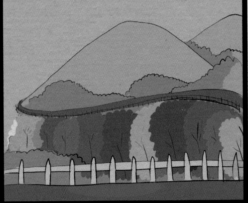

AND THEN WE WON THE WAR.

WHEN MY JOB WITH THE MILITARY WAS DONE, I WAS MORE RESTLESS THAN EVER.

AFTER SPENDING THE LAST FEW YEARS RUNNING MESSAGES, I NEEDED SOMETHING NEW TO DO. SO I HEADED ABROAD.

I DECIDED TO GO SEE FOR MYSELF WHAT ALL THE FUSS WAS ABOUT. I WANTED TO VISIT ALL THOSE COUNTRIES THAT WE HAD BEEN FIGHTING FOR AND AGAINST.

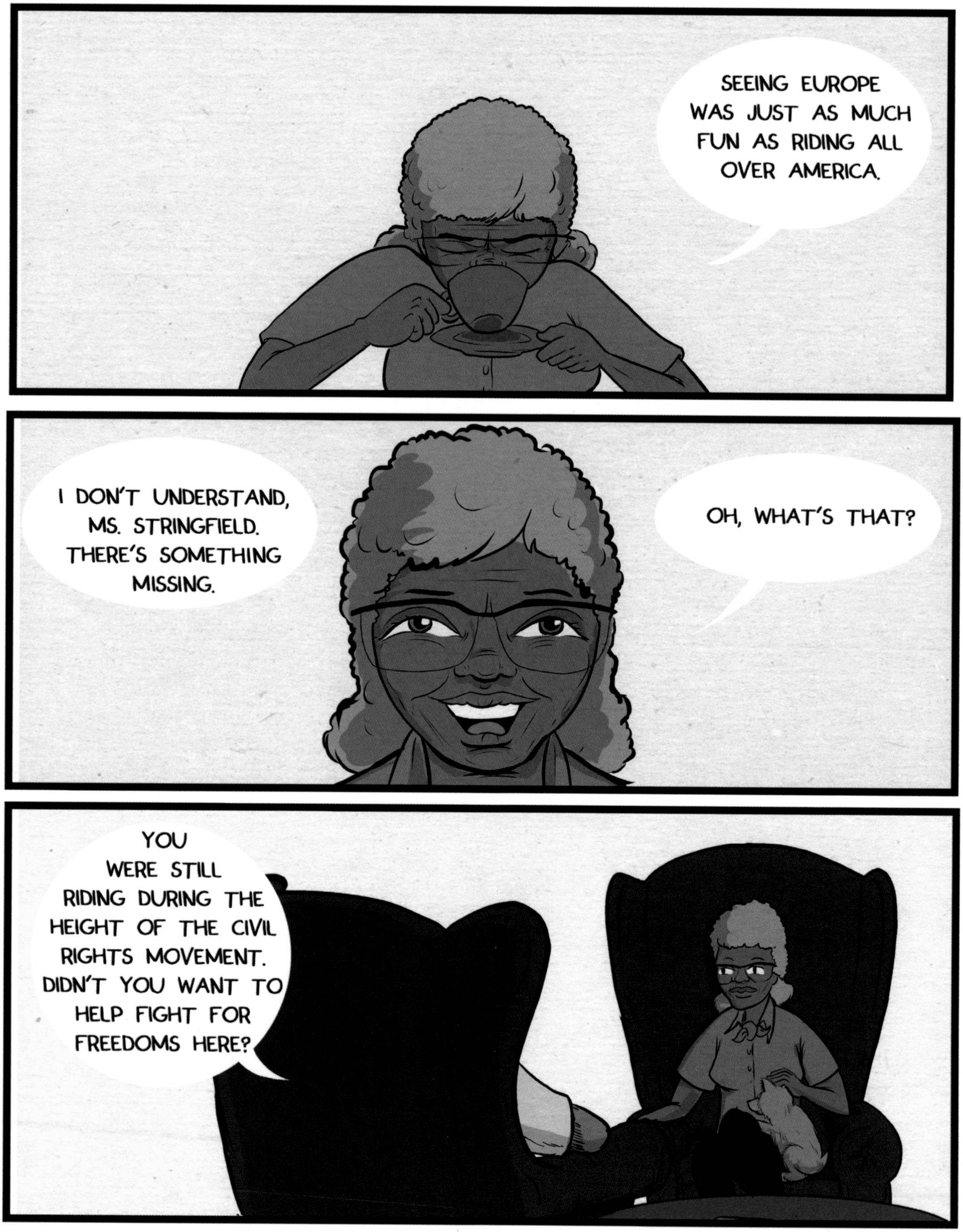
SEEING EUROPE WAS JUST AS MUCH FUN AS RIDING ALL OVER AMERICA.
I DON'T UNDERSTAND, MS. STRINGFIELD. THERE'S SOMETHING MISSING.
OH, WHAT'S THAT?
YOU WERE STILL RIDING DURING THE HEIGHT OF THE CIVIL RIGHTS MOVEMENT. DIDN'T YOU WANT TO HELP FIGHT FOR FREEDOMS HERE?

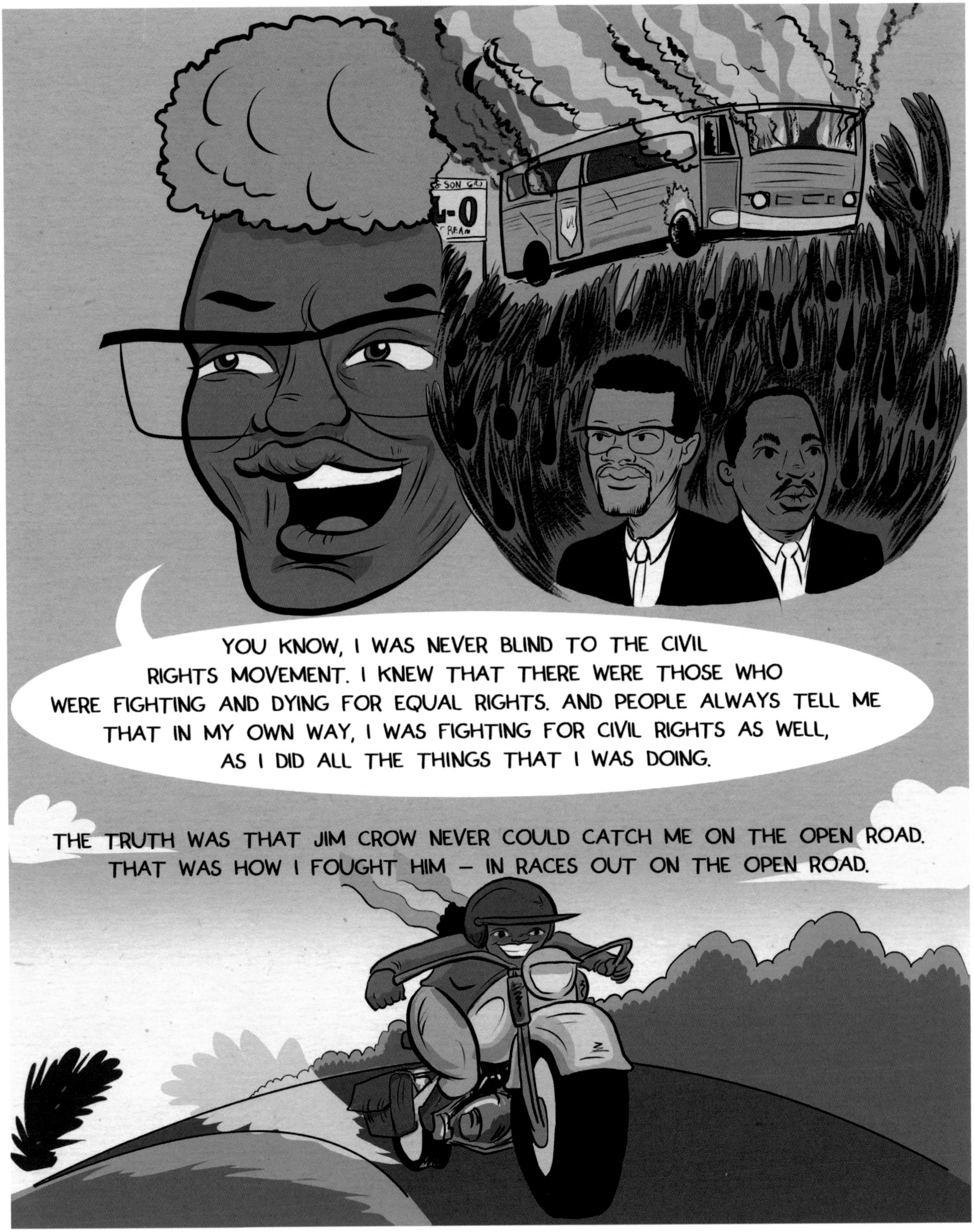
YOU KNOW, I WAS NEVER BLIND TO THE CIVIL RIGHTS MOVEMENT. I KNEW THAT THERE WERE THOSE WHO WERE FIGHTING AND DYING FOR EQUAL RIGHTS. AND PEOPLE ALWAYS TELL ME THAT IN MY OWN WAY, I WAS FIGHTING FOR CIVIL RIGHTS AS WELL, AS I DID ALL THE THINGS THAT I WAS DOING.
THE TRUTH WAS THAT JIM CROW NEVER COULD CATCH ME ON THE OPEN ROAD. THAT WAS HOW I FOUGHT HIM – IN RACES OUT ON THE OPEN ROAD.

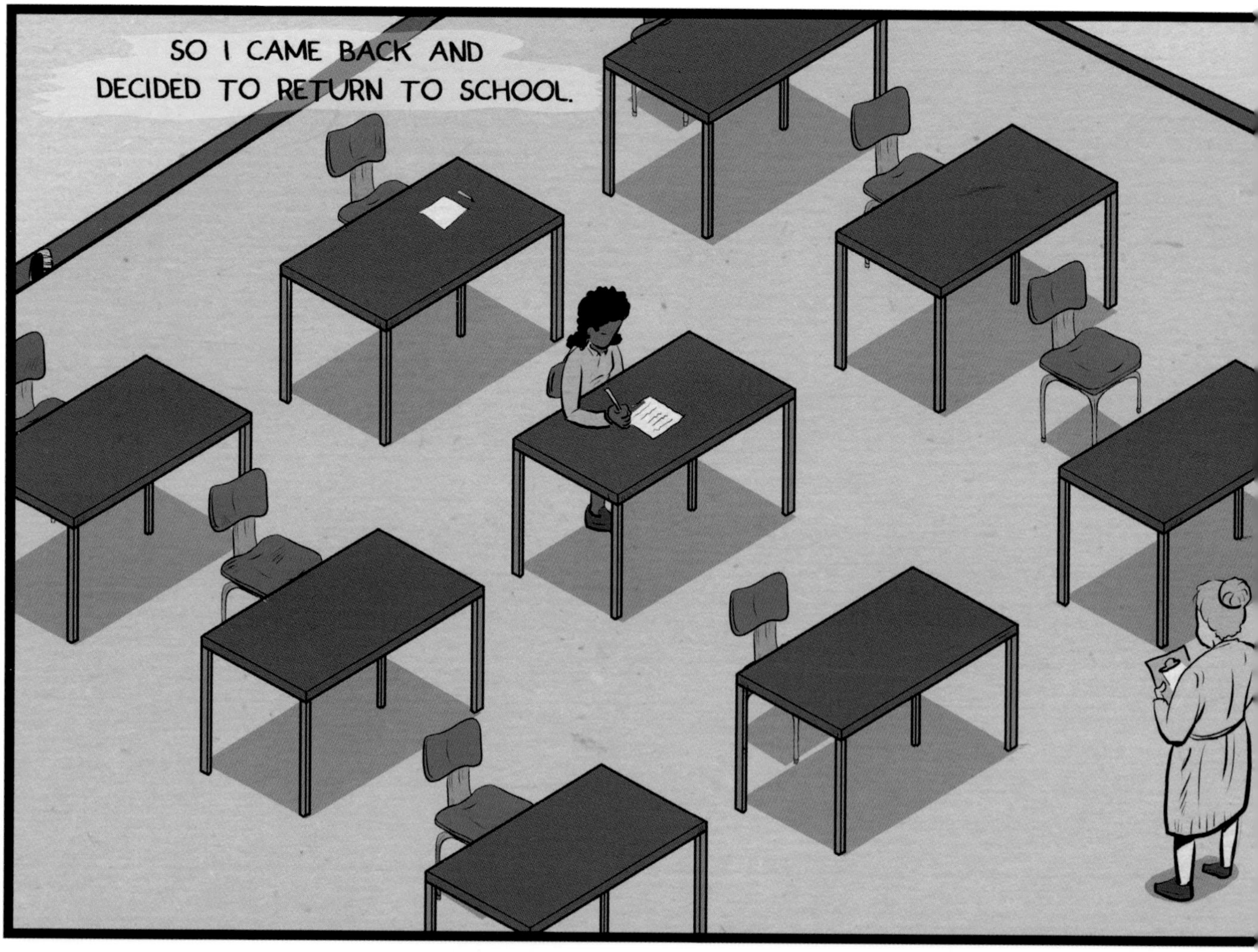
SO I CAME BACK AND DECIDED TO RETURN TO SCHOOL.

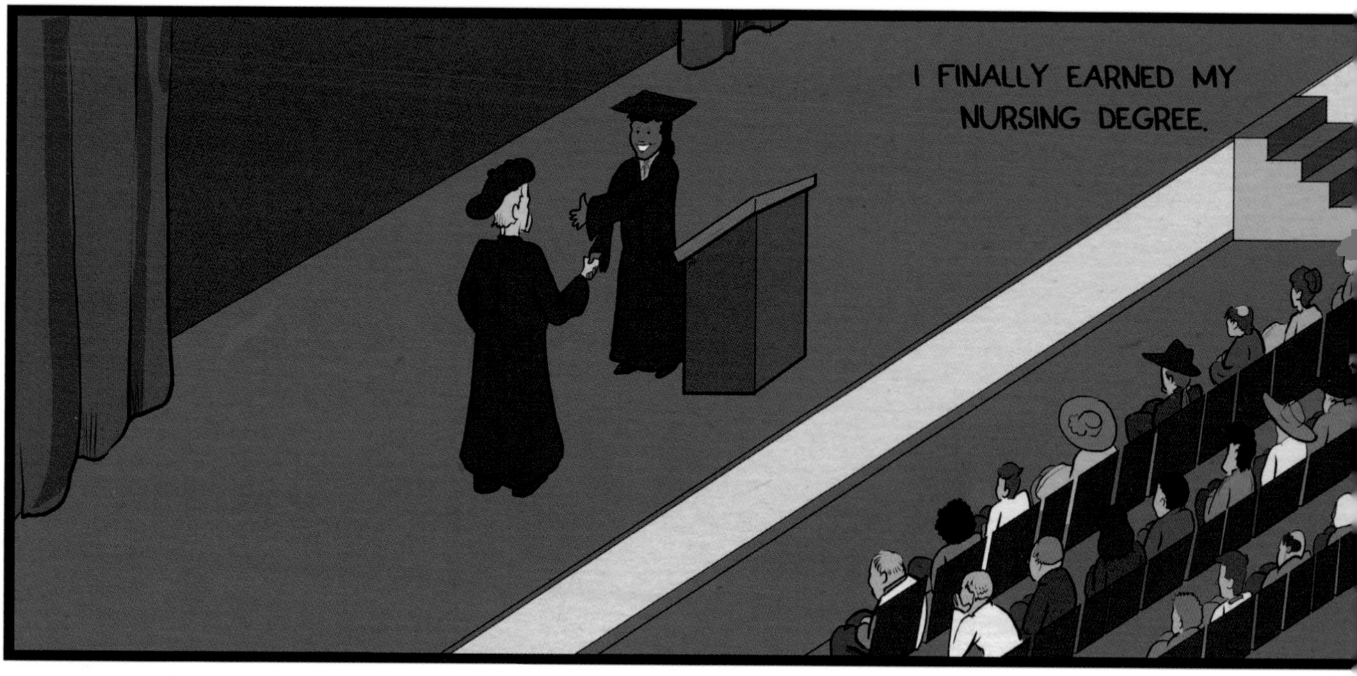
I FINALLY EARNED MY NURSING DEGREE.

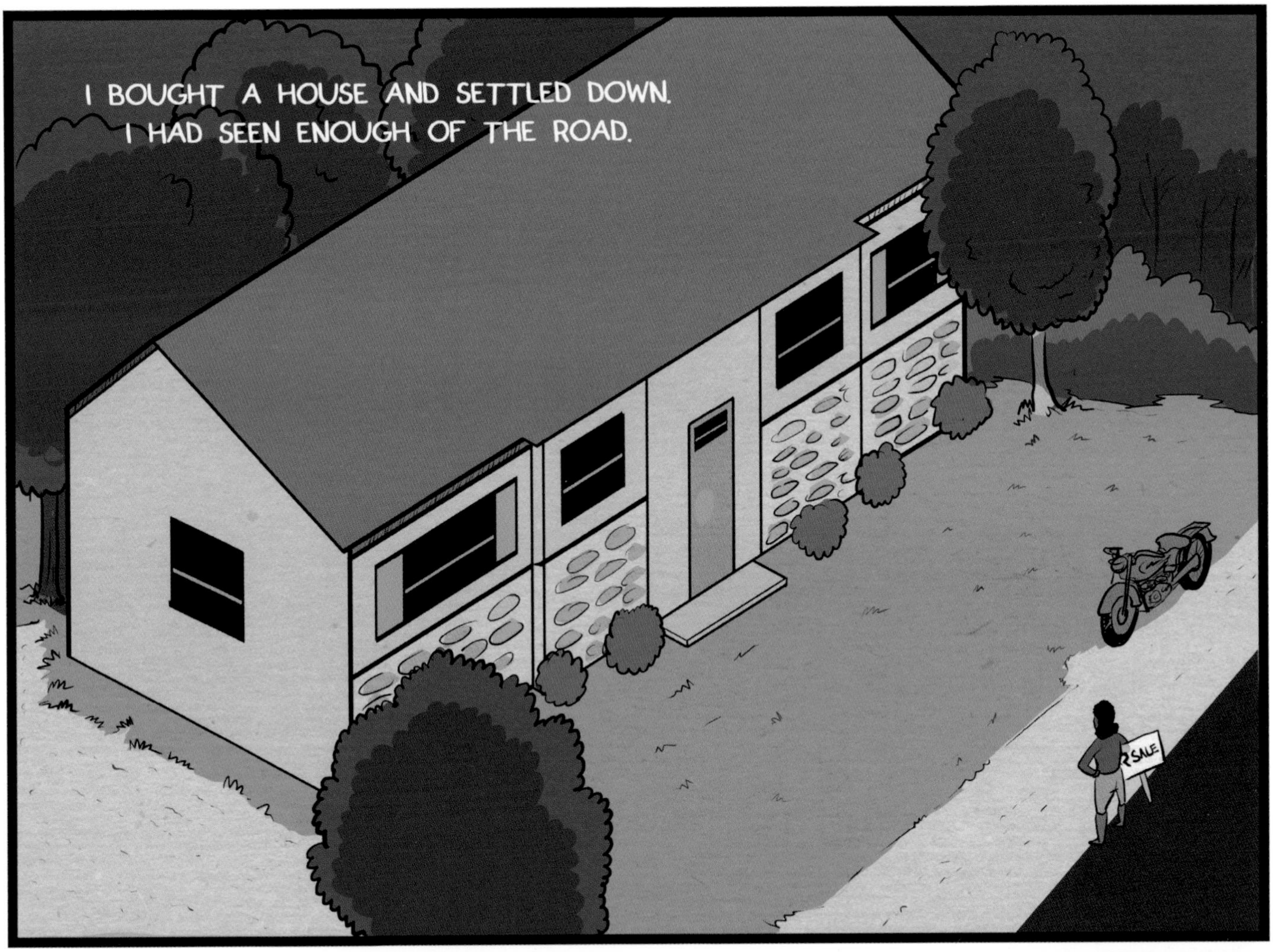
I BOUGHT A HOUSE AND SETTLED DOWN.
I HAD SEEN ENOUGH OF THE ROAD.
SALE

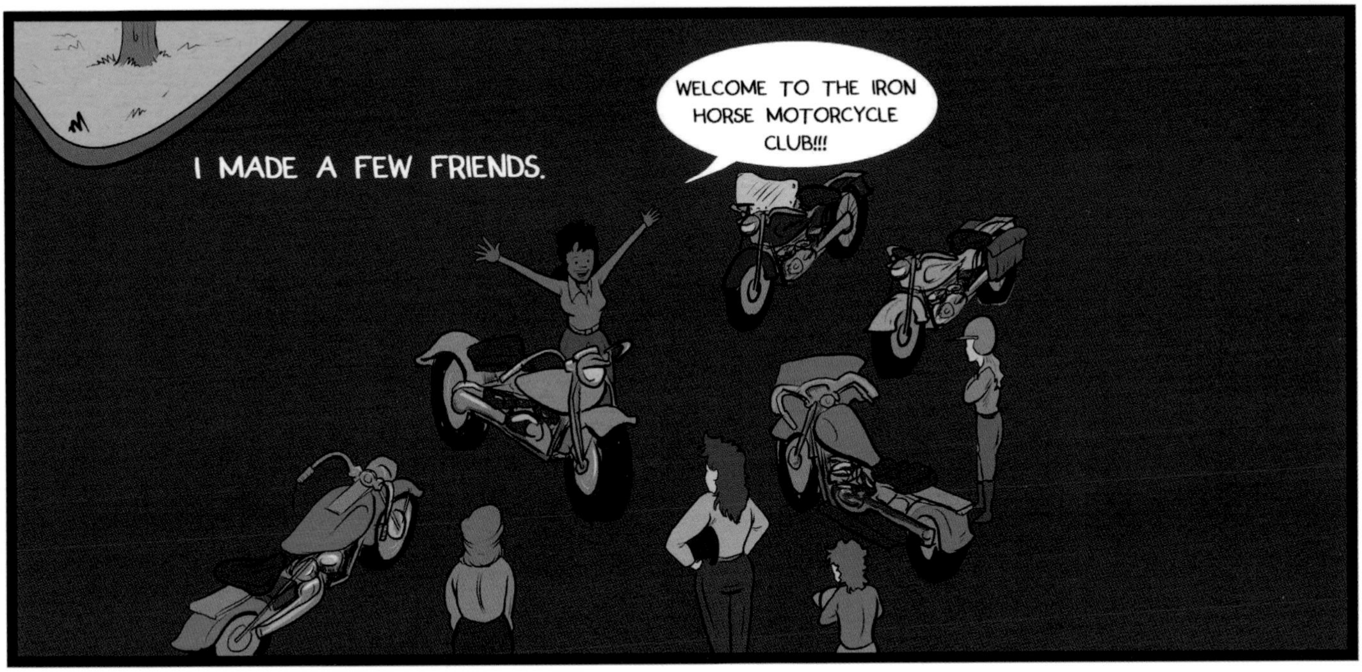
I MADE A FEW FRIENDS.
WELCOME TO THE IRON HORSE MOTORCYCLE CLUB!!!

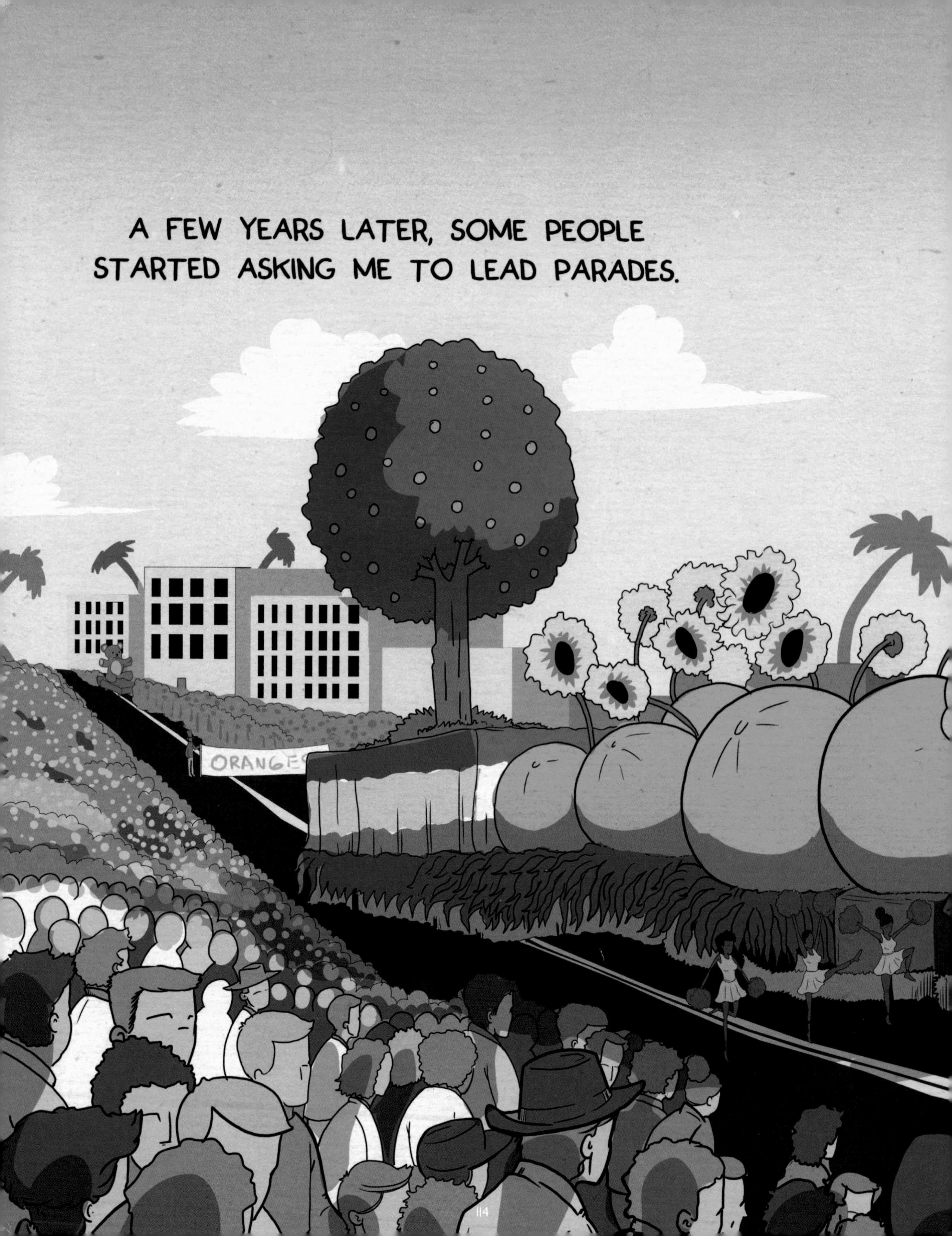
A FEW YEARS LATER, SOME PEOPLE STARTED ASKING ME TO LEAD PARADES.

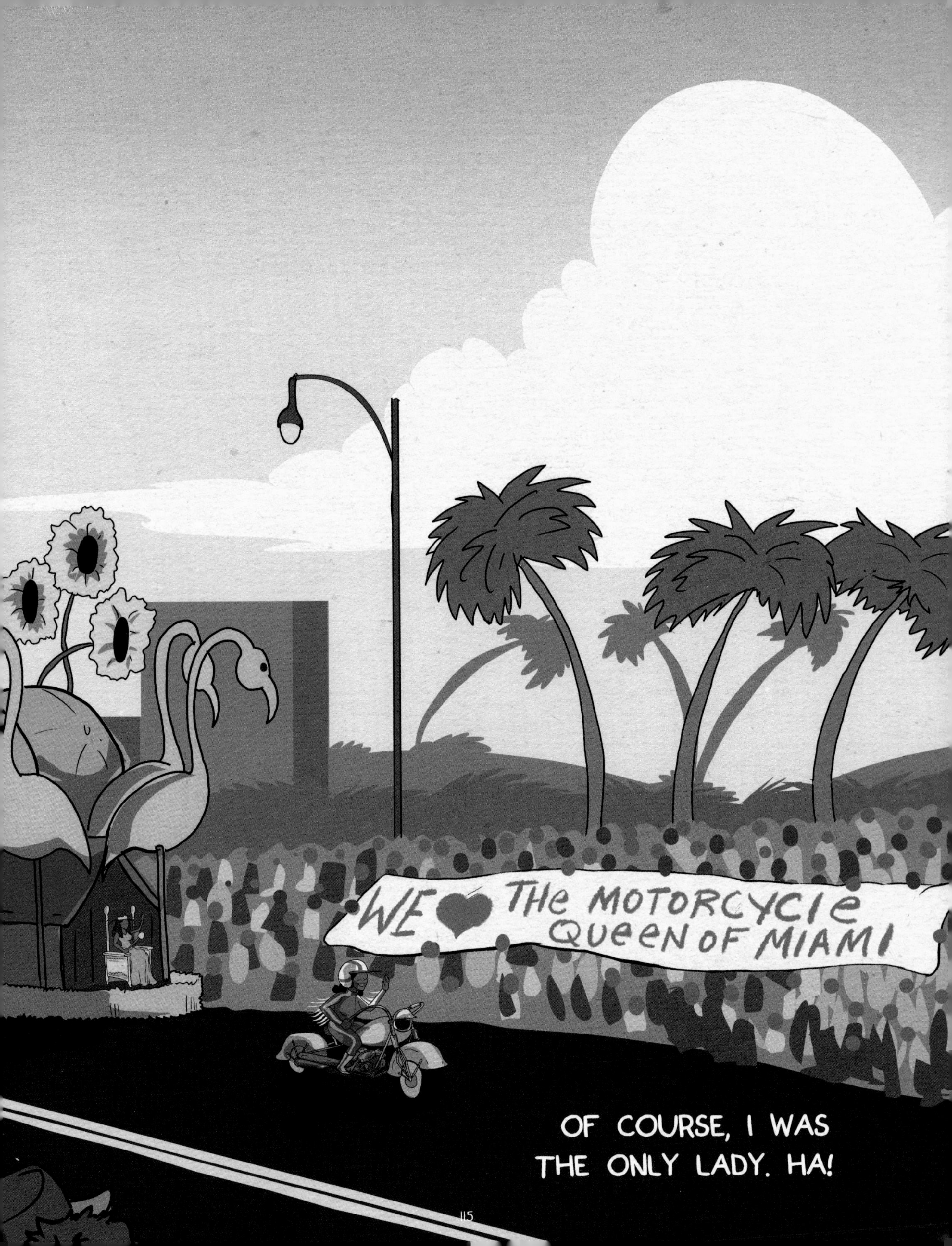
WE ♥ THE MOTORCYCLE QUEEN OF MIAMI
OF COURSE, I WAS THE ONLY LADY. HA!

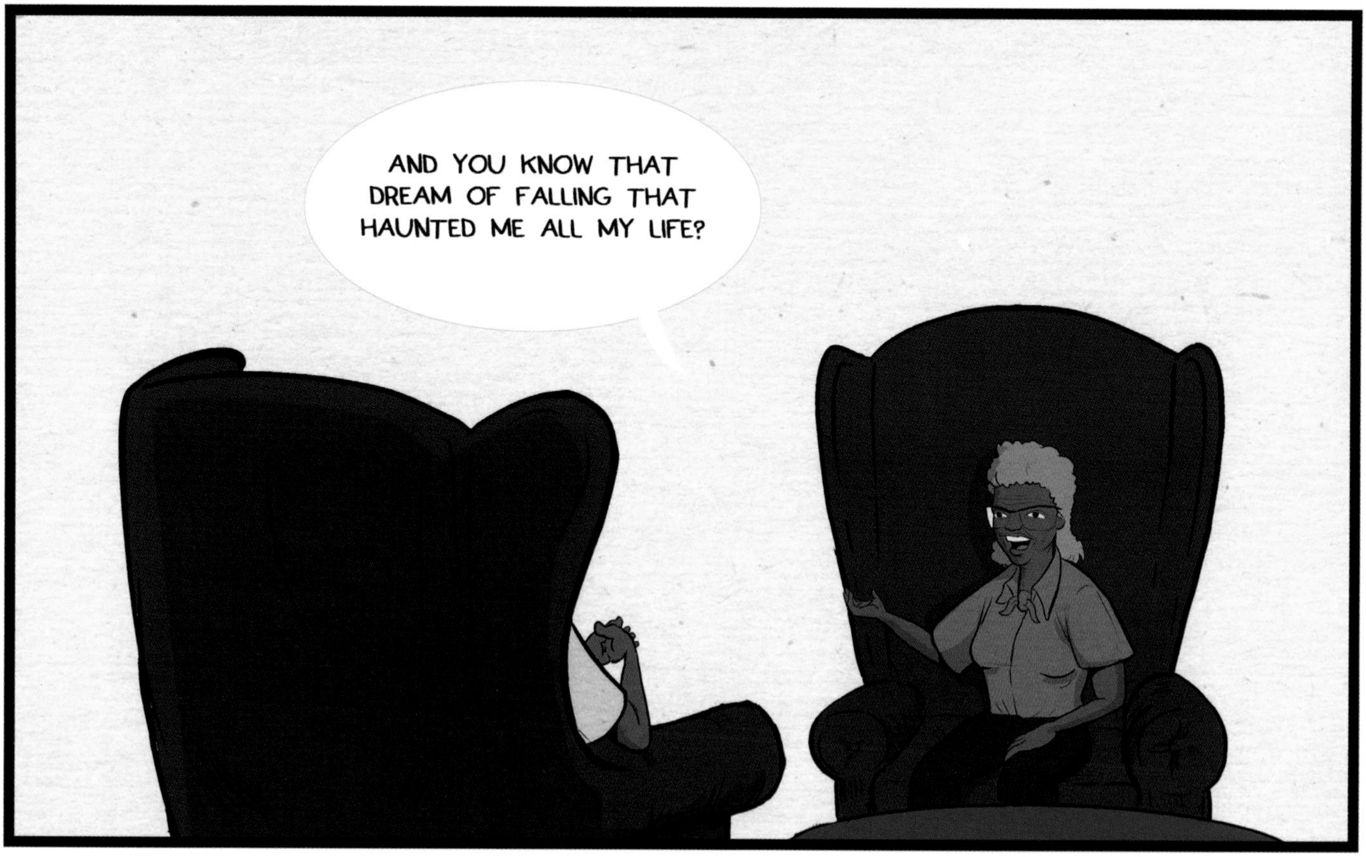
AND YOU KNOW THAT DREAM OF FALLING THAT HAUNTED ME ALL MY LIFE?

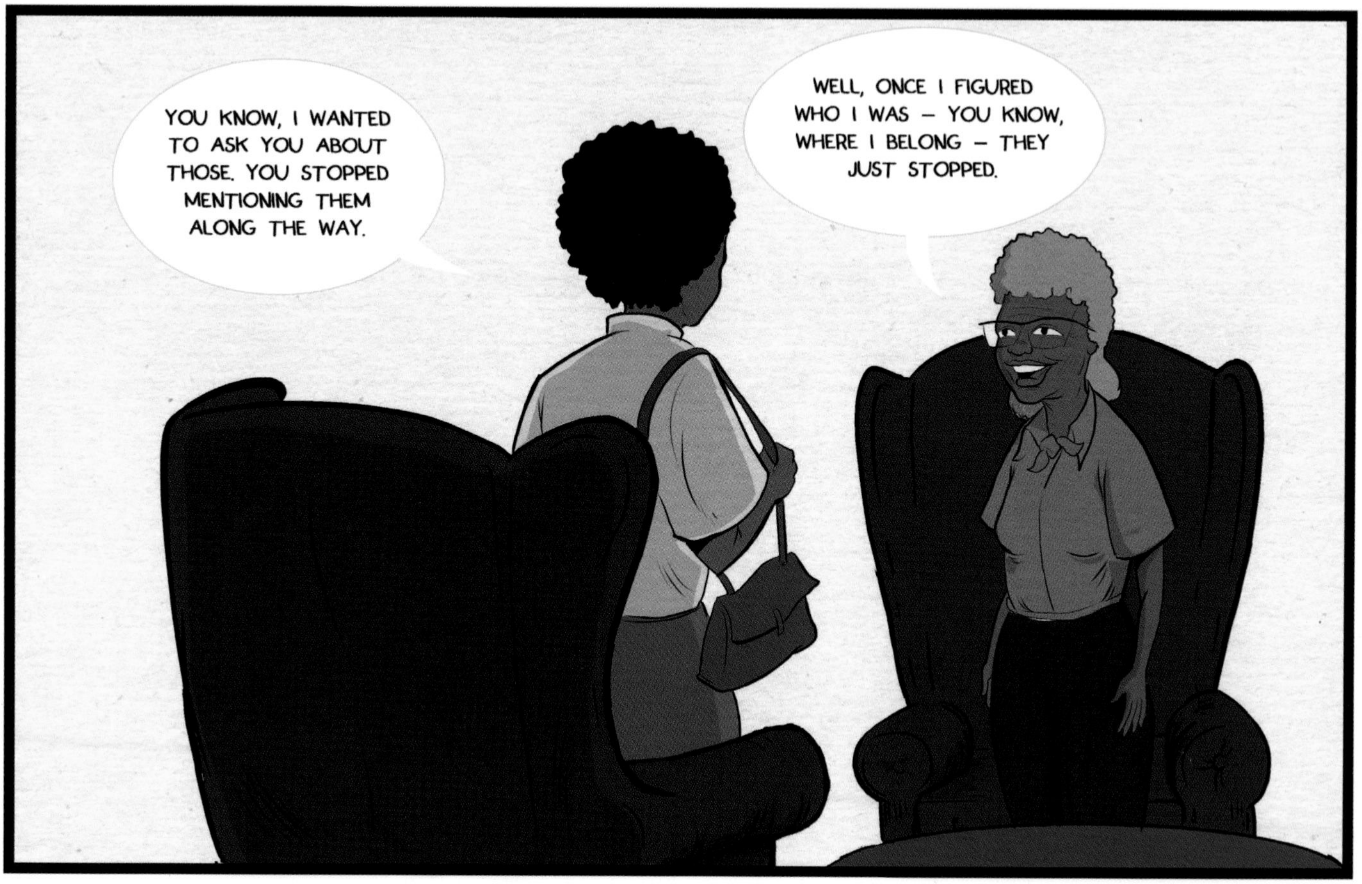
YOU KNOW, I WANTED TO ASK YOU ABOUT THOSE. YOU STOPPED MENTIONING THEM ALONG THE WAY.
WELL, ONCE I FIGURED WHO I WAS – YOU KNOW, WHERE I BELONG – THEY JUST STOPPED.

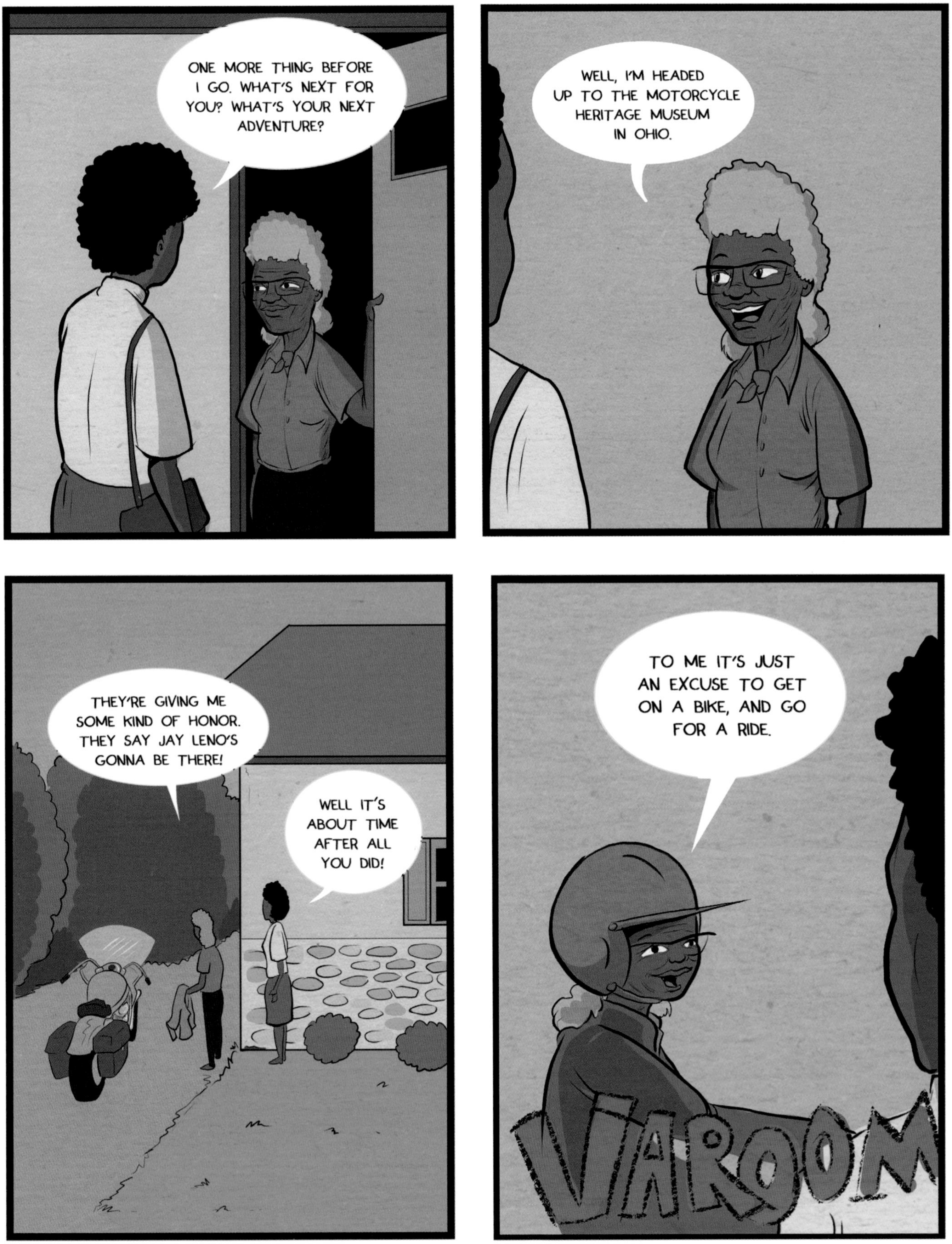
ONE MORE THING BEFORE I GO. WHAT'S NEXT FOR YOU? WHAT'S YOUR NEXT ADVENTURE?
WELL, I'M HEADED UP TO THE MOTORCYCLE HERITAGE MUSEUM IN OHIO.
THEY'RE GIVING ME SOME KIND OF HONOR. THEY SAY JAY LENO'S GONNA BE THERE!
WELL IT'S ABOUT TIME AFTER ALL YOU DID!
TO ME IT'S JUST AN EXCUSE TO GET ON A BIKE, AND GO FOR A RIDE.
VAROOM

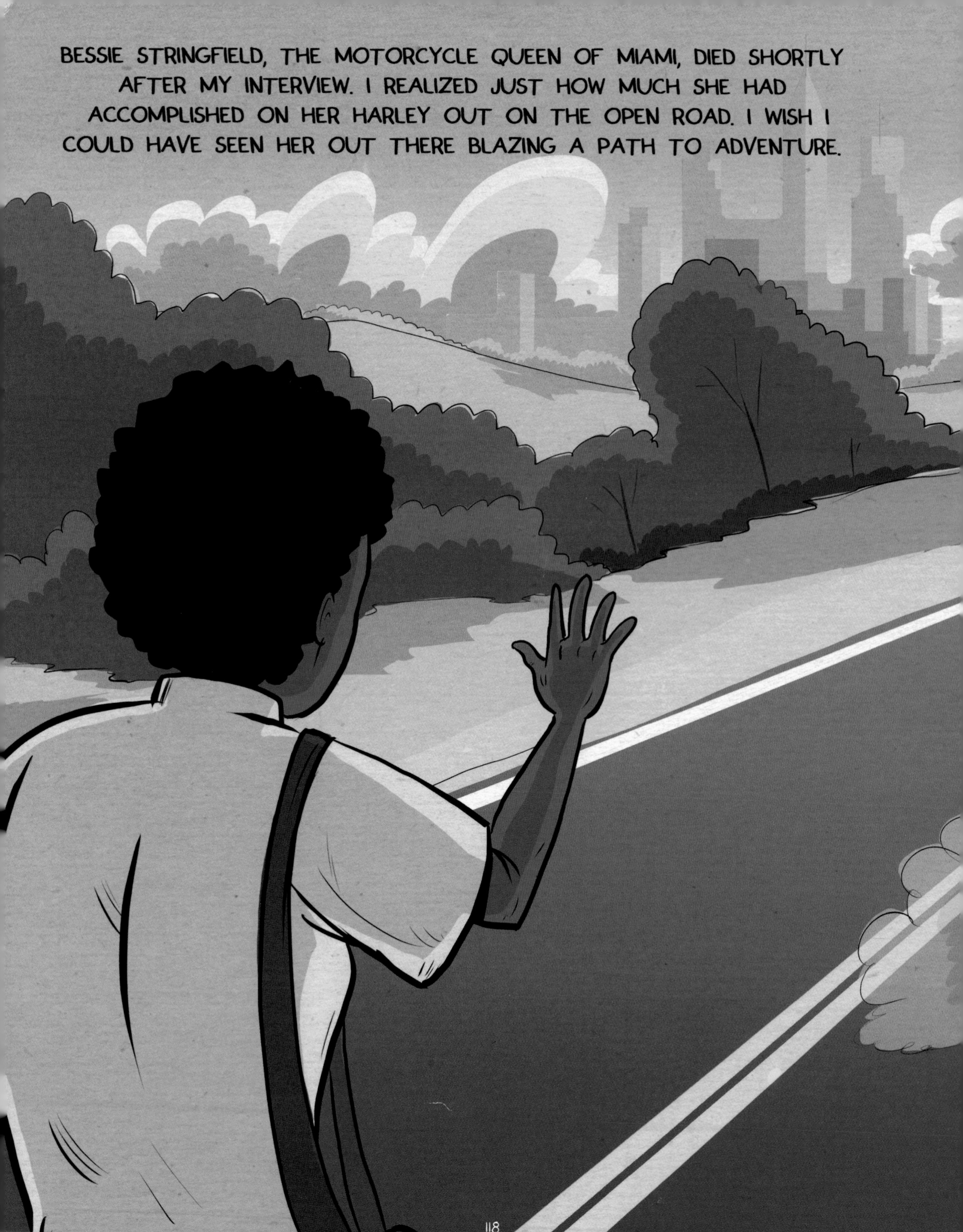
BESSIE STRINGFIELD, THE MOTORCYCLE QUEEN OF MIAMI, DIED SHORTLY AFTER MY INTERVIEW. I REALIZED JUST HOW MUCH SHE HAD ACCOMPLISHED ON HER HARLEY OUT ON THE OPEN ROAD. I WISH I COULD HAVE SEEN HER OUT THERE BLAZING A PATH TO ADVENTURE.

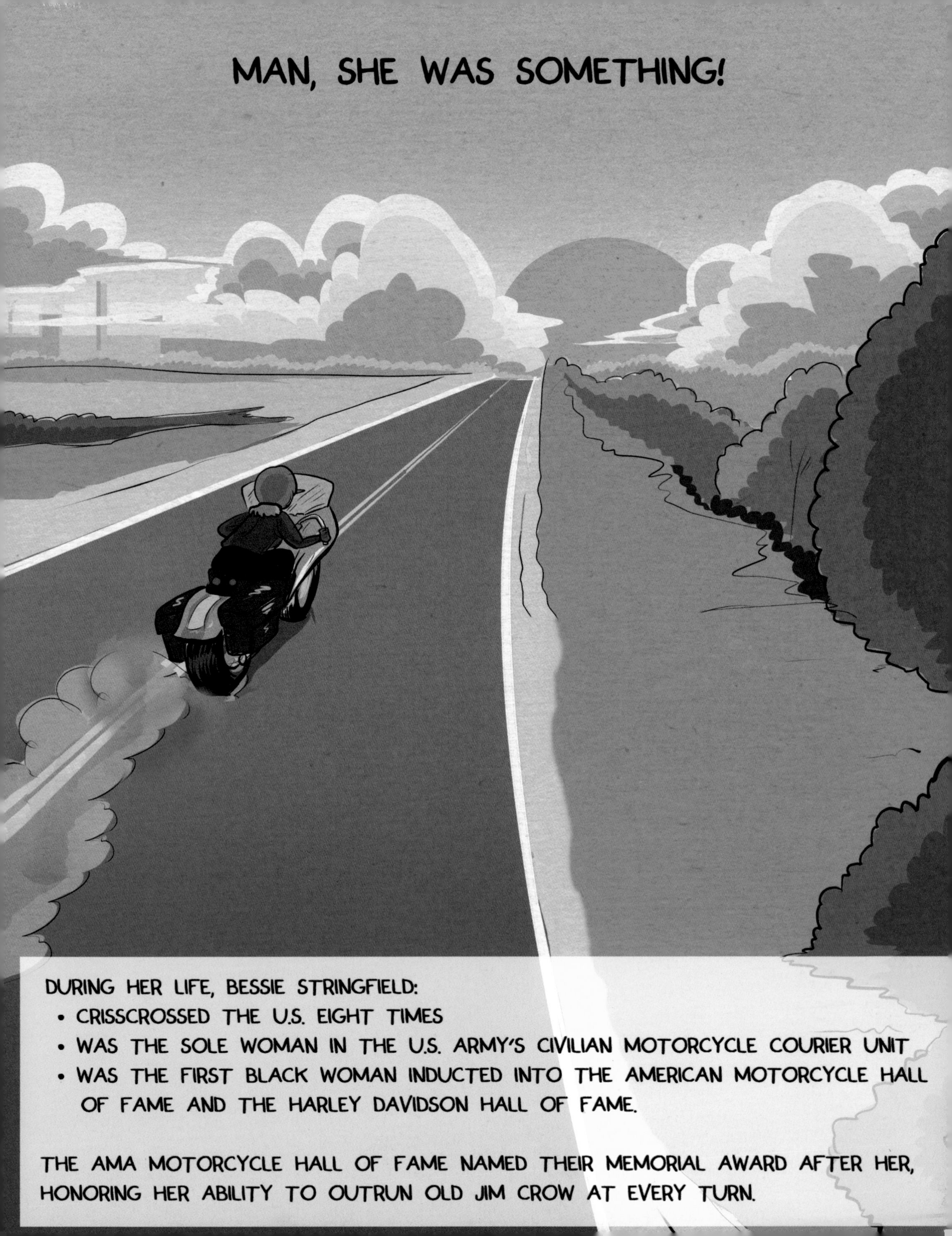
MAN, SHE WAS SOMETHING!
DURING HER LIFE, BESSIE STRINGFIELD:
• CRISSCROSSED THE U.S. EIGHT TIMES
• WAS THE SOLE WOMAN IN THE U.S. ARMY'S CIVILIAN MOTORCYCLE COURIER UNIT
• WAS THE FIRST BLACK WOMAN INDUCTED INTO THE AMERICAN MOTORCYCLE HALL OF FAME AND THE HARLEY DAVIDSON HALL OF FAME.
THE AMA MOTORCYCLE HALL OF FAME NAMED THEIR MEMORIAL AWARD AFTER HER, HONORING HER ABILITY TO OUTRUN OLD JIM CROW AT EVERY TURN.

Bibliography

"Bessie Stringfield." AMA Motorcycle Museum Hall of Fame. American Motorcycle Association, n.d. Web: March 25, 2014. http://americanmotorcyclist.com/Riding/Story/ama-bessie-stringfield-award-1.

Camacho, Maria A. "Bessie Stringfield, 81, Rode Her Harley To Church." *Miami (FL) Herald* Obituary sec.: 4B, Feb. 20, 1993. Web: Sept. 9, 2014. nl.newsbank.com.

Ferrar, Ann. *Hear Me Roar: Women, Motorcycles, and the Rapture of the Road.* New York: Crown Trade Paperbacks, 1996.

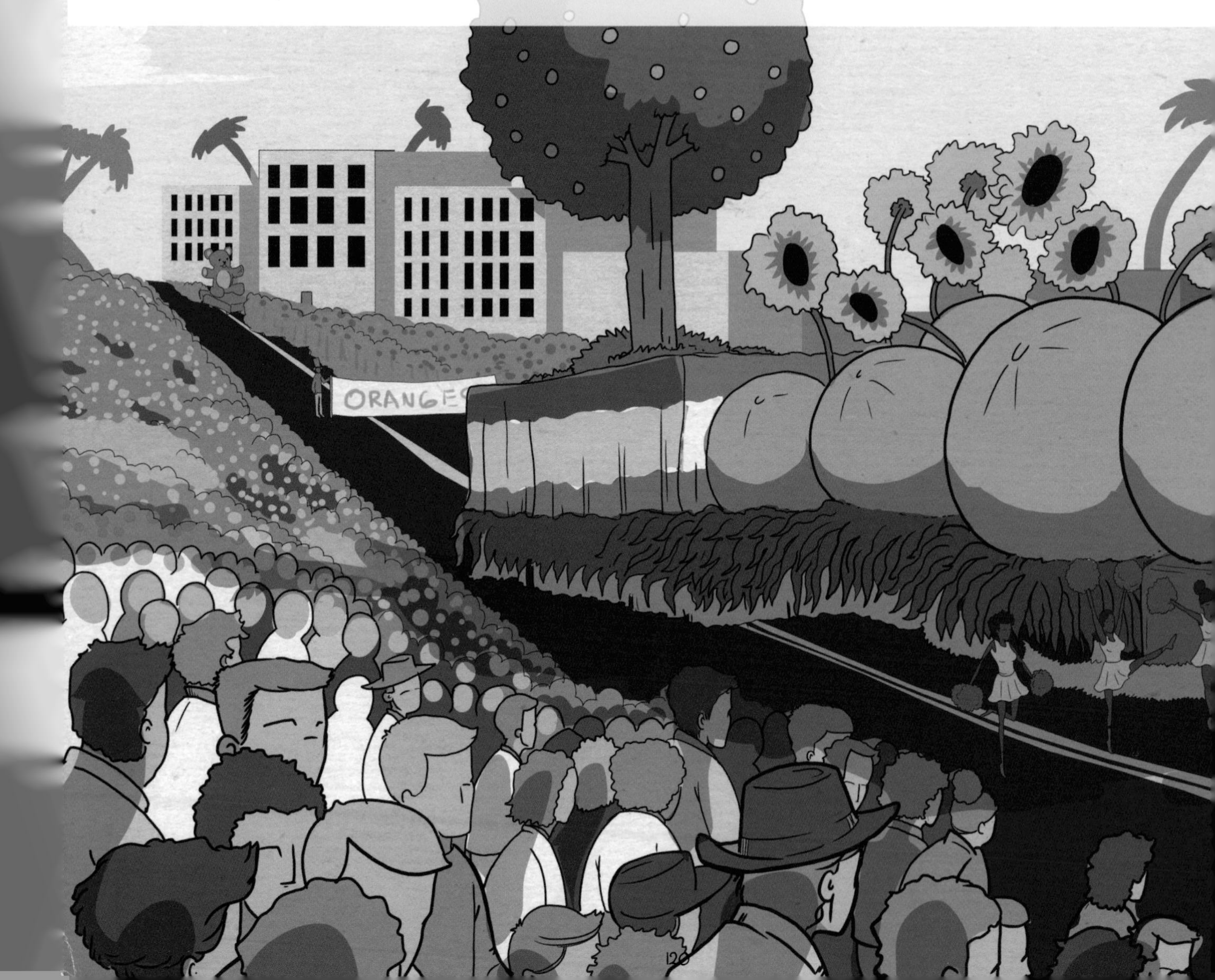
ORANGE

Hines, Bea L. "Bessie Stringfield." Message to the author. E-mail, Feb. 7, 2015.

Jamiol, Paul. "Bessie Stringfield." Message to the author. E-mail, Jan. 8, 2015.

Nielsen, Euell A. "Stringfield, Bessie (1911–1993)." Blackpast.org. Humanities Washington, n.d. Web: May 1, 2015. www.blackpast.org/aah/bessie-stringfield-1911-1993.

"She Paved the Way for Women Bikers." *New Journal & Guide* (Norfolk, VA), 1. Feb. 26, 2003–March 4, 2003.

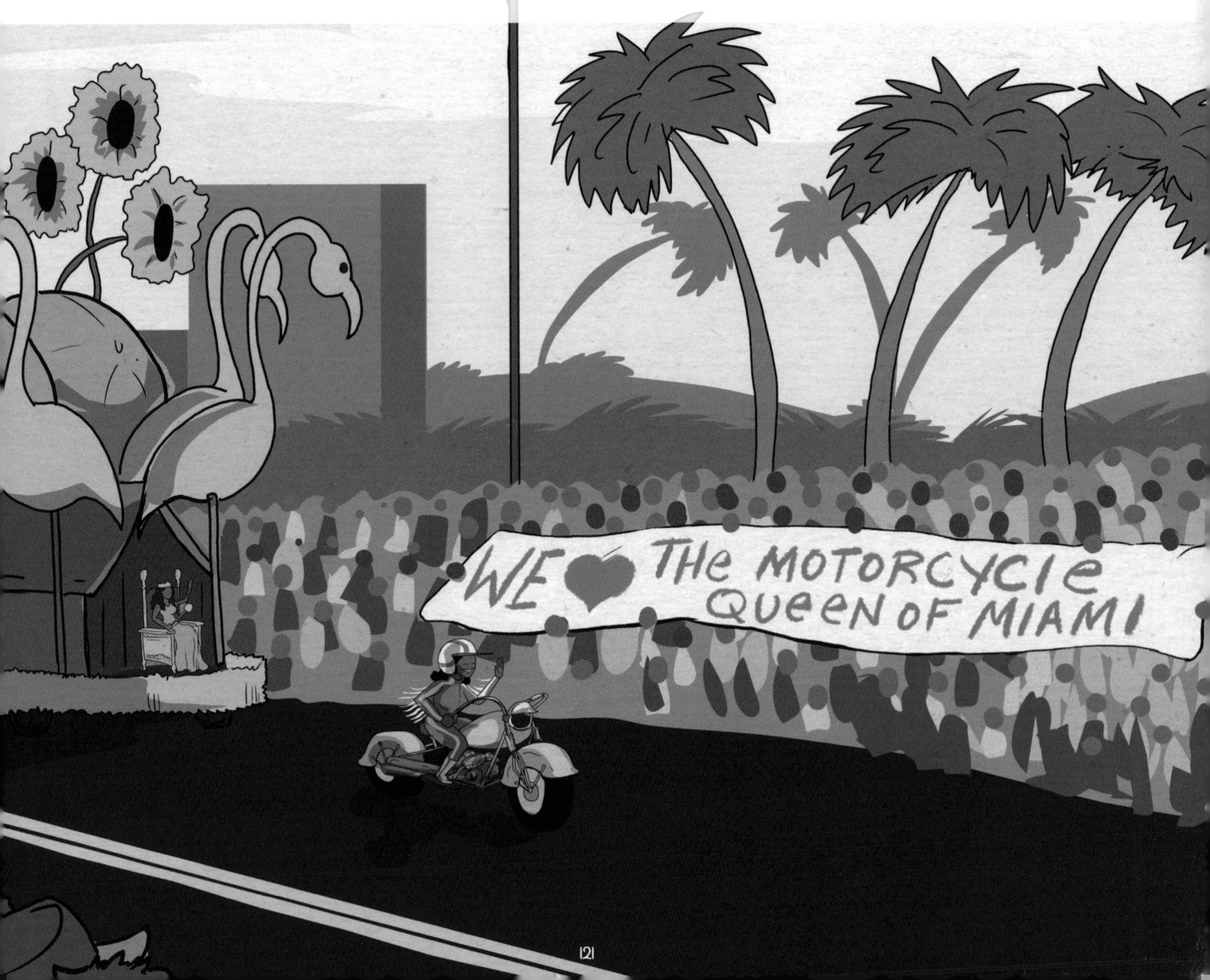
WE ♥ THE MOTORCYCLE
QUEEN OF MIAMI

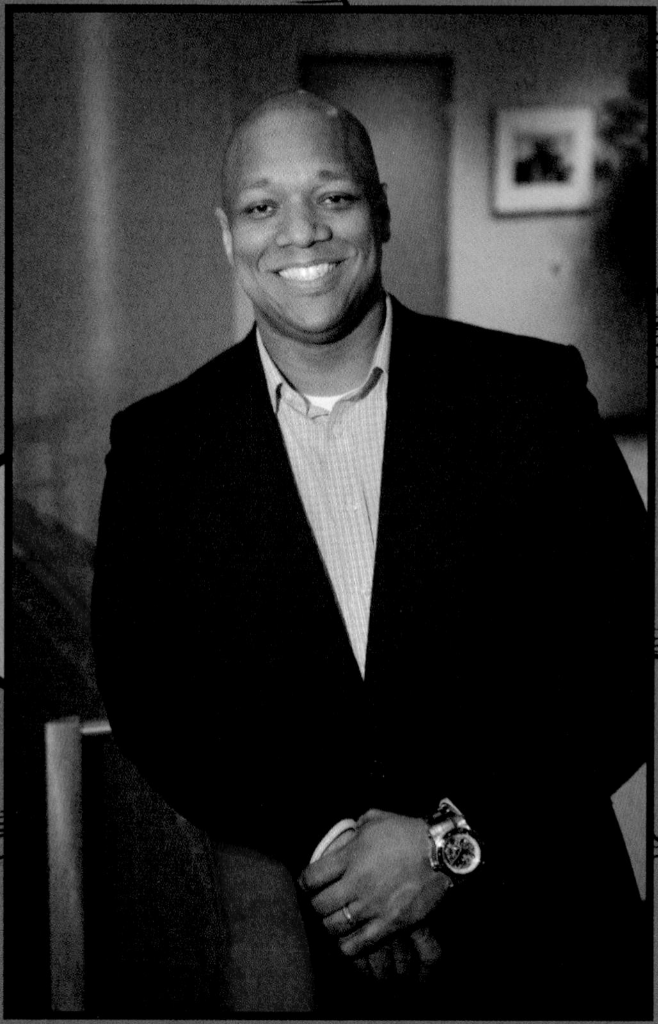

Joel Christian Gill is the Chair of Foundations at the New Hampshire Institute of Art and recipient of the 2016 Boston University College of Fine Arts Alumni Award. He wrote the words and drew the pictures in *Strange Fruit, Volume I: Uncelebrated Narratives from Black History* and *Bass Reeves: Tales of the Talented Tenth, Volume I*. Joel received his MFA from Boston University and a BA from Roanoke College. His secret lair is behind a secret panel in the kitchen of his house (sold separately) in New Boston, New Hampshire where he lives with his wife, four children, talking dog, and two psychic cats.

Visit his website at joelchristiangill.wordpress.com or connect with him on Twitter (@jcg007). Gill believes that 28 days are not enough when it comes to Black History. Join the discussion on social media by following Joel's #28DaysAreNotEnough, his call-to-action about Black History.